Hidden Armies of the Second World War

Hidden Armies of the Second World War

WORLD WAR II RESISTANCE MOVEMENTS

Patrick G. Zander

PRAEGER™

An Imprint of ABC-CLIO, LLC

Santa Barbara, California • Denver, Colorado

Library of Congress Cataloging-in-Publication Data

Names: Zander, Patrick G., author.
Title: Hidden armies of the Second World War : World War II resistance
  movements / Patrick G. Zander.
Other titles: World War II resistance movements
Description: Santa Barbara, California : Praeger, [2017] | Includes
  bibliographical references and index.
Identifiers: LCCN 2017020575 | ISBN 9781440833038 (hardcopy : alk. paper)
Subjects: LCSH: World War, 1939-1945—Underground movements—Europe.
Classification: LCC D802.E9 .Z36 2017 | DDC 940.53/37—dc23 LC record available at
https://lccn.loc.gov/2017020575

ISBN: 978-1-4408-3303-8
EISBN: 978-1-4408-3304-5

21 20 19 18 17   1 2 3 4 5

This book is also available as an eBook.

Praeger
An Imprint of ABC-CLIO, LLC

ABC-CLIO, LLC
130 Cremona Drive, P.O. Box 1911
Santa Barbara, California 93116-1911
www.abc-clio.com

This book is printed on acid-free paper ∞

Manufactured in the United States of America

Contents

Introduction

Shooting broke out from the two sidewalks, as if there were thousands
of men in opposing armies, where were they all hidden? Who WERE
these men, from whom not even a breath was heard?

Diary of Ioanna Tsatsos
Occupied Greece, November, 1943

On August 15, 1944, amphibious personnel carriers filled with anxious
Allied servicemen trundled through Mediterranean waters and rolled
onto the beaches of France's southern coast. They were there as part of the
second phase of the campaign to liberate the continent of Europe from
German domination. Two months earlier the Allies had stormed the
beaches of Normandy on the north coast of France in "Operation Overlord." Now, on the Riviera, the fighting was again fierce, and it would take
weeks before the major cities of the south were liberated. But the invasion,
codenamed "Operation Dragoon," was a tremendous success in military
terms. One crucial reason for that success was that key information had
been provided in advance to the planners of Operation Dragoon by the
French resistance.

 In particular, a married couple, named Albert and Sonja Haasz, had
been critical in assembling that information. Albert and Sonja were French
Jews who lived in terror for their lives every day under Nazi occupation.
They had managed to keep their Jewish identity hidden and simply called
themselves "Hungarians." Searching for some way to fight back against
their oppressors, they had joined the secret French resistance. The resistance was able to ship them to Britain, where they received specialized
training from the Special Operations Executive, the British organization
dedicated to "irregular warfare." With their new skills, they were returned
to France, dropped by parachute under the cover of night. Back home, the
resistance organization directed them to try to infiltrate the German "Todt

Organization," the engineering group in charge of building the coastal defenses for Hitler's "Fortress Europe." Remarkably, they were able to get work, Albert in the Todt Organization, and Sonja, chillingly, in the local branch of the Gestapo, the notorious Nazi secret police. Together they began passing reams of information to the resistance, and Albert began taking meticulous records of the structural details of the coastal defenses. Their harrowing work made possible the creation of a detailed map of all the German fortifications from Genoa to Marseilles.[1] That map, smuggled to the Allied High Command, became the starting point for the planners of Operation Dragoon.

But Albert and Sonja's work also led to resistance bombings of Gestapo offices and German communication stations, and eventually their work caught up with them. Based only on suspicion and hearsay, the German police spied on the two and arrested them. They were brutally interrogated and tortured, the fate that awaited virtually all captured resisters. The Nazi interrogators, in fact, gouged out Sonja's right eye in these sessions. Having admitted nothing, they were deported for questioning to separate concentration camps. Albert was taken to Mauthausen in Austria, while Sonja was taken to the infamous camp at Auschwitz in Poland. There they faced appalling tortures. Albert was hung by his thumbs as SS thugs beat his kidneys with truncheons. Burning needles were shoved underneath his toenails into the quick. He was also subjected to a terrifying round of what historian David Schoenbrun calls the "*baignoire*," which he describes as "repeated drownings in a bathtub, his head held under water until his lungs almost burst."[2] This was the reality that confronted anyone at all involved in resistance activity—arrest, deportation, torture, and, generally, execution. By a miracle, both Albert and Sonja were able to obtain work in their respective camps and so survived to see liberation. Thousands of other resisters, however, were not so fortunate and had to make the ultimate sacrifice in their efforts to free their various nations. Tragically, for the most part their heroic stories died with them.

This book will serve as an attempt to bring the inspiring story of the resistance out of the shadows and into the light for the student and the general reader. It is a story filled with tension, harrowing escapes, secret missions, heroism, and betrayal. It is also a story that is not particularly well known to general readers, military history enthusiasts, or even to specialists who study the world wars. There are important reasons for this. For one thing, the story is extremely complex and covers a vast number of nations, cultures, and languages. To have a thorough knowledge of the resistance operations in World War II means having a detailed knowledge of events in every theater of that war. There were resistance movements operating in North Africa and East Africa, and within the Japanese Empire in Asia. This volume, however, will confine itself to examining the most prominent resistance movements in Europe from 1939 to 1945. But even this narrowed approach presents tremendous challenges. Another practical reason for these challenges is the problem of language. No volume that currently exists provides an archive-based historical study of all the resistance movements in Europe or around the world. For a historian to conduct original research from the archives just in the European theater would require advanced knowledge of all of the following languages: English, French, Norwegian, Dutch, German, Italian, Polish, Russian, Czech, Yugoslavian, Albanian, and Greek. This is simply not realistic. This book, then, is not principally based upon archival sources, although it does use some. A further reason for the difficulty of such broad-based research is simply the depth and complexity of the subject itself. As an example, the most thorough work dealing with the French resistance is the masterwork produced between 1967 and 1981 by Henri Nogueres and Henri Degliame Fouche, *Histoire de la Resistance en France*, which is a five-volume set. The French resistance was indeed an especially vast and complicated case, but each national case could merit a similarly expansive study. A survey like this one, then, must surely be highly selective and limit itself to the most important organizations, events, and individuals. Yet another difficulty facing researchers is the very secretive nature of resistance work. Resistance organizations took meticulous care to cover their tracks and to leave as little documented evidence behind them as possible, for reasons of survival. As a result, documentary records from the organizations themselves are rare. Making this problem doubly challenging is that the institutions that did produce documentary evidence—foreign offices, intelligence agencies, war cabinets, and so on—often made documents on sensitive operations unavailable; until recently, volumes of such records were marked classified and denied to scholars.

With the passage of time, however, the telling of this story as a broader survey has become increasingly more realistic. Gradually, governments have released records, perhaps most importantly the Soviet archives that were opened after 1991. Numerous personal interviews have been conducted over the decades, leading to a growing reservoir of firsthand accounts. Scholars specializing in the history of all of the relevant nations have been conducting archival-level research on resistance organizations, bringing to light many of the individuals, organizations, and operations that had remained obscure. It seems appropriate to bring some of this work together in an effort to provide an overview of all the major resistance movements of Europe. Using archives, secondary monographs, case studies, and numerous personal accounts, this book will give the reader a basic understanding of the realities of occupation, the most important organizations, the key individuals, the largest operations, and the historical issues at stake. This information, along with the bibliographic guide, will also provide specialists and academics a starting point for more in-depth studies. For reasons of length, it has not been possible to chronicle the activities of every resistance organization or the resistance in every European nation. The author has selected those resistance movements that produced the largest organizations and the most consequential operations, and that most deeply influenced the conduct and outcome of the war.

Resistance to dictatorial fascist (or quasi-fascist) regimes did not begin with World War II. While dictatorships in Italy, Portugal, Yugoslavia, Germany, Greece, and Spain (among others) were brought to power often by popular movements, there were always elements of the population who opposed them. One of the trademarks of fascist regimes, however, was the ruthless elimination of all opposition parties in the process of creating a single-party state. Those in opposition parties were often the first targets of a fascist regime and hence were among the first actively to protest. But part of the very essence of a fascist state is the crushing of any resistance to its ideology and its ruling elite. All fascist regimes created elaborate organizations to root out subversion and remove it from society. In Italy this was the task of the secret police agency known as the OVRA (Organization for the Vigilance and Repression of Anti-Fascism), which pioneered many of the techniques of internal terror. The OVRA used phone taps and civilian informers, and it accumulated voluminous dossiers on its suspected internal enemies. These were mostly trade unionists, opposition party leaders, open communists, and socialists. Those considered serious threats were arrested and often sentenced to what was known as *"confino,"* where they were shipped to island prisons or obscure country communities where they lived under surveillance. The OVRA would later be instrumental in helping the Nazi secret police, the Gestapo (*Geheime Staatspolizei*), to establish itself and begin the work of internal espionage and terror in Germany. The Gestapo, like the OVRA, used phone taps, surveillance, and especially a vast network of civilian informers to conduct its work. Recent scholarship suggests that the Gestapo did not so much drive the system of arrests, but was instead struggling to keep up with the numerous denunciations it received from ordinary citizens. These citizens' letters denounced neighbors, personal enemies, or business competitors as "anti-Nazi" or as displaying "antisocial" behavior.[3] The Gestapo arrested such suspicious persons and generally deported them to concentration camps in Germany, which were built and already operating in the first months of Hitler's dictatorship.[4] Later, in the days of the Axis occupation of Europe, these two organizations would be the principal instruments of terror used by Germany and Italy, and the organizations charged with rooting out and destroying the resistance organizations.

But before the Second World War had begun, the ubiquitous nature of the police organizations made mounting a serious challenge to the fascist dictatorships all but impossible. Members of resistance groups could be reported by just about anyone and immediately removed to a concentration camp. Active, violent resistance was almost unheard of except in individual cases. There were some individual acts of violent resistance, but they carried with them the potential for savage reprisals. One example involved a young Jewish man named Herschel Grynszpan, who, outraged at the treatment of his parents in Germany, shot a Nazi diplomat in Paris in November 1938. As a response to this act of resistance, the Nazi hierarchy launched a two-day attack on the Jews of Germany, smashing Jewish shops, destroying property, violently assaulting Jews at random, and burning synagogues. This nightmare is remembered as Kristallnacht for the shimmering broken glass that covered the streets. So small, individual acts of resistance could and did take place, though the potential for deadly reprisals kept them to a minimum. Large-scale organizations, on the other hand, carrying out violent resistance within a fascist state were simply not possible to sustain in such repressive environments.

Still, there were some historically important resistance efforts that offered forceful and even violent opposition to the growth of fascism during the 1930s. Despite the seemingly unstoppable march toward dictatorship, great numbers of the people of Europe did make it clear that they were not willing to accept such a future. The following are some of the most prominent examples indicating that popular movements could work against fascism through peaceful electoral means, through collective physical assertion, and even through the violent means of war.

THE POPULAR FRONT

In Europe during the interwar years, there was a great deal of fragmentation on the political left. After the success of the Bolshevik Revolution in 1917 and the subsequent creation of the Soviet Union in the early 1920s, communist political parties were formed all over Europe. Many of these parties were tied to the Soviet Union through the apparatus of the "Comintern" (Communist International), the Soviet institution created specifically to help spread communist revolution. But there were also numerous other shades of left-wing political groups. These included revolutionary socialists, social democrats, trade unionist groups, and anarchists. These groups tended to establish their own political parties and vote for their own candidates. In the Soviet Union, Joseph Stalin announced that the moderate left-wing groups were splitting the vote and undermining the communist cause; thus, he said, they were actually the greatest enemies of communism and had to be eliminated. After the rise of Adolf Hitler in Germany, however, the policy of Stalin and the Comintern changed. Its officials recognized that fascism was spreading rapidly, and that fascist violence threatened to overwhelm legal, electoral politics. Because of this threat, the Comintern called for a new policy that it called a "popular front." The policy said that all left-wing groups should work together to coordinate their candidates for elections and should publicly endorse their left-wing rivals. By doing so, the hope was that the entire political left wing of an area could vote as a single bloc and thus undermine the far-right (mostly fascist) parties. It was not successful everywhere, but it did produce significant results in France and Spain. Both of those nations were democratic republics with a polarized electorate. In France the many parties of the left struggled to deal with the conservative right wing, as well as a number of fascist and anti-Semitic parties like the *Croix de Feu* (Cross of Fire) and the *Partie Populaire Français* (French Popular Party). But in 1936, the cooperation between the socialists, the communists, and the moderate labor groups produced a victory for a left-leaning government under the socialist prime minister, Leon Blum. In Spain the elections of 1936 produced much the same result, with a left-leaning government elected under the president, Manuel Azana. In parliament the people elected a sizable majority of left-wing deputies, and the government was poised to embark on a program of major reforms. The far right of Spain was horrified by this development, and a group of top generals in Spain's army decided that they must intervene and seize the government. The army's revolt brought about the terrible Spanish Civil War, which lasted from the summer of 1936 to May 1939.

THE BATTLE OF CABLE STREET

In Great Britain the first explicitly fascist political group, the British Fascists, had formed as early as 1923, mostly imitating the strutting and ceremonies of Mussolini's Italian Fascists. Other groups would form in the late twenties, like the fiercely anti-Semitic Imperial Fascist League. But Britain's largest and most visible fascist group was formed by Sir Oswald Mosley in October 1932. Mosley's group, the British Union of Fascists (BUF), put together an extensive political platform, ran a weekly newspaper, and boasted a band of black-shirted ruffians who used violence to "keep order" at the group's numerous meetings. The BUF also got official support from one of Britain's top newspapers, the *Daily Mail*, run by its pro-fascist editor, Lord Rothermere. Despite an initial surge during 1932 and 1933, violence at its mass rallies and Rothermere's withdrawal of his formal support in 1934 sent the BUF into decline. It was after this that the BUF increasingly turned to open anti-Semitism and strident racism. In the fall of 1936, Mosley's group staged a large-scale march that was scheduled to parade through London's East End, where the largest Jewish population was located in the city and where working-class conditions were most difficult. But on October 4, as the march was preparing to move into the East End, legions of people rose up to stop it. Members of Jewish groups, the labor left, and (it must be said) numbers of ordinary citizens built barricades across the streets. They confronted the march with a defiant multitude. While the police mostly helped the fascists (it was, after all, a legally licensed march), the resisters would not yield, and, unable to move forward, the march eventually was terminated. The event has lived on in British history as the "Battle of Cable Street" and stands as a major symbolic victory demonstrating that the majority of the British people would not stand for the prejudice, violence, and intimidation of the fascist cause.

THE INTERNATIONAL BRIGADES OF THE SPANISH CIVIL WAR

The people of France and Spain had spoken in the elections of 1936, and the coordinated program of left-wing cooperation (the Popular Front) had succeeded in keeping the far right out of power. In France tensions escalated and governments broke up routinely, but the French Third Republic remained intact until the outbreak of World War II. In Spain, however, the election of the Popular Front government created a vicious civil war. A group of Spain's top generals, eventually led by Francisco Franco, attempted to launch a military invasion of the capital to seize the government by force. The ordinary people of Spain, however, took up arms to defend the Republican government they had elected. In particular, left-wing labor unions and political parties helped organize the mobilization of tens of thousands of ordinary citizens all over the country, and the Spanish Army was stopped. As the conflict bogged down into a stalemate, Franco appealed for help from both Mussolini and Hitler and received significant material and military aid. Those defending the Republic would now face the troops of Nazi Germany, Fascist Italy, Franco's Spanish army, and foreign legions (mostly Moroccan troops) who came to assist the Spanish "Nationalists." When the Spanish Republic appealed for help to the European democracies—France and Britain—it was turned down. Neither nation wanted to involve itself in another country's civil war. In response to all of this, ordinary people from all over Europe and the world decided to take up arms to help save Spain from fascism. Brigades were organized by the network of communist parties across Europe, and eventually they would be directly controlled by the Soviet Union when that nation agreed to formally join the war on the republican side. Groups from Britain, France, the Netherlands, Canada, Sweden, and the United States, among many others, all came to Spain to put their lives on the line to hold back the tide of fascist dictatorship. The most famous account of life in one of these brigades is the book *Homage to Catalonia*, written by George Orwell, who served in the POUM (or Worker's Party of Marxist Unification) during 1936 and 1937. Perhaps 35,000 individuals went to Spain to aid the Republic, of whom about 15,000 died in combat.[5] In the end their efforts were unsuccessful. The Nationalists prevailed, and Franco would go on to establish his own fascist-inspired dictatorship that lasted until 1975. But it was a demonstration that ordinary people had the courage and the willingness to risk their lives in the fight against fascist domination.

With the outbreak of World War II in 1939 and the succession of successful German and Italian conquests that followed, people all over the continent found themselves under the domination of ruthless oppressors. Those who had enjoyed living in a free republic or constitutional monarchy now found their independence and their political voice entirely erased. Even those who had lived in virtual fascist dictatorships (like Poland or Greece, for example) now found themselves oppressed and subjugated by foreign masters. Eventually, after the nightmare of the initial conquest was over, people from all walks of life began to search for ways to vent their outrage and to find something—anything—they could do to undermine their oppressors. Some would remain unaffiliated and pursue their own private methods for hitting back at the enemy. Others would find each other and agree to form secret informal networks. Still others, like the many military officers or former politicians, would work to form paramilitary organizations to undermine the enemy in any way they could. They understood that although the combat in their country was concluded for the moment, the world was still at war. Thus, anything they could do to reduce the ability of the enemy to wage war was a useful deed, one that might in some way hasten the defeat of the Axis powers. The resistance forces that took shape would find many different methods for this, and listed below are the most important ways that resistance groups worked to damage the Axis and promote an Allied victory.

Peaceful Non-Cooperation

Perhaps the most common form of resistance was practiced by ordinary citizens of modest means. Just because one did not belong to a combat brigade, or did not have the means to blow up a Gestapo office, did not mean that one could not defy the enemy. One could simply refuse to go along with the occupier's policies and refuse to accept his ideology. Particularly the Nazis were determined that in certain places (Norway, Holland, France, and Denmark, for example), the population should be converted to Nazi ideology in order to evolve into an ideal National Socialist state. But all over Europe, the majority of occupied people would have none of it. They wrote graffiti on walls, they demonstrated in the streets, they refused to teach fascist curricula in schools, they went on strike, and they passed out pamphlets that exposed the hate and brutality of Nazism. Their actions were nonviolent, but their resistance was clear. As a result, recruiting those same people into larger armies was impossible, and the Nazi attempt to conscript legions of laborers for the Axis factories was always uneven and problematic.

Spreading of Information

In the process that saw ordinary citizens move from passive subjects to active resisters, the spreading of information played a key role. One of the first activities that potential resisters turned to was the dissemination of information. This served a dual purpose: first, it created an internal system of communication among the occupied population, and second, it served to negate the mass of disinformation and propaganda constantly being circulated by the occupiers. Nazi and fascist occupation regimes produced their own newspapers and publications. They constantly derided resisters as "traitors" and appealed to people to turn them in as their duty. Those Axis publications withheld any negative battlefield information, releasing to the public only what they wanted them to believe. Resisters, though, labored to obtain real information from their communication networks with the Allies and members of their own groups who had obtained first-hand news. They published dozens of resistance newspapers that reassured people that the resistance was in operation, that it was injuring the enemy, and that Allied victory was progressing and imminent. For those suffering under Axis slavery, receiving such news was the best way to keep their hopes—and their defiance—alive. Printing such sheets and distributing them was one way that young people could get involved without immediately being subject to combat conditions.

Undermining of Industrial Productivity

This kind of activity was also nonviolent, though it could border on the violent at times. Tens of thousands of subjected Europeans were conscripted from all over the continent to be sent to German and Italian factories, and there they would labor to produce the armaments and supplies for the Axis war machine. Subject populations were also often made to labor for the Germans in their own lands, as the Axis routinely commandeered the factories and plundered the industrial produce of its occupied territories. As such, one way that outraged workers could strike back was to reduce the output of this industrial production. This could take several forms, but generally it meant slowing down the production process. This could be done through a staged accident, the staged exhaustion of a key raw material, or simply working slowly when out of the sight of supervisors. Another form it could take was the sabotaging of military produce— that is, building faults into key equipment. Again, this could take many forms, such as using faulty wiring in aircraft parts, or misloading powder in shells or ammunition. It is today completely impossible to quantify such activities or to know just how many key parts failed in operation, but personal accounts suggest that such activity on the part of occupied workers was widespread.

Active Industrial Sabotage

For factories that produced especially important materials, the Allies and the resistance organizations often tried to take more direct action. One of the most important, and dangerous, activities that resisters could take on was the destruction of major factory facilities. This generally meant an armed mission. Key factories were almost always guarded by Axis security guards with heavy arms. Resistance teams would have to find secret ways to get past the soldiers, get into the facility, rig a series of high explosives with enough time for escape, and then evacuate to safety. This was often a harrowing mission in military terms, but it was also quite complicated in practical terms. Agents had to be well informed as to the construction of the factory and the function of its machinery. Often agents traveled clandestinely to Britain for specialized training about the factories they planned to target. Resisters destroyed aircraft factories, engine factories, ball bearing factories, chemical factories, cellophane factories, electrical engineering plants, mechanical engineering plants, insulator factories, motor vehicle factories, silk and textile factories, oil refineries, radio factories, precision instrument factories, and rubber works, to name but a few.[6]

Active Sabotage of Communications and Transport Networks

Of the violent categories of resistance activity, the most common and arguably the most important was the destruction of the communications and transport networks inside occupied Europe. This consisted of actions like cutting telephone and telegraph wires, which prevented Axis armies from communicating with each other in real time. This could be quite deadly at times of imminent Allied invasion, when the coordination of divisions was vital to defense. Even more widespread and effective was the destruction of the railway networks. This could be accomplished by blowing up track lines to create large gaps, but also by sabotaging railcars and locomotives as they sat in stations. Ripping out the wiring or pouring sand into the fuel tanks helped to knock locomotives out of service. During 1943 and 1944, when the Allies made multiple landings in Italy and France, the Germans needed lightning-fast decisions and the rapid movement of troops all across Western Europe. With the rail networks heavily sabotaged, however, the movement of arms, supplies, food, and actual troops was often held up for weeks at a time. Every division of German troops that sat in a railway station waiting, or that sat frozen on the tracks in the middle of nowhere, meant one less Nazi division facing Allied soldiers in battle.

Espionage

Another of the extremely valuable contributions of the various resistance organizations was providing information about Axis occupation forces to the Allied High Command. Again, this took many different forms, but common areas of concern were the location and movement of Axis troops, the presence or absence of key personnel, details about fortifications and defenses, schedules of transport, and information on new weapons projects and testing,[7] resistance networks worked to get their agents into key positions that gave them access to Axis information or that put them in direct proximity to key structures or military bases. The information those agents observed would be passed secretly to the heads of their organizations, who then had to get the information to the Allies, usually in London. This was generally done by coded messages sent over wireless transmitters, but it could also be done by sending agents by plane or boat with the relevant information.

Assisting Soldiers and Escapees behind Enemy Lines

It was common during the war for soldiers and officers of Allied armies, or downed airmen, to find themselves stranded behind enemy lines with no direct route to safety. Another common occurrence was the escape of men from prisoner-of-war camps or local prisons. They were outlaws without any identification and could not generally move in public without being detected. Escaped prisoners, stranded soldiers, and downed airmen all faced a perilous situation and needed to get to the nearest neutral territory or the nearest coastline to find a way off the continent. Here the resistance networks did some of its finest work by establishing a string of families and houses that together constituted a safe travel route. An escapee would generally be accompanied by a resistance member to a safe house. There arrangements would be made to prepare fake identification papers or travel documents. Then the two would move by night to the next house, and then to the next, until they reached an airstrip where the men could be flown out of the country, or until they reached the coast, where the resistance generally had local fisherman in its employ. To provide just one example of the numbers involved, "Operation Halyard" was launched in August 1943 to airlift downed airmen out of occupied Yugoslavia. In about a month's time, Operation Halyard evacuated over 500 U.S. and other Allied airmen from the mountains of Yugoslavia.[8]

Killing the Enemy's Key Personnel

Resistance organizations were rarely in a position to face enemy forces in open combat, and so the killing of enemy personnel was often quite difficult. One way to do this was to combine sabotage with armed attack. As an example, a resistance group might choose a railway that ran through a deep forest and blow up the track. When the train stopped for the enemy to repair the track in order to move on, resistance forces could emerge from the forest and shoot as many Axis troops as possible, and then move back into the forests. This was a common strategy in the countryside, but such operations were virtually impossible in urban areas, where all the Axis key staff members were located. There were times, however, when certain individuals in the Axis command were seen as so notorious or so important to the military effort that the decision was made to carry out an assassination. And these assassinations were not limited to Axis officials: Resisters quite often selected for assassination local officials who were collaborating with the enemy. Assassination operations were tense affairs, as most important top officers traveled with heavy security, and the cities under occupation were lined with heavily armed troops. Still, the resistance groups managed to kill a number of such individuals, the most famous being the notorious architect of the Holocaust and governor of the Czech lands, Reinhard Heydrich. Such assassinations carried with them the grim knowledge that the Nazis would respond with brutal reprisals. After the killing of Heydrich, for example, the Nazis killed over 600 innocent Czech civilians and wiped an entire village (Lidice) from the face of the earth.

Armed Combat

Finally, there was the most fundamental form of resistance—open, armed combat. This was exceptionally rare in most of Europe, as it did not fit the circumstances of most resistance groups. In the situation of occupation, a small resistance group in the midst of large occupation army would stand no chance in open combat. There was also the problem of weaponry. The Allies worked to get weapons and ammunition to the resistance groups, but this was extremely challenging and had to be done through secret airdrops or secret shipping. Resistance groups, as we shall see, seemed always to be short of weapons and ammunition. But there were times and places where resistance groups engaged in open combat with the enemy. One of these was the eruption of the Warsaw uprising of 1944, when ordinary people, coordinated by the Polish resistance, took up arms in door-to-door combat with the Germans. Farther east, in the Soviet Union, a special group of brigades was formed, known as the Soviet Partisans. Despite the enormous Nazi invasion in June 1941, the Soviet government had never fallen, and so Stalin's high command worked to supply these groups behind enemy lines with weapons and supplies. Their task was to attack the German rear as much as possible, harassing their communications and transport, but also engaging them in open combat. This was also true of the Communist Partisans in Yugoslavia, who did not hesitate to engage the German troops in the region in combat. To fight pitched battles in open terrain was never the strategy for the resistance groups. Instead they would engage Axis troops emerging from forests or mountain valleys in guerrilla-style attacks, fight it out, and then melt back into the terrain.

In all of these various ways and more, the people of Europe resisted their Axis oppressors. To tell the wide-ranging story of the various resistance movements across the continent, this book has been organized by geographic regions. The first chapter will provide the reader with the background of occupation, describing the extensive list of Axis conquests and the complicated set of political relationships and configurations that they produced. The second chapter will examine the creation of the Allied organizations that labored to build, arm, supply, and direct the various resistance organizations throughout Europe. The first of these branches was Britain's Special Operations Executive (SOE), formed during the summer of 1940. Under the leadership of the Ministry of Economic Warfare, the SOE would recruit and train foreign nationals, provide them with intensive training, and then reinsert them into their various countries. The SOE pioneered many of the innovations of "irregular warfare," such as special weapons, plastic explosives, and customized wireless sets, as well as the tactics of guerilla warfare. It was also one of only two organizations to have intimate contact with nearly all of the resistance movements in Europe. The records of the SOE remain a vital source of information about the various situations and organizations across the continent. The other major Allied resistance organization was the American Office of Strategic

Services (OSS), which was similar to the SOE. The OSS, formed two years after the SOE, used the SOE infrastructures for recruiting, training, and engineering while it gained the experience and expertise of the trade. After the war, the OSS would lay the foundations for the creation of the American CIA (Central Intelligence Agency).

The third chapter looks at the largest and most complex of the national resistance situations—that of France. The French resistance was made up of over 60 different groups, although over time these were gradually incorporated into a larger, more unified organization. Most branches were loyal to the Free French government led by General Charles de Gaulle in London, but not all. This chapter investigates the most prominent of these organizations and looks at some of the key individuals and operations from the occupation in June 1940 until the great Allied invasions of June 1944. The fourth chapter looks at three different nations in the north of Europe. Norway, Holland, and Denmark were all invaded in the very early stages of German expansion, and, as northern Europeans, these populations were governed differently from other occupied countries. Because of their supposed "Aryan" blood, the Nazis granted these states some limited autonomy and tried to promote the evolution of these people into enthusiastic National Socialists. Despite being seen as "racial brothers," the populations of these three nations never remotely accepted Nazism and produced large-scale and effective resistance movements. The fifth chapter looks at a specific group and a specific operation—the Czech resistance and the assassination of Reinhard Heydrich. The Czechs, having been conquered before the war even began, struggled to sustain their small resistance movement and found it difficult to conduct any significant operations. Because of this, and the sense that the Czechs needed to prove themselves, the Czech government-in-exile made the decision to use its agents to kill one of the Nazis' most prominent figures. The sixth chapter looks at the extensive Polish resistance, particularly the activities of the Polish Home Army and the uprising by the Jews confined in the Warsaw Ghetto during 1943. The chapter concludes with a look at the Warsaw uprising of August 1944, when thousands of ordinary people, led and armed by the Home Army, rose up and attacked the German occupation force. The uprising failed miserably and ended in tragedy. It remains highly controversial because of the refusal of the nearby Soviet armies to intervene or help the Poles.

The seventh chapter looks at Nazi Germany itself and the various branches of what became an underground movement. One citizen movement consisted of intellectuals who risked all by circulating information and literature denouncing the Nazis. But generally, the German resistance was made up of political and military elites. There were those who came to believe that Hitler was mad and leading Germany into oblivion. Virtually all of these secret dissidents believed that the only sure way of ending the war and avoiding Germany's destruction was to kill Hitler. The chapter concludes by looking at the most famous attempt to kill Hitler, the "Valkyrie" plot of July 1944. The eighth chapter looks at the Soviet Union and its Partisan movement. Most of the scholarship on the subject since the war has been conducted by Soviet historians projecting the Soviet point of view—that Partisans were all-important to the Soviet war effort and that they were another example of the masses of Soviet people standing up to defend their beloved communist system regardless of the danger. More recent research, after the opening of the Soviet archives in 1991, is producing a modified and more balanced picture of the Soviet Partisan effort. The ninth chapter looks at the resistance movements in the Mediterranean, focusing upon Italy, Greece, and Yugoslavia. The author has combined these nations together in a single chapter first because of their geographic proximity, but also because their fates were so intertwined. It was the Italians who invaded Albania, then Greece, and later much of Yugoslavia. In Greece and Yugoslavia, however, the Germans were forced to intervene due to Italian failures on the battlefield. As a result, Greece and Yugoslavia ended up with both German and Italian (as well as Bulgarian) occupation forces, and hence a very complicated political configuration. This became even more complicated in the late summer of 1943, when Mussolini's dictatorship collapsed and the Italian state eventually joined the Allies. In Greece and Yugoslavia, this instantly changed the enemy targets of the resistance, but in Italy itself the situation became even more difficult. After the collapse of fascism, a vigorous resistance movement took shape there almost immediately, but just as this was happening, the Germans invaded Italy and took control of the northern half of the country. Therefore, Italian resisters found themselves fighting the Germans but also fighting the hardline fascists who remained loyal to Mussolini and to Nazi Germany. It was simultaneously a war against a foreign enemy and a civil war.

The tenth and final chapter of the book deals again with the French resistance as the Allied armies arrived *en masse* for the liberation of Europe. This chapter will look at the role of the resistance in preparing the way for the D-Day landings in June 1944 and the landings in the south of France (Operation Dragoon), which led to the eventual expulsion of the Nazis from French territory. As those Allied armies advanced, however, they fully intended to bypass the capital city of Paris, which they saw as not strategically important, but which would require a large commitment of resources. The French leadership, however, insisted that Paris must be liberated as soon as possible. The resistance groups in Paris forced the issue by launching an uprising against the German occupation troops in Paris. The Allied commanders were thus forced to bring their armies into the city to prevent a bloodbath. This resulted in some of the most symbolic and iconic moments of Europe's liberation.

In every one of the national cases examined, the author will try to bring to life the realities of life under occupation, the tangled political complexity of the various situations, the organizational structures of the resistance groups, and some of the most significant operations. But also important will be the human and emotional side of the story—the agonizing tragedies of arrests, tortures, and executions, the extreme tensions of operations and escapes, the bitterness of internal struggles, the extraordinary mental and physical strength of the agents, and finally the joyous release of liberation.

NOTES

1. For the story of Albert and Sonja Haasz, see David Schoenbrun, *Soldiers of the Night: The Story of the French Resistance* (New York: Meridian, 1981), pp. 403–405.

2. Ibid., p. 405.

3. See Robert Gellately, "The Gestapo and German Society: Political Denunciation in the Gestapo Case Files," *Journal of Modern History* 60 (4) (December 1988); also see Robert Gellately, *Backing Hitler: Consent and Coercion in Nazi Germany* (Oxford: Oxford University Press, 2001).

4. Germany's concentration camps were not built as centers for mass killing as the death camps of the Holocaust would be. Concentration camps subjected inmates to forced labor and a good deal of mental and physical torture, but the death camps of the Holocaust would not begin operation until 1942.

5. See Antony Beevor, *The Battle for Spain: The Spanish Civil War, 1936–1939* (New York: Penguin, 2006), pp. 157–165.

6. See "Evaluation of SOE Activities in France," undated, British National Archives, HS/8/42, 12–13.

7. For example, the Polish Home Army's intelligence network was the first to inform the Allies of the V-1 and V-2 rocket projects at Peenemünde.

8. See Richard M. Kelly, "Behind the Enemy Lines: Operation Halyard," *Blue Book Magazine* 83 (4) (1946).

1

The Axis Conquest of Europe
(1938–1941)

In the first year and a half of World War II, there seemed to be no end to the parade of conquests amassed by the Axis powers in Europe. Nazi Germany, and after June 10, 1940, fascist Italy, marched to victory after victory, taking control of virtually the entire continent. Along the way there had taken place a few meaningful Allied victories—the moral victory of the evacuation at Dunkirk, the Greeks temporarily holding back the Italians, the liberation of the Italian-held region of Abyssinia (Ethiopia), and the vital victory in the air during the Battle of Britain. But despite these few victories, it was clear that the aggressive campaigns of the Axis had been overwhelmingly successful. If one looked at a map of continental Europe in early June 1941, one confronted a truly frightening prospect.

The vast majority of the continent by that time was occupied by Nazi troops, or was operating under some variation of puppet government cooperating with the Nazis. This was the case in Poland, France, Belgium, the Netherlands, Luxembourg, Denmark, Norway, Slovakia, Hungary, Romania, Bulgaria, Yugoslavia, and Greece. The Soviet Union and Nazi Germany were treaty partners and had cooperated in splitting Poland between themselves. The Baltic nations were by now also under Soviet control. Fascist Italy occupied most of Greece, all of Albania, parts of southern France, and large areas of Yugoslavia. In France's "unoccupied" and supposedly independent rump state (known as Vichy France after the new capital city), an extreme right-wing government had been assembled under the leadership of Henri Philippe Pétain. His government aided the Nazis in numerous ways, and his Vichy state bore frightening similarities to the fascist dictatorships. Spain was now under the dictatorship of Generalissimo Francisco Franco, who was busy consolidating his own power

The Axis occupation of Europe by December 1941. (ABC-CLIO)

after the nightmare of the Spanish Civil War. He stunned the Axis powers by remaining a noncombatant in the war, he but provided aid to the Axis powers in a number of secretive ways. Though no friend to Nazi Germany, Portugal was also under the quasi-fascist dictatorship of Antonio Oliveira de Salazar's Estado Novo and was officially a noncombatant nation. Only Switzerland and Sweden were officially designated "neutral" countries. After June 1940 the only nations left at war with the Axis powers were the United Kingdom and its imperial allies. In general terms, Europe was a continent under complete control by ruthless dictatorships implementing the policies of their pitiless ideologies—Nazism, fascism, and Stalinist communism. The future for the people of Europe looked quite bleak indeed; as for despised minorities and ethnic groups like Jews, the Roma, and Slavs, among others, they were facing a future of mass enslavement and extermination. If the United Kingdom were to reach an agreement with the Axis powers, or to finally succumb to military defeat, the war would be over and there would be no stopping whatever murderous programs the Axis decided to implement. The outside world would be facing an entire continent under the control of totalitarian dictatorship. The implications of such a prospect are chilling to imagine.

THE AXIS CONQUEST OF EUROPE 1938–1941

How did the European continent come to be dominated by the fascist dictatorships of the Axis powers? The process began before the Second World War actually commenced and began to take shape soon after Adolf Hitler came to power in January 1933. Hitler's government invested tremendous amounts of economic resources into the national project of rearmament. This was expressly prohibited by the Treaty of Versailles, the agreement imposed upon Germany by the victorious powers after the conclusion of the First World War. Convinced that Germany's aggressive militarism had been the primary cause of the Great War, the victorious powers at the Paris Peace Conference imposed highly restrictive conditions on Germany. The treaty assigned all blame for the war to Germany and her allies, removed Germany's overseas colonies, reduced the size of the German nation, required crushing reparations payments, and imposed strict limitations on Germany's armed forces. Germany's army would be limited to only 100,000 men; its navy was reduced and submarines prohibited; Germany was also strictly prohibited from establishing a military air force.[1]

An essential component of the Nazi political program had always been to dissolve the Treaty of Versailles and to free Germany from such restrictions. Hitler and his Nazis ranted against Germany's virtual slave status and demanded that Germany must build its military strength in order to recover its rightful level of self-determination. As such, when Hitler was appointed chancellor in January 1933, he almost immediately began steps to rebuild Germany's military strength. The process had actually been going on in secret ways during the days of the Weimar Republic but had realized only modest gains. The requirements of secrecy forced the Germans to take surreptitious steps, like building surplus civilian aircraft that could one day be converted to military purposes if necessary. Under Hitler, however, rearmament became open and public by 1935. In that year Germany signed the Anglo-German Naval Agreement with Great Britain, which allowed Hitler to expand his navy. Later that year he announced to the world that Germany was creating a military air force—the Luftwaffe. Also during 1935, Hitler had reinstated conscription to increase the size of all of Germany's armed services. By early 1938 the Nazi war machine was becoming formidable. Hitler now began to use his growing power to intimidate neighboring states and to bring about another cherished objective of Nazi ideology: the reunification of the German people into a single German political state. After the Great War, the negotiations at the Paris Peace Conference had resulted in the creation of new nations within Central and Eastern Europe. With the dissolution of the Austro-Hungarian Empire and the reduction of the size of Germany, ethnic Germans found themselves living in nations like Czechoslovakia, Poland, the Austrian Republic, and even Italy. Nazi ideology, championed by a furious Adolf Hitler, demanded that all these ethnic Germans be reunified into a greater German Reich.

In the spring of 1938, Adolf Hitler began translating that racially based ideology into political reality. He began by resuming his efforts to bully the Austrian government into renouncing its own independence and forming some kind of amalgamation with the German Reich. Exactly what form this amalgamation would take never was clearly defined, but through the agents of the Austrian Nazi Party, Hitler's government created demonstrations, riots, and street violence to escalate tensions. Eventually Hitler's demands increased with his insistence that prominent Austrian Nazis be appointed to key positions in the Austrian cabinet. With tensions at a boiling point, Hitler invited the Austrian chancellor, Kurt Schuschnigg, and his diplomatic corps to his residential complex at Berchtesgaden for talks. In these talks Hitler intensified his bullying tactics, even openly threatening to send a military invasion. Cowed and browbeaten, Schuschnigg agreed to increased levels of Nazi participation in his cabinet, but after returning to Austria, he came up with a masterstroke of his own. Since Hitler insisted that the Austrian people have the freedom to choose a union with Germany, Schuschnigg announced that there would be a great plebiscite on the matter—The Austrians would have the chance to cast their votes. This greatly alarmed Hitler and sent him into a rage. After all, if the Austrians voted against unification with Germany, then Hitler's efforts would be seen by the world as the naked aggression they certainly were. Rather than allow any vote to take place, Hitler sent his troops rolling into Austria on the morning of March 13, 1938. On the heels of the tanks were the men of the SS, who quickly rounded up and arrested the key leaders of the anti-Nazi community: socialists, trade union leaders, Jews, and so on. Afraid of a pointless bloodbath, the Austrian government gave the order for no military resistance to take place. As a result, Hitler was able to absorb Austria into Germany with remarkable ease. Mussolini's Italy, once the champion of Austrian independence, now made no step toward intervention. Mussolini had strained relations with the democracies and taxed his own resources in his conquest of Abyssinia. Realizing that he needed good relations with Germany more than ever, Mussolini let Hitler know that Italy would take no steps to protect Austria. Once the German military had secured Austrian territory, the passage of a few laws formally dissolved its government, and Austria ceased to exist as a sovereign nation. It was now merely an administrative district of the German Reich.[2]

Later in the year, Hitler began to make threatening references about the German-speaking peoples in the borderlands of neighboring Czechoslovakia. In these areas bordering Germany, known as the Sudetenland, there was a German-speaking majority, many of whom longed for incorporation into the German nation. The Czechoslovakian government, unsurprisingly, was adamantly opposed to losing sovereign territory and some of its most important military fortifications. Hitler, however, continued exploiting the tensions between the Czechs and the Sudeten Germans to demand that these German-speaking peoples be given their rights of "self-determination." The tensions with Czechoslovakia were even more strained because of treaty obligations between France and Czechoslovakia. Great Britain also had treaty agreements with France, and so the possibility loomed that a German invasion of the Czechoslovakian Sudetenland could trigger a general European war. But Hitler was convinced that the French wanted no part of an armed conflict over Czechoslovakia and would find any excuse to slip out of their obligations. Nor did he think that the British government supported any level of armed conflict over issues in Eastern Europe. His conclusions about the democracies proved correct. As his ultimatums to the Czechoslovakian government intensified and the date fast approached for Hitler's threatened military action, last-minute talks were arranged. Brokered by Mussolini, negotiations were held at Munich involving Britain, France, Italy, and Germany. Czechoslovakian representatives were barred from participation. The parties reached an agreement whereby France and Britain would allow Germany to annex the Sudetenland into the German state without honoring their obligations to aid Czechoslovakia. In return, Hitler gave verbal assurance that this would be his last expansionist move in Europe—that this would complete his efforts to reunify the German people. The British prime minister, Neville Chamberlain, returned to a hero's welcome in Britain and announced that war had been averted. Later that day, at 10 Downing Street, he spoke to the public again and assured them that he had "returned from Germany brining peace with honor. I believe it is peace for our time. We thank you from the bottom of our hearts. Now I recommend you go home, and sleep quietly in your beds."[3]

Chamberlain's efforts to avert a conflict are a matter of intense debate even today. There were some critics at the time, like Winston Churchill for example, who criticized the democracies harshly for backing away from a situation that demanded resolve. But generally, the Munich Agreement that Chamberlain helped to secure was seen as a miraculous diplomatic coup, preserving peace in an almost impossible situation. But events only months later made the Munich Agreement and Chamberlain's hopeful words about "peace for our time" seem darkly ridiculous. Hitler moved into the Sudetenland in early October, whereupon the Czech president, Edvard Beneš, resigned in protest over the dismemberment of his state. A few months later, during early March 1939, the Germans pressed their occupation farther into the remaining territories of Czechoslovakia. The regions of Bohemia and Moravia, which included the capital city of Prague, were made into a "protectorate" of the German state under a colonial governor. The Slovakian region was allowed to create its own Nazi-friendly government, which remained a German ally throughout the war. The Nazi Empire had begun to take its initial shape. By the spring of 1939, two sovereign European nations had disappeared from the map and were under Nazi domination.

The appeasement policies of the French and British governments had been shown to be a disastrous failure, and any commitments made by Hitler had been proven worthless. While outrage grew in the democracies over the Czech fiasco, by March 21 Hitler was making new demands. This time Hitler was aiming his threats at the nation of Poland and the free city of Danzig. Poland had been reinstated as a sovereign nation as a result of the Paris Peace Conference. To give Poland access to the Baltic Sea, the diplomats at Paris granted to Poland a long tract of territory running through the German nation. At the Baltic coast, that strip of territory ended at the formerly German port city of Danzig. This strip of territory, which divided Germany into two non-contiguous pieces, came to be known as the "Polish Corridor." Now Hitler demanded that Danzig be returned to Germany and that the Polish Corridor be modified to allow German access to the city. Hitler's diplomats insisted that the Poles would be given the right to use the port, but the Poles saw the entire issue as a

German bullying tactic to encroach on Polish territory. Distressed at Germany's aggression with Austria and Czechoslovakia, both France and Britain now publicly pledged to defend Polish independence in the case of German aggression.

In the face of the pledges by France and Britain to protect Polish independence, Adolf Hitler searched for a foreign policy move that could neutralize the commitments of the democracies. If he could secure a visible alliance with another major power, when he attacked Poland the democracies would face a war against two nations, rather than just Germany alone. To this end, Hitler persuaded Mussolini and his government to sign a defensive and economic alliance on May 22, 1939. The formal title of the agreement was "The Pact of Friendship and Alliance between Germany and Italy," but it soon became known by the very fascist-sounding title "The Pact of Steel." While committing the two nations to an enhanced economic and diplomatic relationship, the most significant stipulation was in Article III, which committed each nation to help the other in the event of "military complications."[4] Now if Hitler invaded Poland and Britain and France decided to intervene, they would be fighting both Italy and Germany. Hitler felt sure that this would intimidate those two countries into backing away from their pledges of Polish support.

The extreme tensions generated by the Polish situation and the growing fear of war overshadowed another territorial expansion that took place only a week after the democracies pledged to defend Poland. In the south of Europe, Mussolini launched an invasion to formally conquer the nation of Albania. Italy had worked to assert influence over Albania through the 1920s and 1930s. Mussolini had signed the First Treaty of Tirana (1926) and the Second Treaty of Tirana (1927) to engineer a defensive alliance with the Albanians. He had given monetary loans to aid the Albanian government and had sent Italian advisors to help shore up the Albanian armed forces. Albania's King Zog, however, recognizing the acquisitive tendencies of the fascist dictatorships, began to stiffen his resolve to maintain Albanian independence. He refused to renew the Tirana treaty and signed trade agreements with Yugoslavia and Greece in a bid to reduce Italian economic influence. As Hitler moved to occupy Czechoslovakia and threatened Poland, Mussolini was acutely aware of the increasing power of Germany and the appearance of Italian weakness; it was becoming clearer that in the alliance between the two dictatorships, Italy was the junior partner. To remedy this problem of diminishing prestige and to solve the problem of King Zog's resistance, Mussolini decided to invade and conquer Albania. Italian troops moved in on April 7 and within two weeks had defeated the tiny level of armed resistance. The Albanian army was sabotaged by its Italian advisors, who disabled the army's large guns and removed ammunition. As a result, most of the resistance was organized by

Albanian civilian patriots and armed police. Only about 700 Italians were killed in the conflict, and by April 12 all of the port cities, the capital city, and the military facilities were in Italian hands. King Zog fled into exile in Greece, and Albania became part of the Italian fascist empire.[5]

The summer of 1939 was extremely tense, but no significant move was made by a major power. Then, on the morning of August 24, people all over the world awoke and read a remarkable story in their newspapers over breakfast. Hitler's Nazi Germany and Stalin's Soviet Union had signed a formal agreement of "non-aggression." This was a stunning development. Since its inception, the Nazi Party had railed against Marxism of all shades as the most dangerous threat to Western civilization. Nazi ideology sought to eliminate all traces of Marxist influence in Germany and supported all efforts to undermine communism and socialism anywhere. Hitler had also written in his book *Mein Kampf*, in 1925, that it was Germany's historic destiny to attack and conquer the lands of Russia for the expansion of the German race. The vast areas of *Lebensraum* (living space) could be secured for German racial expansion, the Soviet Union's vast natural resources could be appropriated, and the fountainhead of world communism could be eliminated forever.[6] Likewise, Marxists in Europe, whether revolutionary socialists, democratic socialists, or Soviet-style communists, saw fascism as the most lethal of the enemies of the people. Communist ideology interpreted fascism to be the last desperate attempt of the forces of big capital to preserve their system. Communist and fascist ideologies were supposedly diametrically opposed, and each was out to eliminate the other. But now Nazi Germany and the communist Soviet Union had signed an agreement of alliance. The Nazi–Soviet Non-Aggression Pact simply said that neither nation would move to intervene against the other in the event of the other nation making any kind of military or expansionist move. There was, however, a secret protocol in the pact that was only revealed after the end of the Second World War. This secret section divided Poland and the Baltic nations into German and Soviet "spheres of influence." In essence, the western part of Poland would become German territory and the eastern regions would revert to Stalin's Soviet Union. Also, the Baltic nations were set aside as a Soviet "sphere of influence." With the Pact of Steel in place with Italy, and now the Non-Aggression Pact signed with the Soviet Union, Adolf Hitler felt he was sufficiently protected to move forward with his plans for the conquest of Poland.

In the last week of August, the British were once again attempting last-minute negotiations with Hitler's government to appease Germany's demands regarding Danzig and the corridor. The British yet again were amenable to German demands. They thought, however, that Hitler's insistence on a Polish representative to immediately appear and sign these demands into reality was unreasonable. From here the negotiations broke down. This was no disappointment for Hitler; despite a few arguments against war from his inner circle, Hitler decided that the time was right to move into Poland with all his nation's might. On September 1, 1939, German troops crashed across the Polish border. The invasion of Poland was massive in scale and involved numerous tank divisions and a devastating aerial bombing attack. The Polish armed forces were significantly outnumbered and possessed vastly outdated weapons and tactics relative to the German Wehrmacht (the regular German army). Film footage still exists recording Polish mounted horse cavalry charging German tanks and being blown to pieces. The Polish defensive effort was pushed back at every front. By September 17 the Poles were forced to withdraw deep into the eastern or southern regions of the country, but on that very day the Soviet Union launched its own massive invasion of eastern Poland. The Soviets sent in an army of 800,000 men—a number that easily overwhelmed the already devastated Polish force. German forces were finally able to take Warsaw, Poland's capital city, on September 29. By October 2 the last Polish stronghold at Hel was overrun and the campaign essentially over. The western side of Poland was in German hands, the eastern under Soviet domination. In the years to come, the Polish people would suffer perhaps more than any other in the war—forced from their homes, forced into slave labor, randomly executed. For the Jews of Poland, they would be hunted down and segregated into urban ghettos, or more often gunned down in mass executions and tossed into mass graves. By 1942 the effort to exterminate Jews was intensified and refined into the industrialized system of death camps, gas chambers, and incinerators known as the Holocaust.[7]

What role did the British and the French play in stopping the conquest of Poland? Those nations played no significant role. Both France and Britain demanded that Hitler remove his troops after September 1; each nation pledged that war would be inevitable if he did not. Hitler did no such thing, and as a result, both France and Britain declared war on Germany by September 3.

In Chamberlain's radio address to the people of Britain, he sounded like a man defeated, but he did spell out the reality of the situation. His words have mostly been forgotten, especially in the wake of Winston Churchill's far more inspiring rhetoric to come later. But on September 3, Chamberlain told the British people,

> This morning, the British ambassador in Berlin, handed the German government, the final note, stating that unless we heard from them, by 11 o'clock, that they were prepared at once, to withdraw their troops from Poland, a state of war would exist between us. I have to tell you now, that no such undertaking has been received, and that consequently, this country is now at war with Germany. . . . We have a clear conscience; we have done all that any country could do to establish peace. The situation in which no word

given by Germany's ruler could be trusted, and no people or country could feel itself safe had become intolerable . . . Now may God bless you all. May He defend the right. It is the evil things we shall be fighting against—brute force, bad faith, injustice, oppression, and persecution—and against them I am certain that the right will prevail.[8]

But with war declared, what did France and Britain offer Poland in terms of tangible military assistance? Very little indeed. Geography was part of the problem. To get troops and equipment into the area, Britain and France would have to pass through Germany itself on land. Poland was such a distance away that flying into the area was terribly problematic, and using ships in the Baltic would mean battles at sea. There was no sure way to get assistance to the Poles. The only real assistance that either power could render was to launch a massive attack on Germany itself from the west. Neither side felt it was prepared for such an attack, and so Poland suffered its brutal defeat, all the time praying for reinforcements from its allies that never came.

In the months to follow, a strange stillness moved across Europe. The Nazis began the process of "reorganizing" Poland but did not launch any attacks anywhere else. Likewise the French and British scrambled to prepare their military forces, build equipment, and train soldiers, but initiated no attacks. This rather surreal state of war, with no combat, continued through the end of 1939 and into March 1940. In British discourse this period became known as the "Phony War." But, although this was the case between these three powers, there did take place a major conflict in the far northeast of Europe. The months of the "Phony War" were not entirely silent.

In the secret protocols of the Nazi–Soviet Non-Aggression Pact, the area of Finland was designated to be within the Soviet sphere of influence. By the late 1930s, Joseph Stalin had reversed his earlier Soviet policy of alliance with Finland and acknowledgement of existing borders. Stalin became convinced that for improved security, the Soviets needed to reclaim vast parts of Finland that had once belonged to Imperial Russia. Efforts at negotiations with the Finns in the late thirties had amounted to nothing, with the Finns firmly rejecting any Soviet claims even to Finnish islands in the Baltic. Now, with the war under way and with the assurance that Germany would not intervene, Stalin made his move against Finland. On November 30, 1939, a massive Soviet invasion crossed into Finnish territory. Immediately upon doing so, Stalin created a puppet government at the first major city to be captured, Terijoki. From that point this duplicate, Soviet-sponsored government became known as the "Terijoki government." But the official Finnish government remained in Helsinki and conducted the defense against the Soviets. The Finns surprised the world with their tenacious resistance. The Soviets eventually had to pour significant resources into the so-called Winter War, until they reached a ratio of four men to one. Eventually they wore down the Finns, and they negotiated a peace by March 12, 1940. The Soviets now claimed large tracts of Finnish territory in the southern region of Karelia and, in the north, the region of Salla. The Soviets also claimed a number of islands in the Gulf of Finland. Certainly, Adolf Hitler took careful notice of the ineptitude of Soviet military forces, and the limited gains that the Soviets were able to claim.[9]

Hitler was very busy with his generals at this time, planning his next major moves in the west of Europe. Those plans were unleashed early on the morning of April 9, as the Nazis put Operation Weserubung into action. Weserubung was the code name for the simultaneous invasion of both Denmark and Norway. Norway was a vital area for Nazi Germany because of its production of iron ore, along with Sweden. Those Scandinavian iron ore centers were in the extreme north, and the ore was shipped from the Norwegian port of Narvik. So crucial was this supply of raw materials to Germany's war effort that the British had been discussing for some time how to block German shipments, through mining its waters or even outright occupation. Hitler became convinced that Germany must preempt any Anglo-French move in Norway, and this would have the added benefit of providing important naval bases for German operations against the British in the North Sea and the Atlantic. Denmark offered no significant supplies to Germany but occupied a key piece of geography. Denmark would be needed as a staging area for the invasion of Norway, and it provided important air bases for control of Northern Europe. Finally, there was the simple fact that if Denmark remained neutral, it could provide a staging area for Germany's enemies immediately on her northern border. For all these reasons, Hitler had insisted, sometimes against the protests of his military planners, upon going ahead with the invasions together. At around 4:00 AM on April 9, German troops moved across the borders of Denmark and approached a series of principal Norwegian ports, with naval support from troop carriers and its U-boat fleet. In Denmark, the aerial bombing attacks on Danish airfields and the advance of German troops convinced the king of Denmark, Christian X, that serious armed defense was folly. In a matter of hours, he and the rest of the Danish government agreed to capitulate to the Germans. Their only condition was to keep their independent government in place to handle Denmark's domestic affairs. The Germans ultimately agreed, and so because of this almost immediate surrender, the Danes received quite lenient treatment relative to the other areas of occupied Europe.[10]

In Norway, the Germans sailed into a number of important Norwegian ports, landing on that morning of April 9. In rapid succession they hit Oslo, Kristiansand, Egersund, Stavanger, and Bergen in the south, Trondheim on the northern coast, and Narvik in the far north. Armed Norwegian ships put up resistance but were quickly overcome and sunk. On land, the Germans were dropping large numbers of paratroops (this was the first opposed paratroop operation in military history), and though brave, the Norwegian military was no match for the German troops. Most of these areas fell within the day, and by the evening of April 9, the pro-Nazi politician Vidkun Quisling announced by radio that he and his followers had taken the government in a coup d'état. In fact, he had discussed this with leading Nazis before the invasion took place, and it was agreed that a Norwegian government should immediately seize power. The legitimate government of Norway was sent into hiding, including its monarch, King Haakon VII, and others from the royal family.[11]

The British responded immediately to the German invasion of Norway, sending numerous ships to engage with the German navy and large numbers of ground troops to assist the Norwegians on land. There was serious land combat in all the major Norwegian centers including Oslo, Trondheim, and Narvik (where in fact the town was temporarily taken back from the Germans). The fighting lasted through April and into late May. The British were assisted by a contingent of French soldiers, sent by the French government in early May, and also by groups of Polish soldiers who had escaped in 1939, and who had agreed to continue fighting against the Nazis. Eventually, though, the Allied armies were forced to withdraw. By the last week of May, Allied forces were almost entirely gone, and the legitimate Norwegian government was facing the agonizing reality that it would have to leave the country. On June 7 the members of the Norwegian cabinet and the royal family departed for England on the British battle cruiser *Devonshire*, where they would now work to establish a Norwegian government-in-exile. One of the principal reasons that the Allies had withdrawn from the Norwegian fight so early, and without expanding operations there, was that Hitler had already launched another, even more frightening invasion during May: the invasion of the Low Countries, and of France itself.

On May 10, 1940, Hitler's Germany launched its most audacious attack to date. In a mass movement of troops, the German army moved into the Netherlands, Belgium, Luxembourg, and France in a virtually simultaneous series of invasions. While Hitler had pulled off numerous coups by this time, France stood out as his greatest gamble. France was considered one of the world's "great powers" and considered to have the strongest military forces in continental Europe. It was no surprise that the Netherlands, Belgium, and Luxembourg could put up only token resistance—but France was expected to make a convincing stand against Germany. Great Britain had been sending troops into France since the opening days of the war, but by March 1940, it had expanded its British Expeditionary Force (BEF) to some 316,000 men. The French, during the interwar years, had invested the bulk of their defense budget into developing a long line of defensive forts along the German borderlands. It was a technological miracle of the age, featuring massive guns, concrete forts built into the hillsides, underground facilities for huge numbers of troops, and even an underground rail system for troop transport. Named after a French minister of war, André Maginot, the "Maginot Line," as it became known, seemed to be impenetrable. But where the northeast French border with Germany ended and the border with Belgium began, the French ended their line of fortifications. In that borderland area lay the vast and dense Ardennes Forest. Military planners believed that no military force could make a rapid advance through terrain so densely forested; so for French planners, the forest acted as an extension of the Maginot Line of defense.[12]

On May 10, 1940, when Hitler launched the great offensive commencing the Battle of France, however, the German armies were able to move through the Ardennes Forest without great difficulty. The German High Command had adopted new philosophies of battle strategy during the 1930s, based on emerging new technologies. The Germans had been rapidly mechanizing their forces, including the newest models of tanks, bulldozers, and large trucks for the movement of troops, though they still used large numbers of horses as well. The Germans were able to sweep through the Ardennes in a relatively short time and overwhelm the small numbers of French and British troops in that region. The Germans were then able to force French and British troops west, surrounding them and forcing them eventually into a small pocket on the far northern French coast. At this point nearly the entire BEF and large numbers of French troops might have been obliterated by German bombing, or simply taken prisoner. But Hitler called a halt to the advance for his armies to reorganize and regroup. In this brief window of time, the British were able to move their navy quickly into position and to begin requisitioning every available vessel on the British seacoast. Little trawlers, merchantmen, fishing boats, and even yachts were employed in this emergency operation to evacuate the troops from the beach at the French city of Dunkirk. The evacuation at Dunkirk from May 26 to June 4, code named "Operation Dynamo," rescued nearly 340,000 British and French soldiers, who would live to fight again.

The Battle of France was already coming to a close in the early weeks of June. With so many British and French troops out of the way, the Germans began to close in on Paris. The capital surrendered on June 14, and the Germans staged a visible and humiliating spectacle by marching past the Arc de Triomphe and down the Champs-Élysées. The French government, meanwhile, had fled Paris and was making its way to Bordeaux to attempt to carry on the fight. But it soon became apparent that further efforts were futile. France's prime minister, Paul Reynaud, resigned his office on June 16 and was replaced by Henri Philippe Pétain. Pétain, one of France's greatest living heroes from the Great War, believed that defeat was inevitable, and he announced to the nation over the radio that he intended to ask the Germans for an armistice. When notified that Pétain hoped to sign an armistice, Adolf Hitler immediately replied that the meetings would take place in the Forest of Compiègne; this was where the Germans had been forced to sign an armistice in November 1918, in a French railroad car. Now Hitler's staff located the exact railroad car in a local museum and had it brought to the historic location. On June 22, Pétain and his staff were forced to sign humiliating peace terms in the same railcar and in the same location where France had humiliated the Germans 22 years earlier. Germany had her revenge.[13]

The political and geographic consequences of the collapse of France and the Low Countries were as follows. The Netherlands, Belgium, and Luxembourg were all put under German occupation, and their respective governments fled the continent. As the Nazis were swiftly defeating their opponents in this operation, Benito Mussolini decided to declare war on France and Britain on June 10. He initiated attacks in the South of France and would take small portions of French territory along the Italian border in the southeast. The Germans took formal possession of the northern half of France and the entire region along the Atlantic coast, ruling as an occupying power. This gave the Nazis the prestige of controlling Paris and the ability to create defensive fortifications all along the Atlantic coast—a system that became known as the "Atlantic Wall." But Adolf Hitler allowed the nation of France to continue to exist in the southern half of the country. France's ragged collection of politicians moved their capital to the small resort city of Vichy. The sitting president, Albert Lebrun, appointed Pétain as premier, with the full powers and responsibilities of the head of state. From this point Pétain would go about reforming the French government under his own fascist-style dictatorship. Vichy France, as it was called, would now function as a quasi-fascist state and aid the Nazi war effort in several crucial ways, including industrial supply, raw material supply, labor supply, and even lending help to Nazi policies of racial oppression. Although France was still technically a sovereign nation, this small "rump" state was, by necessity, friendly and helpful to the Axis. These were some of the darkest days in French history, and to thousands of despairing French people, it must have seemed that there was no hope for the future. But in the chaos of the defeat, among the thousands of French soldiers that managed to flee, one of France's top tank commanders had escaped to Britain. His name was Charles de Gaulle, and as the undersecretary of war at the time of the French collapse, he refused to accept France's surrender. In Britain he would make his claim to be the head of the French government-in-exile. His organization, "Free France," emerged, through tremendous difficulties, to be the leading organization of the

French resistance and continued to fight the Nazis until France's ultimate liberation in 1944.

The only nation now left opposing the Axis powers was Great Britain, though she could still rely on several of her imperial allies. To bring the war to an early end, Adolf Hitler needed either to reach an agreement with the British or to defeat them. But reaching an agreement now seemed highly unlikely. In May, just as the Battle of France was commencing, Britain had experienced a change of government. Neville Chamberlain had been forced out, and Winston Churchill was now prime minister. Churchill's policy was clear and defiant: Britain would fight the Nazis "in spite of all costs, in spite of all terror." To Churchill and his supporters in Britain, the fight against the fascist dictatorships was a struggle for the future of civilization. There would be no surrender, and there would be no deals with Hitler. So, as Hitler considered options for ending the war, it appeared that Germany would have to attack and conquer Great Britain. The German military plan to accomplish this was code-named "Operation Sea Lion," and its first phases commenced during the summer of 1940.

The German High Command had decided that attempting to land a German ground force to attack Great Britain would be impossible, given the strength of Britain's Royal Navy. In order to be able to launch such an invasion, they decided that significant air attacks on Britain's fleet would be necessary. But in order to neutralize the Royal Navy through air power, Germany had to have control of the skies—in other words, Britain's Royal Air Force (RAF) had to be taken out of the picture before such an operation could be launched. With this in mind, the Germans began to send waves of bombing aircraft across the English Channel to attack Britain's centers of aircraft manufacturing and especially to attack the airfields and facilities of the RAF. The Battle of Britain had begun.

All through July and August German bombers, escorted by fighters, came across the Channel to bomb Britain's industrial cities and air facilities. Britain, of course, fought back using its fleets of fighter planes (the famous Hurricanes and Mosquitos) to attack German aircraft as soon as they were identified. It should also be noted that during this period, British bombers flew missions to Germany and dropped bombs on that nation's industrial centers and air facilities. Both sides caused numerous civilian deaths in their attempts to break the will of the other. But in the skies over Britain, despite their own serious losses, the British were inflicting serious damage on the German air fleets. One crucial reason for this was that the British had a kind of secret weapon in its early stages of operation. This was radar, and the British Air Ministry had been developing the technology since 1935. By 1940, radar stations had been set up along the Channel and North Sea coasts, and radar technicians could identify enemy fleets at a considerable distance. By plotting the eventual location of these fleets,

British fighter planes could be scrambled to ambush the German formations. This was far more difficult during night raids, but still the British inflicted heavy losses. But by the end of the summer, the British numbers and facilities were running extremely thin. In late August, British planes began intensively bombing industrial targets in the German capital city of Berlin. This produced significant civilian casualties and eventually convinced an enraged Adolf Hitler to authorize mass bombing of the city of London, which began in early September. The intensive bombing of London has been forever remembered as "the Blitz," and it continued through September, October, and November. Still, the aims of the German High Command—to terrorize the British and cripple their industrial capacity— were never realized. The shift to bombing London, and away from British airfields, allowed Britain's Fighter Command to recover and continue its attacks. The enormous costs to Germany's Luftwaffe, in terms of the numbers of planes and pilots lost, convinced Hitler to formally postpone Operation Sea Lion by mid-October. By December Hitler decided to call off the invasion of Britain indefinitely.[14] He was determined to focus on a larger and more important project—the future invasion of the Soviet Union— and was concerned that continued action over Britain was threatening the resources needed for that invasion. The British survived the ordeal, and far from breaking British spirits, the Battle of Britain seemed to strengthen the resolve of the British public. It also began to shift American opinion, as several U.S. politicians and military men now believed that Great Britain would survive and should be helped in any way possible.

The war now moved into 1941, and with the immediate threat to Britain removed for the moment, the Axis powers were about to embark on another round of conquests in the east of Europe. On October 28, 1940, while the Battle of Britain was coming to a close, Mussolini invaded Greece, intending to conquer that nation formally and make it part of his empire. Both Mussolini and Hitler saw the future of fascist Italy as the master of Mediterranean and southeastern Europe. "Il Duce" was also becoming increasingly angry and humiliated by Hitler's running the war without consulting him. He famously remarked to his foreign minister and son-in-law, Count Galeazzo Ciano, that "Hitler always faces me with a *fait accompli*. This time I am going to pay him back in his own coin. He will find out from the papers that I have occupied Greece!"[15] And so Mussolini hoped to expand the Italian Empire and startle Hitler with a bold invasion that would command respect. Italian troops poured into Greece on the morning of October 28, 1940, from the Italian-occupied nation of Albania. The Italian ambassador in Greece presented Greece's own quasi-fascist dictator, Ionnis Metaxas, with a set of outlandish demands, including rights for the Italians to set up military bases and occupy Greek territory. Unsurprisingly, Metaxas flatly rejected these demands. With that, the invasion escalated, but the Greeks put up surprisingly strong resistance and eventually pushed the Italians back to the Albanian border, where the battle lapsed into stalemate.

At this point, Adolf Hitler felt he was obligated to intervene in the Greek situation. Far from gaining respect for Mussolini's armed forces, Hitler felt that their bungling failure in Greece had now put German security at risk. Hitler had been pleased when, at the beginning of the war, the Metaxas government had declared Greek neutrality. With Albania occupied by Italy and Greece neutral, this meant that Germany's expansion in Eastern Europe was protected from Allied invasion from the southeastern Mediterranean. But now with the Italian invasion of Greece, the British had responded (per their treaty obligation) by sending troops and air support to defend the Greek mainland. Greek and British forces were successful in holding back the Italian advances, and it looked quite possible that British forces would be in Greece for the foreseeable future. That meant Greece could now be used as a staging area to attack Germany's territories in Eastern Europe. Hitler believed he had to take action.

While Hitler and his staff were planning their intervention in Greece, the situation became more complicated. The nation of Yugoslavia had been under the government of Prince Paul, a member of the Yugoslav royal family, since 1934, when the king, Alexander, had been assassinated. Prince Paul did not claim the throne but instead ran the country as a regency, which operated in reality as a virtual dictatorship. When World War II broke out, the Yugoslavs attempted to remain neutral. But three of their prominent Balkan neighbors—Hungary, Romania, and Bulgaria—all eventually signed onto the Tripartite Pact, the treaty that bound Nazi Germany, fascist Italy, and Imperial Japan. Their accession to this alliance made them Nazi allies, and the German government was increasing the pressure on the Yugoslavs to sign on as well. Eventually, on March 25, 1940, Prince Paul's government signed the documents to become part of the Pact, though this caused tremendous outrage and protest throughout the country. Two days later, a group of top-ranking officers in the Yugoslav air force carried out a coup d'état and seized power. General Dušan Simović took control and immediately announced that his new government refused accession to the Tripartite Pact, and hence the signature was void. Yugoslavia would remain neutral. Hitler was outraged by this development and issued directives that Yugoslavia was to be invaded and conquered as a hostile enemy. As this was only days away from his anticipated invasion of Greece, German plans were modified to launch the invasions of the two nations simultaneously.

On the morning of April 6, 1941, an enormous German invasion rolled into both Yugoslavia and Greece. In Yugoslavia, the battle lasted only about two weeks, with the members of the newly installed government fleeing to safety in Britain. In the course of about 20 days, British and Greek forces were overwhelmed in Greece, Athens was taken, and the Greek king and his government fled to take refuge on the island of Crete. The majority of the British Expeditionary Force also retreated to Crete. On May 20, however, the Nazis launched another major operation invading Crete, this time using large numbers of airborne paratroops. The battle was ferocious but lasted only a week's time. After seven days the British forces began to withdraw, and Greece's King George II fled to British Egypt. By June 1 both Greece and Yugoslavia were in Axis hands. Yugoslavian and Greek territory was divided up, with Germany taking control of most of the central Serbian territory in Yugoslavia but only some of the northern territories of Greece, and most of Crete. The Italians were given the majority of the Greek mainland to occupy and the western and southern regions of Yugoslavia. Now two more nations had been wiped off the map, replaced with a patchwork of "occupation zones." The Yugoslav government-in-exile established itself in Britain, the exiled Greek monarchy in Egypt.[16]

Even with this stunning string of victories, Adolf Hitler had not yet realized his most grandiose dream: the conquest of the Soviet Union. With the Balkan campaign over by the end of May 1941, Hitler could return his full attention to the enormous plans for a Soviet invasion. The great enterprise would be code-named "Operation Barbarossa," and it would represent the largest ground campaign in history. It is worth reminding ourselves that the Soviet Union and Nazi Germany were still alliance partners, having signed the Nazi–Soviet Non-Aggression Pact in August 1939. Hitler, of course, had only agreed to this treaty for the sake of expediency, but his permanent ambitions in Russia had remained unchanged. Now, in June 1941, he would move. At 3:15 AM on June 22, the invasion commenced with legions of German bombing planes hitting Soviet defenses and cities. Tanks and ground troops then rolled across the Soviet borders. The story of the Nazi–Soviet conflict is enormous in scale, and it is well beyond the scope of this brief overview to delve into its details. But the initial phase of the Nazi invasion was spectacularly successful and captured vast tracts of Soviet territory in a very short time. The Soviets certainly had been preparing defenses along their border, but they were nowhere near prepared for an invasion of this scale. They were overrun and overwhelmed. Joseph Stalin, the Soviet premier, had been informed by his intelligence services that German forces had been moving into position for weeks prior to the actual invasion. But Stalin refused to believe that Hitler would attack the Soviet Union at this time. Whether he believed that he could truly trust Hitler seems doubtful, but certainly he was convinced that an invasion was not imminent as long as Britain remained a combatant in the west. Seven days into the invasion, Stalin acted very mysteriously and withdrew from operations to a small dacha. For a few days, no one knew where he was or even if he was alive. Was he having health problems or a nervous breakdown of some sort? Or was he creating a situation where his political colleagues and commanders had to come beg him to lead them? As his biographer Robert Service tells us, "The truth will never be known since Stalin never spoke of the episode."[17] Eventually Stalin emerged and continued to work with his commanders to deal with the German invasion as best they could. The war in the Soviet Union would be unspeakably savage. Hitler had given orders that no quarter was to be given to the people he considered subhuman. And so entire towns were razed, entire villages were gunned down, and individual atrocities of sadistic cruelty were encouraged. In the end, our best estimates indicate that some 26 million human beings were killed by the Nazis in the Russian campaign, the vast majority of them civilian casualties. Germany lost close to 4.5 million military dead. It was the largest scale of any of the theaters in the Second World War.[18]

But initial penetration by the Nazis into the Soviet Union in the summer of 1941 represents the point of maximum extent of the Axis domination of Europe. By that terrible summer, all nations on the European continent, save Switzerland, Sweden, and Great Britain, were under the domination of fascist dictatorship in some fashion. But now Great Britain and the Soviet Union had been forced together as allies against the Axis powers. And all over Europe, people were hard at work to try to undermine the Axis in any way they could. All over Europe the resistance networks were taking shape, arms were being stashed, and missions of espionage, sabotage, and outright guerilla fighting were under way.

"EUROPE'S LIFEBOAT": BRITAIN AND THE GOVERNMENTS-IN-EXILE

During the painful period of Axis aggression and conquest from 1935 to 1941, one by one, a number of European governments were dissolved and ejected as Nazi Germany and fascist Italy occupied their nations. But in nearly all cases, the members of these governments worked to hold their organizations together and to establish a base of operations outside their native lands. Some began their operations in France, but after the Nazi conquest of that country in the spring of 1940, like virtually all the governments-in-exile, they ended up in Great Britain. This chapter will close, then, with a brief overview of the various governments-in-exile established after the conquests of their respective nations. The list will be itemized in chronological order, and it will include a general description of the political situation in each home country and of the exile government organization, and list some of its key officials. Given the number of these exiled governments, it can be difficult for students and scholars alike to keep track of the complex array of organizations and individuals. But a basic understanding of the government-in-exile situation is important for a thorough understanding of the complex resistance picture within Europe during the war.

The various governments-in-exile operating during this period were often a source of irritation and frustration for British authorities. These governments were given facilities and financial assistance from the British treasury. This was certainly merited, and sustaining those governments was part of Britain's wider strategy for winning the war—and also for establishing an orderly peace settlement afterward. The Foreign Office continued to be the primary organ of the British government managing the relations with the governments-in-exile, but inevitably issues of war needed to be handled with the exiled officials. The governments-in-exile regularly campaigned for increased levels of resources and higher levels of influence in policy that would affect their home countries. Naturally, this led to conflict at times, as British (and later American) military planners were working with their own set of top priorities. One of the leading responsibilities taken on by the governments-in-exile was to manage the resistance activity in their respective nations under occupation. Here, they worked mostly with the newly created Special Operations Executive (SOE), which will be discussed in the following chapter. Again, SOE priorities and those of the exiled governments often clashed. But later in the war, as these nations were liberated, many of the governments-in-exile were able to return and establish regimes friendly to Britain and America, and to "Western values" in general. As we shall see in subsequent chapters, this did not work in every case. In some cases the resistance movements themselves were able to capitalize on popular support and eliminated their exiled governments altogether.

Below is a list of the nine various governments-in-exile and a brief overview of their situations, along with a few other nations that had similar situations of Axis occupation but did not create a formal government-in-exile.

1. The Czechoslovakian Government-in-Exile

During the Czech crisis of the autumn of 1938, the status and future of Czechoslovakia were very much in question. Adolf Hitler had made clear his intention to annex the German-speaking region known as the Sudetenland and had been working to foment disaffection and agitation in the region. The Munich conference of late September 1938 saw both France and Great Britain agree to allow Hitler to annex that region, without any military intervention on their part—despite French treaty obligations.

Czech prime minister Edvard Beneš had not been allowed to take part in the discussions. The Nazis eventually seized the Sudetenland but then, during the spring of 1939, took the rest of Czechoslovakia by armed invasion. In the Czech-dominated areas, they established the Protectorate of Bohemia and Moravia and put the former Nazi foreign minister Konstantin von Neurath in power as its governor. In the Slovak territories, the Nazis worked with local leadership and allowed a nominally independent Slovakian state to establish itself as a dictatorship under Monsignor Jozef Tiso. Slovakia remained a Nazi ally for most of the war.

The Czechoslovak government was legally disbanded in this process, and the prime minister, Beneš, fled to America, where he took up an appointment as a university professor in Chicago, Illinois. But his former government colleagues soon convinced him to return. They were working together in Paris to establish a government-in-exile. They first created a committee they called the Czech National Liberation Committee, and then they began negotiating with various other European governments to gain formal recognition. The French government, however, was quietly noncommittal when it came to recognizing the Committee as a formal continuation of the old Republic of Czechoslovakia, though the French did allow the Committee to begin reorganizing a Czech army on French soil.

With the fall of France in June 1940 and the ascent of Winston Churchill in Britain, the Committee was able to relocate to London, where it found formal, unambiguous recognition as the legitimate Czechoslovak government. By the end of 1941, both the United States and the Soviet Union had also recognized the Beneš government as the legitimate Czechoslovak government-in-exile. Beneš took the position of president of the republic, with Jan Šrámek acting as prime minister and Jan Masaryk as foreign minister. The government took up residence in a tiny hamlet known as Aston Abbots in the county of Buckinghamshire, in the old church abbey.

2. The Polish Government-in-Exile

On September 1, 1939, Nazi Germany launched its massive invasion of Poland. This is the moment that most consider to be the starting point of the Second World War. As we saw above, the Polish resistance was courageous but doomed to failure by a lack of resources and modern armaments. By early October the fight was essentially over, Poland having been left to its fate by its allies. In the process, the existing president of the Polish Republic, Ignacy Mościcki, resigned and named a successor, the marshal of the Senate, Władysław Raczkiewicz. Raczkiewicz had already escaped to Paris and so immediately upon notification took the oath of office in the Polish embassy in Paris and named a prime minister.

The prime minister, Władysław Sikorski, would emerge as one of the most important Polish leaders of the war. General Sikorski would also take on the responsibilities of supreme command for the Polish armed forces, which continued to fight in several theaters throughout the war. The foreign ministry was given to another prominent figure in Polish history, Edward Raczyński. Like the Czechs, the Poles first established their government in France but then fled to Britain as France collapsed. But unlike the Czechs, the Poles would need to manage a large military force. As Poland collapsed under Nazi attack during September 1939, thousands of Polish soldiers were able to escape by fleeing into neighboring countries and then making their way to France and Britain. As a result, when the Polish government-in-exile was established, it had a political organization and a prominent military organization. Polish troops would fight in numerous campaigns including Norway, France, North Africa, Italy, and in Operation Market Garden at Arnhem. In addition to managing a full army, the Polish exile government also worked to manage relations with the functioning underground resistance within Poland itself. This organization was known as the Polish Home Army or Armia Krajowa. To direct operations in the Polish underground, the government would have to work initially through the SOE, but later through cooperation with the Soviet Union.

3. The Norwegian Government-in-Exile

After the Nazi invasion of Denmark and Norway in early April 1940, Denmark capitulated almost immediately, while the Norwegian campaign struggled on through May. When the Norwegian military was forced to surrender and the Expeditionary Forces had returned home, Norway was officially placed under Nazi occupation. In Norway there was a pro-Nazi political group known as the National Unity Party, under the leadership of Vidkun Quisling. Quisling collaborated with the Nazis and by 1942 was installed as the leader of a puppet dictatorship. The Quisling government was hostile to any resistance efforts and used its resources to track down and suppress those organizations. The Norwegian government in place before the Nazi invasion had been forced to evacuate and took up residence in Great Britain. Norway had been a constitutional monarchy with a prime minister and cabinet from Norway's Labour Party. The entire sitting government left Norway on a British warship on June 7, 1940. This included Prime Minister Johan Nygaardsvold and his full cadre of cabinet ministers as well as Norway's king, Haakon VII and his son, Crown Prince Olav. They took up residence in the Kingston House Estate apartment block in the Knightsbridge area of London and stayed there throughout the rest of the war. The Norwegian government was able to return to Norway on May 31, 1945, after the war in Europe had ended.

4. The Danish Government under Occupation

In Denmark, the Nazi invasion had been so swift and effective against the tiny Danish resistance force that Denmark's king, Christian X, had decided that further resistance was doomed and pointless. Threatened with massive aerial bombing of the civilian population in the capital city of Copenhagen, he formally communicated the nation's surrender on the first day of the attack. His early surrender earned Denmark fairly lenient treatment. The Nazis would occupy Denmark and make use of its natural resources, industry, and strategic advantages, like airfields, but Hitler allowed the Danish government to remain in place. The Danish king and his government continued to function and did not escape to form a government-in-exile. Despite this situation, a robust resistance effort would take shape in Denmark.

5. The Dutch Government-in-Exile

The Netherlands was a country also with a constitutional monarchy in place when the Second World War broke out. It also had reasonably strong relations with Germany. But, this did not stop Hitler's armies when he launched his great invasion of France and the Low Countries on May 10, 1940. Dutch resistance was tiny in comparison to the invading German forces, and the Dutch government surrendered by May 15. Soon after, Holland's Queen Wilhelmina escaped across the Channel to Britain with the sitting Dutch government under Prime Minister Dirk Jan de Geer of the Christian Historical Union Party, and his ministers. There they were installed at the Stratton House apartments on Piccadilly across from Green Park in central London. There was extreme tension in the Dutch government-in-exile between the queen and her prime minister. De Geer was convinced that the war could never be won, and he urged the Dutch government to sign an alliance of friendship with the Nazis (essentially making themselves a subject state to Hitler in exchange for returning home). The queen was adamant that the government would fight on and support the Allies in any way possible, including resistance activities. She eventually dismissed de Geer and replaced him with Pieter Sjoerds Gerbrandy. Gerbrandy worked with the queen and the Allies to use the resources of the Dutch Empire to aid the Allied cause. De Geer would go on to be considered one of the Netherlands' most notorious traitors, returning to the Netherlands where he was a conspicuous collaborator.[19]

6. The Belgian Government-in-Exile

Belgium was attacked as part of Hitler's massive invasion of France and the Low Countries on the morning of May 10, 1940. The Belgians had mobilized quite a large force given the small size of their nation, and memories of German atrocities from the First World War were still fresh in the minds of Belgian citizens. They fought on until May 28, when it was clear that they had been defeated. Belgium was a constitutional monarchy, but its king, Leopold III, elected to surrender himself along with his armies to the German High Command. He was arrested and held in prison until the end of the war. The rest of the Belgian government escaped to the city of Bordeaux on France's southern Atlantic coast. Soon after, it was forced to move to the French city of Limoges. Here the Belgians would try to obtain friendly treatment from Henri Pétain, the new head of state of Vichy France and a collaborator with the Nazis. Pétain ordered the Belgian government to dissolve itself, making it clear in his decree that this was a directive from Nazi Germany. There was a period of internal dissent in the government, and more than one member had escaped to Britain and tried to claim himself the new Belgian "government-in-exile." Finally on October 22, 1940, the elected prime minister, Hubert Pierlot, and a few of his ministers arrived in London. The Belgian government-in-exile was made up of only four ministers, but they were original ministers from the last elected government in Belgium. For this reason the British and other Allied governments formally recognized them. The small Pierlot government took up residency in offices in Eaton Square in the Belgravia district in central London and continued to administer its colony in the Belgian Congo and to aid the Allies however it could, including resistance activities.

7. Luxembourg's Government-in-Exile

The tiny Grand Duchy of Luxembourg was invaded as part of Hitler's great invasion of France and the Low Countries, which commenced on May 10, 1940. The invasion of Luxembourg was met by only the tiniest token resistance and was essentially complete within a matter of days. The head of state, Grand Duchess Charlotte, other members of the ducal family, and the majority of her government ministers fled the country on the day the occupation started, seeing the inevitability of Nazi rule. They left behind a small committee to run the country on a provisional basis and to negotiate with the Nazis, with the aim of retaining Luxembourg's independence. This was dismissed by the Germans, and on July 29, 1940, a Nazi official was made a military governor of Luxembourg and all institutions of Luxembourg's sovereign government were declared dissolved. The grand duchess and her government fled first to Paris, and then after the defeat of France, to Lisbon. Eventually, the government settled in Great Britain, where it was formally recognized as an official government-in-exile. The government was given offices in Belgravia in London at 27 Wilton Crescent, where it remained headquartered through the duration of the war. Today, that building functions as the Luxembourgian embassy to the United Kingdom.

8. The French Government-in-Exile or "Free France"

France was overrun by a massive Nazi invasion by early June 1940. As discussed above, the French government fled to Bordeaux and then fell apart as the Nazis demanded terms. Henri Philippe Pétain was named head of the government, whereupon he announced to the French people that further resistance was futile. He agreed to talks with Germany and capitulated. At this point the sitting president of France, Albert Lebrun, resigned his position, naming Pétain as premier with full powers. It was Pétain who would then put together a new French government that would rule over the southern half of "unoccupied" France, while the Nazis occupied and governed the north of the country and the Atlantic coastline. Pétain's rump state became known as "Vichy France," because the capital had been moved to the small spa town of Vichy. While these events had been going on, however, two other crucial events took place. First, nearly 150,000 French troops were evacuated to Britain in the Dunkirk operation in late May and early June. Second, a member of the French government, the undersecretary for war, Brigadier General Charles de Gaulle, had escaped to Great Britain. De Gaulle quite simply refused to accept the capitulation of France by Pétain. In Britain, he was given the facilities to broadcast a radio message to the French people via the BBC on June 18. In that now-legendary message, he announced that he represented an organization of the "Free French" who were continuing the fight against the Axis, and who would not cooperate with the Pétain regime. This was the clarion call to the French people to begin the process of resistance. It also began de Gaulle's own work on building up an organization to carry on the fight. De Gaulle was able to gain recognition and support from Winston Churchill, and so he established offices at Carlton Gardens in London. Here he would go through the painstaking work of recruiting soldiers to fight alongside the British and later the Americans, to recruit others for government posts, and to recruit those who would work on resistance inside France. Although de Gaulle was the first and most famous figure to announce "Free France," both Winston Churchill and Franklin Roosevelt found him extremely difficult to work with, and both had worries about his political ambitions after the war. Thus, the British and the Americans supported another

French general who had escaped to French North Africa, General Henri Giraud. After the Allied landings in North Africa (known as Operation Torch), there were serious tensions as the British and the Americans both tried to wedge Giraud into control of the Free French effort. Eventually, in January 1943 a conference was held at Casablanca between the Allied leaders, and both Giraud and de Gaulle were invited. A compromise of sorts was worked out as the Allied leaders declared the two men joint leaders of French North Africa, and this led to the creation of the French Committee of National Liberation (CFLN). The new committee served to unify all French imperial territory under the administration of the CFLN and set up the apparatus for the committee to govern those territories. It would also command the Free French military forces that would fight alongside the other Allied armies. Finally, it would seek to manage the resistance operations inside occupied France. Under this new format, however, Giraud's erratic behavior and distaste for politics caused him to fade into the background as de Gaulle emerged as the clear leader of Free France. De Gaulle's organizations had also done the most by far to coordinate and manage the resistance activities within occupied France. By war's end, the French people rallied around de Gaulle as the clear choice to lead the nation into its new era of liberation.

9. The Greek Government-in-Exile

In Greece, a quasi-fascist dictatorship had been in place since April 1936 under Prime Minister Ioannis Metaxas. Greece, like Italy, was a constitutional monarchy. The Greek monarch, George II, had appointed Metaxas and supported his regime, which became known as the "4th of August Regime," for the date when it was formally announced. The Metaxas regime took most of the standard steps of fascist dictatorships— eliminated political parties, eliminated trade unions, made strikes illegal, and censored the press. Despite the kinship in political systems, however, Mussolini bullied the Metaxas regime into war after October 1940. Metaxas died during the conflict, of a throat condition in January 1941. But Greek resistance held the Italians at bay into the spring of that year. At that point Nazi Germany intervened and moved in an overwhelming force that would see Greece occupied by both Germany and Italy. It was in the early phases of the Nazi invasion that the Greek monarch, George II, and his key ministers fled to Crete. The subsequent Nazi invasion of Crete in May 1941 forced the Greek government to move to Cairo in Egypt, then part of the British Empire. It was here in Cairo that the Greek monarchy would spend most of the war. The British government gave King George and his government formal recognition and constantly worked to support the monarchy for its reinstatement after the war. But within Greece two major resistance movements developed, one communist, the other democratic republican. Hence, the monarchy had virtually no influence on events inside the country. Popular support for the monarchy all but disappeared within Greece during the war, and the monarchy found itself irrelevant at war's end, as the Greek people moved into their own civil war.

10. The Yugoslavian Government-in-Exile

Yugoslavia was also a constitutional monarchy in the years leading to World War II. It was a country riven by political, ethnic, and religious differences. Its leaders had tried unsuccessfully to negotiate an independent status in the new fascist order for Europe. The country was attacked and invaded by the forces of Nazi Germany in early April 1941. Its 17-year-old head of state, King Peter II, and his key ministers left during April, taking refuge in a string of locations—Greece, Palestine, Egypt, and finally Great Britain. In London, King Peter and his government would take up residence in Claridge's Hotel, where they remained throughout the war. King Peter's initial government included Dušan Simović as his prime minister, but there would be five prime ministers in office before the end of the war. Back in Yugoslavia, the Axis powers divided up Yugoslavia into a number of states, some administered by Italy, others by Hungary and Bulgaria, and with the most significant portion of the Serbian state under Nazi occupation. Later, elements of the Yugoslav army came together in a resistance movement, led by the royalist general Draža Mihailović, who was anti-Axis but also anticommunist. At the same time, there developed a large communist resistance movement under the leadership of Josip Broz Tito, known as the Partisans and tied to the Soviet Union. This would lead to deeply complicated relations with the British and the Americans, who did not wish to see a communist regime take power in Yugoslavia after the war, but who were also determined to use the Partisans (who were extremely effective) against the Axis. Mihailović's Chetniks, as they were called, often fought the Partisans more vigorously than they did the Axis, and in fact they were known to cooperate with the Germans against Tito at times. Popular support of the monarchy began to fade seriously during the war inside Yugoslavia, and increasingly it became apparent that Tito's communists provided by far the most influential leadership of the general population. The British government helped arrange a settlement in June 1944 between the royal government and Tito's Partisans. King Peter sent his prime minister (Ivan Šubašić, by this time the leader of the Croatian Peasant Party) to the Adriatic island called Vis, where he met with Tito. The two governments signed the Treaty of Vis (also known as the

Tito–Šubašić Agreement), which created a hybrid government. The king remained head of state, while Tito became prime minister in a coalition government, with Šubašić taking the post of foreign minister. The British government pushed the agreement enthusiastically, hoping it would ensure a parliamentary democratic government at war's end. This did not happen, however, as Tito and his supporters were able to take control of the government and create a communist state in the postwar era.[20]

NOTES

1. See Patrick G. Zander, *The Rise of Fascism: History, Documents, and Key Questions* (Santa Barbara, CA: ABC-CLIO, 2016), pp. 129–132. See also Margaret Macmillan, *Paris, 1919: Six Months That Changed the World* (New York: Random House, 2003), pp. 459–483.

2. Perhaps the best description of the progression of the Anschluss remains the classic work by Gordon Brook-Shepherd, *Anschluss: The Rape of Austria* (London: Macmillan, 1963).

3. David Faber, *Munich, 1938: Appeasement and World War II* (New York: Simon and Schuster, 2008), p. 7.

4. Zander, *The Rise of Fascism*, pp. 164–167.

5. Denis Mack Smith, *Modern Italy: A Political History* (Ann Arbor: University of Michigan Press, 1997 [1959]), pp. 398–399.

6. Adolf Hitler, *Mein Kampf*, trans. Ralph Manheim (New York: Houghton Mifflin, 1971 [1925]), pp. 654–655.

7. For an overview of the Nazi and Soviet invasions of Poland from September 1 to October 6, see Antony Beevor, *The Second World War* (New York: Little Brown, 2012), pp. 22–39.

8. Robert Self, *Neville Chamberlain* (Burlington, VT: Ashgate, 2006), p. 381.

9. For an overview of the Winter War, see Beevor, *The Second World War*, pp. 40–51.

10. See David Lampe, *Hitler's Savage Canary: A History of the Danish Resistance in World War II* (New York: Skyhorse, 2011).

11. For a detailed analysis of the Norwegian campaign, see Gerri H. Harr, *The German Invasion of Norway: April 1940* (Annapolis: Naval Institute Press, 2009).

12. Beevor, *The Second World War*, p. 77.

13. For a full description of the Battle of France, see Beevor, *The Second World War*, pp. 79–121.

14. See Roy Conyers Nesbit, *The Battle of Britain* (Stroud, UK: Sutton, 2000).

15. Galeazzo Ciano, *The Ciano Diaries, 1938–1943* (Garden City, NY: Doubleday, 1946).

16. See Sabrina P. Ramet, *The Three Yugoslavias: State Building and Legitimation, 1918–2005* (Bloomington: University of Indiana Press, 2006), pp. 113–162. For a description of the invasion of Greece, see Mark Mazower, *Inside Hitler's Greece: The Experience of Occupation, 1941–1944* (New Haven: Yale Press, 1993).

17. Robert Service, *Stalin: A Biography* (Cambridge, MA: Harvard University Press, 2004), p. 414.

18. For a detailed description of the Russian campaign, see Beevor, *The Second World War*, pp. 186–206.

19. During the period of exile, de Geer was sent by the Dutch government-in-exile on a mission to the Dutch colonies in the East Indies (today's Indonesia). On the trip he contacted the Germans and arranged safe passage back to the Netherlands. There he became a notorious collaborator and wrote a small book on how the Dutch people could best cooperate with their Nazi occupation force. After the war he was tried and jailed. He died in 1960, still protesting his innocence.

20. For a discussion of the transition of the immediate postwar arrangement to a communist dictatorship under Tito, see Phyllis Auty, *Tito: A Biography* (New York: McGraw-Hill, 1970), pp. 229–245.

2

Setting Europe Ablaze

Britain, the United States, and the Creation of the Allied Resistance Organizations

Throughout the period from September 1939 to June 1941, as we have seen in the previous chapter, the Axis powers achieved an astonishing string of military conquests. In conquering and occupying most of Europe, the Axis had eliminated France from the war all together. As of June 1940, only the United Kingdom and its empire remained as combatants against the Axis. As the political and military leadership in Britain confronted an occupied continent and faced the terrifying possibility that their own island might soon be invaded, they began to consider new and "irregular" forms of warfare. Britain was fighting the enemy openly on sea and in the air. But without a British presence on the continent, how could the war be pressed against the Axis from behind the lines? In answering these difficult questions, Great Britain would create two new and unprecedented organizations. One was devoted to resistance and sabotage inside Britain in case of the unthinkable—a German invasion of Britain itself. The other organization, the Special Operations Executive (SOE), would be devoted to creating and coordinating resistance, subversion, and sabotage to be carried out by the peoples of all the occupied countries. The foundations of resistance in World War II were laid within these two British organizations, both created in the summer of 1940. Another important Allied organization would come into being after the United States was forced into the war in December

1941. Recognizing the advanced state of the British intelligence and subversion organizations, the United States created its own Office of Strategic Services (OSS) by June 1942. Together, the SOE and the OSS would work with numerous resistance organizations all over Europe to build resistance groups, arm them, and coordinate their activities in order to inflict the maximum level of damage to the Axis powers' ability to make war.

WAITING FOR "CROMWELL": BRITAIN'S "AUXILIARY UNITS"

The first formally organized resistance group of World War II, designed to harass the enemy through stealth, sabotage, and guerilla tactics, was never called into use. In the earliest days of the war, as the British government contemplated the possibilities of a German invasion, its leaders decided that a special group should be created to attack and harass the invader from the rear. As the British and French efforts to repulse the Nazi invasion of Norway dissolved into a defeat, the question became increasingly urgent—would the Nazis attempt to invade Great Britain? The next great Axis offensive, as we have seen, took place in France and the Low Countries throughout May and into June 1940. It was during this period, as the reality of a French collapse was becoming clear, that steps were taken to create a special force in Britain.

At the urging of the War Office, the Inter-Services Projects Board met in April 1940 to discuss the concept. The Board had representation from the Admiralty, the Air Ministry, the War Office, the chiefs of staff, and the Secret Intelligence Service (SIS). They proposed creating a force with a multipurpose mission, but whose primary mission was "to co-ordinate projects for attacking the enemy by irregular operation."[1] The unit was formally approved by May 27, and it was decided that the group would be organized as a top-secret branch of Britain's "Home Guard." The Home Guard was the force responsible for managing home defense, including preparation of physical defenses, observation, and direction of the public during enemy raids. The new secret branch of this service, then, as a branch of that service, was designated the Home Guard "Auxiliary Units."

The commander in chief of Britain's home forces was General Edmund Ironside, and as he looked around for a capable man to lead this new secret force, he decided upon a man with whom he had served in the past. Colonel Colin Gubbins and Ironside had served together in Russia in the days of the Russian Civil War. At that moment Gubbins was just returning from commanding troops in Norway, where he had distinguished himself, and Ironside knew him to be a master of the techniques of irregular warfare. Gubbins took up the post in June 1940 and immediately began to build a secret resistance infrastructure. As Gubbins understood his mission, it was to create a force that would be virtually invisible to the Germans if they invaded. If the Germans were able to move an invasion onto British shores and then move into the interior, the job of the "Aux Units," would begin. They would, according to Gubbins, "act offensively on the flanks and in the rear of any German troops who may obtain a temporary foothold in this country."[2] They would also provide intelligence to the government and military forces on the status of any enemy troops and equipment movements. It was decided that if a German invasion were detected, the Aux Units were to be put into operation with the announcement of the code word "Cromwell." If such orders came, the units were to go underground and prepare for action.[3]

To accomplish this mission of attacking and harassing an occupying enemy, the first step after recruiting staff had to be to establish secret facilities. The Aux Units devised a network of astounding bunkers throughout the country. These hideouts were dug underground, often lined with metal, and furnished in bare fashion to provide cover for agents and storage for supplies they needed. To avoid identification, the Aux Units came up with ingenious hidden access points—a visible steel door or manhole in the middle of the countryside was a sure giveaway. So they used fake tree stumps, thickets of shrubs, and the bottoms of water troughs in the grazing lands of sheep and cattle.[4] Even British military staff out to inspect the facilities were unable to find them. With these facilities established (and so well hidden), the next step was to accumulate the supplies needed to accomplish the mission. The hideouts could be stocked with bare amounts of canned foods for agents in emergency, but their principal purpose was to house the small arms and explosives needed. Handguns, Sten guns (small submachine guns), hand grenades, and particularly plastic explosives were supplied for the Auxiliaries and stored in large caches in these underground holes, just waiting to be used when the time came. Agents in the Auxiliary Units were organized into small, local cells of no more than ten. Cells generally were not aware of other cells or the locations of other facilities—a practice that would be continued in resistance organizations on the continent. Should a member be captured, it was imperative that he or she had no knowledge of other groups that the Nazis could extract under torture.

In the end, of course, the British Auxiliary Units were never put into use; the Germans were never able to stage a ground invasion of Great Britain. By November 1944, with any invasion threats long over, the Auxiliary Units were disbanded. Not all of their weapons caches, though, were dismantled, and strange and worrying discoveries of these weapons supplies continued into the 1960s. The first chief of the Auxiliary Units, Colin Gubbins, had gotten the group established during the summer and fall of 1940.

But in November 1940, Gubbins, the master of irregular warfare, was assigned to a newly established group that would be concerned with resistance not in Britain but instead in the Axis-occupied territories around the world. It was in this new agency that Gubbins and his approach to war would fulfill their full potential; he had been seconded to the Special Operations Executive.

SETTING EUROPE ABLAZE: THE SOE AND THE INFRASTRUCTURE OF RESISTANCE

One organization, more than any other, came to be involved in the entire spectrum of resistance activities during the Second World War. The British named this organization the Special Operations Executive, or SOE, and it was the one organization that touched nearly all the geographical and functional areas of resistance. It was created just as Hitler was consolidating his occupations in the early summer of 1940, and it endured, through multiple crises and setbacks, until the end of the war. The Special Operations Executive operated within all the European areas of resistance (though its activities in Poland and the Soviet Union were quite limited), in Africa, and also in the Far Eastern theater against the Japanese. The men and women of the SOE pioneered and developed new methods of subversive warfare, recruited the agents to carry it out, established the training infrastructure to prepare those agents, moved them into the theaters of conflict, supplied the technical equipment, and helped create and expand the numerous organizations all over Europe that would carry on the covert war against the Axis. The work was exceedingly dangerous, and the casualty rates for secret agents were appallingly high.[5] Agents who were caught were invariably tortured brutally for their information and then executed. To take on an assignment for the SOE in occupied territory was an act of extreme courage and patriotism.

The reasoning behind the creation of the SOE stretched back to World War I. As European tensions increased during the late 1930s and Britain's military and political experts began to contemplate the nature of a new war against Germany, they focused on some of the lessons from 1914 through 1918. Most military experts thought that another conflict based on mass armies of infantry was highly undesirable and unrealistic. They concentrated more on the use of air and sea power and the new technological weapons at their disposal. But they also believed that another form of warfare would be crucial in any new conflict: economic warfare. Certainly, Germany had been squeezed to the breaking point during the Great War, particularly by Britain's naval blockade, which deprived that country of raw materials, war materiel, and food. This had been one of a few decisive factors in the German defeat.[6] British planners believed that "in the end Germany had only succumbed as a result of the collapse of morale and economic disintegration caused by the British blockade." And if this was true, they asked, "Why should not this weapon now play an even more important role?"[7] This thinking dovetailed with some of the existing beliefs among Britain's political leadership about the stability of the Nazi regime. Prime Minister Neville Chamberlain was convinced that the moderates in Germany were dissatisfied with the radicalism and aggression of Hitler's government and could possibly be convinced to stage a coup and bring him down. Even after the war had begun, Chamberlain continued to hope that "Hitler might be overthrown by moderate forces in Germany under the impact of economic pressure."[8] This was a serious misreading of the situation. As history has shown, Hitler's regime had established itself absolutely, and the "moderate forces" in Germany were either dead, languishing in concentration camps, or cowed into silence and cooperation. Still, in Britain, according to historian David Stafford, the belief in economic warfare as "the *primary* instrument of war and the means to victory was the conventional wisdom of the day, and the mainstay of official strategy."[9]

This conventional wisdom was put into practice as early as 1938 with the formation of three new branches of service. First, a new branch of the General Staff of the War Office was established named GS(R). Later changed to MI(R), this group was tasked with investigating and developing new techniques of "irregular" warfare. The second group was created within the already existing Secret Intelligence Service (SIS), which was under the leadership of the Foreign Ministry. The SIS had been in existence since before the Great War and was the nation's principal organization for collecting foreign intelligence. It would eventually evolve into the famous MI6 of the Cold War era. But in 1938 SIS created a new department called "Section D" to develop strategies for covert operations in enemy territory—that is, to find "how could enemies be attacked, otherwise than by the usual military means."[10] Within SIS a third new group was established that same year as the Department of Propaganda. It soon became known as Department EH because of its headquarters building at Electra House. Its brief was to develop strategies of "black propaganda" and misinformation to be spread in enemy territory to undermine an enemy's war effort. These three departments would form the base of what would one day become the SOE. All three commenced operation in 1938.

After Hitler's violation of the Czech agreement, with German troops moving into the rest of Czechoslovakia, these three groups were directed to begin activities. The same day that Britain formally declared war on Nazi Germany, September 3, 1939, a new ministry was formed called the Ministry of Economic Warfare. Its purpose was to plan and develop strategies for economic pressure and to coordinate the various resources available to apply that pressure, under the leadership of the conservative politician Sir Ronald Cross. The Ministry of Economic Warfare attempted to work with this new group of agencies, but their plans and activities were quite small, underfunded, and ineffective. Operations such as the attempts to disrupt shipments of oil to Germany from Romania were failures.[11]

But priorities changed with the coming of Hitler's spring offensive of 1940. Denmark, Norway, the Netherlands, Belgium, Luxembourg, and then France all fell in rapid succession. By June 1940, Europe had changed dramatically, with much of Western Europe now under Axis domination and with Italy having joined the war on the side of the Nazis. Now as those British military planners considered the role of economic pressure, they were forced to think about injuring the German war effort *outside* Germany—within its occupied territories. On May 19, 1940, with the Nazi conquest of France in process, Britain's chiefs of staff discussed the needs for increased pressure behind the German lines if France were to fall. A strategic analysis paper was produced that defined the kind of effort needed and the kind of organization required to make it happen. The paper was given a very vague title, "British Strategy in a Certain Eventuality," but was clear about what would be required. It read, "A special organization will be required and plans to put these operations into effect should be prepared, and all the necessary preparations and training should be proceeded with as a matter of urgency."[12]

By the time this paper was circulating, there had been a drastic change in Britain's situation. Neville Chamberlain had been forced to step down, and after a brief but intense period of struggle, Winston Churchill had emerged as the choice to take his place as prime minister. It was Churchill's new War Cabinet that eventually concurred with the recommendations of the paper and, in a meeting on May 27, agreed to create the new organization, with Churchill himself a strong proponent. Despite general agreement to create the new organization, there ensued a struggle over the issue of what ministry would control it. The Foreign Office, Military Intelligence, and the Ministry of Economic Warfare all made their cases. In Churchill's new War Cabinet, he had appointed a new man as minister of economic warfare. This was the Labour fireball Hugh Dalton. A member of parliament since 1924 and a prominent Labour voice in economics and foreign affairs, Dalton was able to convince the War Cabinet to place the new Special Operations Executive within his ministry and keep it separate from the War Office. In a letter he wrote to Lord Halifax, the foreign secretary, he made his case for a separate group under his leadership:

> This "democratic international" must use many different methods, including industrial and military sabotage, labour agitation and strikes, continuous propaganda, terrorist acts against traitors and German leaders, boycotts and riots . . . It is quite clear to me that an organization on this scale and of

this character is not something which can be handled by the ordinary departmental machinery . . . What is needed is a new organization to co-ordinate, inspire, control and assist the nationals of the oppressed countries who must themselves be the direct participants . . . [T]he organization should, in my view, be entirely independent of the War Office machine.[13]

By July the charter for the SOE had been completed and the organization formally approved. With this done, Winston Churchill is said to have turned to Dalton and given the instruction, "And now, set Europe ablaze!"

This was the initial spirit driving the SOE, and certainly it reflected Dalton's own ambitions. He and the organization's supporters dreamed of creating large fighting armies, creating constant combat in the enemy's rear, and routinely pulling off acts of sabotage against the enemy's military machine. But this vision faded very quickly. The SOE found itself faced with innumerable limitations. First of all, the realities of the German and Italian occupation forces would not allow for such highly visible and wide-spread subversion activities. If resisters did instigate open acts of violence against the Nazis or fascists, the reprisals were savage, with huge rounds of arrests, trials, tortures, and executions. The Nazis were known for executing entire organizations or sometimes murdering all individuals in a particular village. The SOE found that the various governments-in-exile were adamant about limiting any possibilities for such horrors to be brought upon their people back home. While the SOE was constantly trying to come up with plans for devastating assaults on the Axis, the governments-in-exile were just as consistently insisting that the SOE do nothing to provoke the Axis forces into further atrocities.

Other severe limitations on the SOE vision had to do with the conflict between organizations, some of which saw the SOE as a departmental rival or as a frivolous waste of resources. In the many studies that have been carried out on the history of the SOE, this is a prominent theme—the constant wrangling between government agencies over the SOE's operations. The governments-in-exile, as mentioned above, constantly urged limiting any major operations that might provoke massive Axis reprisals. The SIS (Secret Intelligence Service) was another source of tension. That organization had labored for decades to build up carefully placed agents and networks for intelligence gathering. But active resistance activity—blowing up railroad lines or firing on Nazi troops—put enemy authorities instantly on alert, generating investigations in areas where SIS agents would immediately be put at risk. The last thing the SIS wanted was to bring the attention of the Gestapo to the organizations or geographic areas where their agents were silently gathering sensitive information. This is certainly understandable. Still, from the point of view of the SOE, this would seem to suggest that active subversion could never take place; SIS agents were everywhere. An SOE report on activities in France began by listing the obstacles to SOE activities. The number-one obstacle listed was "Foreign Office limitation preventing any sabotage, limiting activity" and "preaching the gospel of 'go slow.'"[14] SOE historian M. R. D. Foot writes that Foreign Office influence was both "strong and inhibitive," and that they encouraged the "doctrine of 'no bangs without Foreign Office consent.'"[15] The result was a constantly negotiated and often tense relationship between the SOE and the SIS. The ministry that oversaw the SIS, the Foreign Office, often had its own diplomatic reasons for wanting to restrain SOE activity. If a foreign government became aware of British spies and agents operating within its borders, this could do serious harm to the formal diplomatic relations between the nations. This is why the Foreign Office strictly prohibited SOE operations in places like Spain, an ostensibly neutral country (despite its regular aid to Axis nations), where such activity could be highly sensitive.

Another source of difficulty for the SOE was the key issue of logistics and the fact that the SOE was left to rely on help from outside services to get its means of transport to the various theaters around the continent. Given that Britain is an island, there were only two modes of transport that would allow the SOE to move agents, materiel, and information in and out of Europe: air and sea transport. The SOE worked to develop its own sea networks, as will be discussed below, but for air support it had to rely on the RAF. For its needs like the transporting of personnel, parachute drops, or heavy loads of supplies, the SOE needed bombers with heavy payload capacities. Fighter planes were virtually useless. But Bomber Command was quite averse to parting with aircraft it needed to fulfill its own military objectives of bombing Axis cities and facilities. The head of Bomber Command, Sir Arthur "Bomber" Harris (also known as "Butcher" Harris to his critics), was convinced that the accuracy and effectiveness of British bombing were making a direct contribution to winning the war with every mission. Diverting bomber planes to the SOE to build a resistance network that might take shape within months or years, or that might never launch any meaningful assault on the enemy, seemed to him unjustifiable. Also, the SOE's requirements could not always be quantified with a great deal of notice. This tension comes out in a memorandum sent from an RAF analyst to Harris. In it, the author hopes that the RAF might

> try and tie down SOE to reality . . . the resources of SOE at present are so slender that they cannot hope to take on more than a very small portion of their elaborate plans . . . From our point of view . . . we should like to have their requirements at least one month ahead in order that we may try and fit them into our own operation and to divert aircraft for their work. . . . In the past, however, SOE do not appear to have had more than a day to day idea of their requirements.[16]

In the margins there is a penciled response, presumably from Harris, that reads bluntly, "Give them no more aircraft." Later in the war, it became apparent that Bomber Command's efforts were far less effective than they may have thought. The famous "Butt Report," released in August 1941 (named after the civil servant who compiled the research), found that the vast majority of Britain's bombs did not come within even five miles of their targets.[17] In fact there were many examples of "SOE's superiority to Bomber Command in attacking pin-point targets in occupied territory."[18] But all the same, it was true that Bomber Command was focusing its aerial terror on the primary enemy nations (Germany, Italy, and Japan), while the SOE found that it could not operate in those nations with any effectiveness. So the contest between the SOE and Bomber Command continued.

Despite the numerous practical limitations, like transport and the lack of support from other organizations, the SOE began constructing a working organization. Dalton named Sir Frank Nelson as the first director of the SOE in August. Nelson then set about hiring the staff to create the infrastructure of the organization. Perhaps his most important hire in November 1940 was his seconding of a man named Colin Gubbins, who had established the Auxiliary Units. Gubbins would soon be assigned to head up both the SOE's operations and the training areas. If there was a single personality that most characterized and shaped the SOE, it was Gubbins. He is the man who conceived the training structure of the organization and primarily constructed its training syllabus—that is, the actual training given to recruits. It was Gubbins who was primarily responsible for conceiving the kinds of operations that would be used to undermine the enemy—he was a true expert and pioneer in the art of "irregular warfare." Here there is a historical debate regarding the traditional story of the SOE. The traditional view about the SOE was that Gubbins and his colleagues conceived the arts of "irregular warfare" virtually on their own, out of necessity and without any precedents. This view has been recently challenged by A. R. B. Linderman in his book *Re-Discovering Irregular Warfare: Colin Gubbins and the Origins of Britain's Special Operations Executive* (2015), which puts forth the argument that Gubbins and his staff used a number of historical examples (some from their own experience) to assemble the strategies for the SOE. The techniques of resistance and irregular operations came from past examples like T. E. Lawrence and the Arab Revolt during World War I, the Russian Civil War, the terrorist operations of the IRA, terrorist operations from the Indian independence movement, the Spanish Civil War, and the Chinese Civil War, among others.[19]

That the SOE operations and research staff used historical examples for inspiration in their planning takes nothing away from their accomplishment in building a large-scale, functioning resistance network throughout the world. Out of almost nothing they built an organization with high levels of training, pioneering new technologies and an administrative structure for direction and control. While historical examples may have existed for inspiring strategies, virtually no organizational structure or pool of talent existed when the organization was created. As Gubbins was later to recount, "There was ... practically nothing existing, just one explosives school and a dozen officers and civilians . . . There was no contact with anyone in the occupied countries, no wireless, no personnel, no special equipment, no aircraft—in fact—blank. All this had to be built up from scratch."[20]

The head offices of the SOE were established in London at 64 Baker Street, and by 1943 most of the buildings on the west side of the street had been requisitioned by the various subgroups of SOE.[21] This earned its employees the nickname of the "Baker Street Irregulars." The initial organization of the SOE was separated into three sections but did not last long. The first section (SO1) was devoted to developing propaganda and misinformation and was made up mostly of the staff from the Foreign Office's former Department of Propaganda. The group never really gelled with the organization and was later moved from the SOE to a newly created organization specially devoted to propaganda, known as the Political Warfare Executive (PWE). The second section of the SOE was SO2, which was devoted to operations and training. SO3 was the section devoted to research and planning. Within a year it was seen that SO3 was overwhelmed with paperwork and was losing its productive relationship with those in operations. Thus, SO3 was merged into SO2.[22] What had begun as SO1, SO2, and SO3, by 1941 had become a more unified single organization, simply known as the SOE. The new SOE was itself organized into three new sections. The first area consisted of the various "country sections," each devoted to an occupied territory and responsible for developing the networks inside it and for conducting the operations in that territory. Secondly, there was the Intelligence and Planning Section, which had the dual function of conceiving and planning operations and strategies with the various country sections. It also sorted and organized all the intelligence gathered through operations and distributed it to the various government departments to whom it was meaningful (especially the SIS and the War Office). The third section was the Training Section, which was responsible for operating all the training facilities, and for delivering the instruction to all recruits.

With the organization taking its shape over the first twelve months or so, the next step toward building an effective resistance force was to recruit suitable agents. These agents would take on the extremely challenging task of beginning to build a resistance force within the occupied country. They needed to be highly familiar with the country in question, and usually a native of that country was the best candidate. There were certainly exceptions. Sometimes a candidate might be found who had spent a number of years in that country, perhaps attending school or university there, and who had a command of the language and customs. If a candidate was deemed to have the requisite level of familiarity with a country (language, customs, geography, etc.), then the person would have to possess the needed skills to operate within the country, or be seen to have the intelligence and enterprise to learn those skills. If the SOE's recruiters felt they had a candidate who possessed these qualities, assuming the candidate had the desire, they would be sent into an intensive training course that lasted nearly two months. The SOE constructed a training program that was at first delivered all in the same location, at a stately private home in Hertfordshire. The recruits learned how to handle explosives, to use weapons of all kinds, and to operate covertly in a foreign land (known as "tradecraft"). The first class was matriculated as early as October 12, 1940, with a class made up of Frenchmen, Norwegians, Belgians, and one Scot.[23]

The SOE soon found it was better to separate classes of trainees, often by nationality if possible, and to create separate facilities for specific training. From this a four-stage process emerged, with facilities requisitioned in both England and Scotland. Stage 1 put the recruits through a kind of basic training, where they trained in physical fitness, map reading, and the basic use of firearms. Throughout the training, evaluators watched the recruits to see how their personalities were suited to secret work. For example, a well-stocked bar was available at the end of the day, and evaluators watched to see who was vulnerable to drinking to excess and who might spill secrets or betray their identities under the influence.[24] Such violations were grounds for not passing the course. Stage 2 included training in mountaineering, small boat sailing, armed combat, unarmed combat (including silent killing), and raiding techniques. Weapons training included arms from all the major belligerent nations and major makes of weapons. The challenges at the school included a mission to blow up actual railroad tracks and trains without detection. According to historian A. R. B. Linderman, "As many as a third of the recruits would fail this course."[25] For those that did pass the course, Stage 3 was parachute training at RAF Ringway, a base in Cheshire (near Manchester) that emerged as the principal parachute training school for all the British armed services. For the recruits that could pass parachute training, they were finally briefed on the real purpose of their training. They were given the choice at this point as to whether they were willing to go into an occupied country as an operative. For those who accepted, they moved into a final school for refining their training. Stage 4 was conducted in a group of country houses in Hampshire, each house devoted to a specific territory. Here recruits learned the finer points of tradecraft, including cover stories, avoiding detection, use of codes, forgery of documents, safe-breaking, and even the use of enemy uniforms. To pass out of these "finishing schools," the recruits were given missions for a small team. They had to pull off operations locally, like planting explosives in a specific location in the town, breaking into a factory undetected, or stealing equipment from a nearby police station. To make things even more challenging, the SOE evaluators gave the local police some knowledge about the operations, and even some general descriptions of the recruits. Though this was just practice, a candidate would have to exercise extreme care to avoid detection. If recruits were caught by local authorities, they went to jail, and only the use of a memorized telephone number could get them out.[26] Some recruits would go on to a fifth stage if specialized training was needed for their specific missions. Skills in this final stage could include specific challenges of seamanship, the operations of particular kinds of factories, or how to operate underground printing operations for spreading subversive publications.

This network of schools for the training program was spread across a number of facilities across Britain, most of them private houses with large grounds requisitioned by the military. Eventually, however, the SOE would open training facilities in Palestine, India, Ceylon, Australia, and Canada. In all, the SOE trained at least 6,810 student recruits. Of these, only about 480 were British; the others were generally natives of the countries to which they would soon be assigned.[27] The SOE also was not averse to using women in its resistance operations; as we shall see throughout this book, women played a vital role in resistance all over Europe. The SOE employed around 3,200 women within its administrative and operational personnel.[28]

Finally, the SOE would also comb police and prison records to find criminals with the kinds of specialized skills that were needed for such work. The criminal class was "a social stratum SOE neither neglected nor despised . . . indeed sometimes found most useful." In fact, says Foot, "SOE's forgery section would have got nowhere at all without help . . . from some recently released professionals."[29]

Once recruits had been trained, the challenge was to move them into the specific theaters of operations in the occupied countries. Again, this was accomplished by either sea or air. As we have seen above, resources from the RAF were often quite limited and difficult to predict. Therefore the SOE developed a network of sea transport, including a group of fishing vessels that moved across the English Channel to France, though Nazi security kept this to a minimum. Other locations were easier to manage, such as the fishing boats on Gibraltar at the mouth of the Mediterranean. Here the SOE built a "fleet" of boats that carried operatives to the south coast of Spain (although this was technically prohibited), and more importantly conducted at least 36 separate missions landing agents in France. This was stopped, however, by November 1942, when the Nazis occupied the south of France and fortified the coastline.[30] Perhaps the most important of the sea routes into occupied territory was the fleet of disguised military and fishing vessels that moved across the North Sea between Britain and Norway. The Nazis did not build significant fortifications and defenses along the Norwegian coast, as they had on the "Atlantic Wall." Its crenellated coastline with deep fjords made such defenses nearly impossible. As such, the SOE put together a regular service using expert fisherman, both British and Norwegian, to make the frightening crossing to move agents in and out of occupied Norway. This crossing was far more dangerous than sailing in the Mediterranean or even the English Channel, because of the often terrifying conditions in the North Sea. But it was those same hostile weather conditions that made sea passage all the more necessary, as airplanes simply could not function in such storms. Despite these conditions, the SOE developed an almost regular system of transport from the Scalloway base in the Shetland Islands to the coast of Norway. The transport operated so regularly that it became known as the "Shetland Bus."[31] Over the course of the war, the "Shetland Bus" line would transport nearly 150 tons of supplies and some 84 agents to Norway, and bring out 26 agents and 109 refugees.[32] The SOE's branch in Cairo also developed small and discreet fleets of fishing boats that operated in the Eastern Mediterranean, based out of Egyptian ports. These flotillas, mostly operating to Albania, Greece, and the Eastern Mediterranean coast, became known as the "Levant Fishing Patrol."[33]

Despite what the SOE managed in building up a network of sea transport, it was always aircraft that played the primary role in transport for that organization. They relied on bomber aircraft for their transport of large groups and for large cargoes of supplies and arms. The primary bomber the SOE used was the Armstrong Whitworth Whitley bomber, which had gone into operation in 1937 but was nearly obsolete as a bombing aircraft at the outbreak of war. Although it had two engines, it could not hold altitude if one of the engines stopped functioning. Still, the Whitley was used as a bomber by the RAF through 1941. By 1942 most Whitleys were being converted to cargo and transport use, and the SOE was able to get more aircraft for its purposes. The other principal aircraft used by the SOE was the Westland Lysander, a single-engine plane with a multiple-person cockpit and room in its fuselage for light bombing capability. The plane was first operational in 1938, but it was found generally ineffective as a light bomber in the early years of the war. But for the SOE it had a number of advantages. Because the SOE got exclusive use of some Lysanders, these were painted flat black and so were extremely hard to detect by sight. The plane could hold a few passengers, and there was room for modest amounts of cargo. But its principal advantage was its ability to

The Westland Lysander, with its ability to take off and land on short runways, was the most versatile aircraft for Resistance operations. (United Kingdom National Archives)

take off and land using very short runways. This was crucial behind enemy lines, where runways were often extremely short and tucked away in forest clearings and flat meadows. Lysanders could get in and out very quickly.

When an agent was going to be transported, there were some mandatory steps to be taken for their safety. The first of these was the preparation of fake identification papers. The SOE made the effort to have these prepared some time before departure so that the agent could become intimately familiar with the information in them, and also to "wear" the papers a bit to give them a realistic worn look. A report on French operations, though, revealed that this was not always accomplished, with papers sometimes only arriving just before an agent was departing, and "as a result (they) were unable to check them." Other agents "complained that they were not able to 'wear' the papers enough before departure and so they were too new."[34] In addition to false papers, clothing had to be just right. One needed the clothes to match the role of the identity one would be playing out in enemy territory: authentic workers' clothes for blue-collar types, French tailored suits for businessmen, and so on. This was a challenge, and the SOE had special staff devoted to making certain that clothing could not reveal the true identity of the agent, for example sewing authentic labels into the clothes rather than leaving British labels in place. A British label in a French workingman's dungarees could instantly reveal his identity. A final and thorough search was conducted before agents climbed on the boat or plane that would take them to their destination. The SOE staff searched for any clues in clothing, hats, papers, shoes, keys—anything. But once again, reports showed that the SOE did not have a perfect record in its final quality-control checks: "All agents were supposed to be searched before dispatch. Six report that they were not. In one case an agent found on arrival in the field a card with his real name and that of a tailor on it in his suit pocket!"[35]

Once a trained agent was transported into his or her theater of action—either landed on a coast by boat, landed on the ground by a Lysander, or, as was so often the case, parachuted behind the lines in darkness—what kinds of operations did they take on? Most of the rest of this book will discuss the various types of missions taken on by secret agents in the various movements across Europe. But in a general sense, there was a kind of schedule of operations. First, agents were dropped into enemy territory, especially at the beginning of the war, with the job of finding others who would be willing to get involved in resistance and then building a resistance network. As a report on SOE operations said in March 1941, those trained by the SOE "are trained in all forms of sabotage and paramilitary work, and *those of the best type are given additional training as organizers of subversive warfare.*"[36] For those individuals who showed extraordinary qualities, the SOE assigned them to begin the process of building the actual organizations inside their country. As we shall see in several cases throughout Europe, some resistance organizations were already coming into form by the time SOE operatives arrived, and in the case of France, several of those resistance organizations chose not to work with the SOE. But in general, SOE-trained personnel did the initial work to put together networks of people who were courageous enough, skilled enough, and discreet enough to help.

With a group of individuals in place and willing to work in a resistance network, there was a set of important structural elements to put into place. First, the group had to establish a network of safe houses—facilities (peasant homes, taverns, barbershops, etc.) where operatives could meet and hide when necessary. These were most often the homes and businesses of the members of the resistance group themselves, and of those who were sympathetic to the cause. Very often resistance networks were used to transport agents across the country, and especially to hide downed airmen or escaped prisoners. They had to be able to move across the country unseen and find safe places to sleep and hide out along the way. Eventually these kinds of "underground railroads" would lead to the coast or to country runways, where SOE aircraft could land and get them out.

With a group of safe houses in place, the next great task was to establish a system of communications with the SOE in Britain. Little could be accomplished if resistance networks could not relay information back to the organization, specifying supply needs, locations of drop zones, and targets for bombing, and of course relaying sensitive intelligence; communications were essential for resistance to function. To make these communications possible, it was necessary to put wireless transmitters (W/T sets) in places where Axis security hopefully would never find them. Most often this was in people's homes, hidden out of sight and when necessary taken out and set up in attics or basements. This was another exceedingly dangerous risk to take for a private individual, for Gestapo agents were constantly on the lookout for families harboring transmitters. The British eventually developed a W/T set called "Wireless Set A" that could be housed in a suitcase, but other cover had to be developed as well, or the German security forces would know exactly what to look for. The W/T sets had knobs for locating prearranged frequencies, and then transmitters would use Morse code to send their messages. A preestablished set of codes would also be used to ensure that the transmission was really their agent rather than a Gestapo agent. But even this was not always a guarantee of security. As we shall see later in the book, Gestapo agents were sometimes able to capture wireless operators and force them to give up the codes, which meant that the Gestapo could send misinformation to London and decode any important information the SOE sent. The W/T sets came with a very lengthy aerial wire of nearly 60 feet, and to get decent reception, it had to be strung. Operators would string the aerial around their houses and roofs, and often from their house to a tree; 25 feet of aerial was considered the absolute minimum for getting reception. This, of course, made the operator highly conspicuous, and disguises had to be thought of, like using the aerial as a home's clothesline in the yard. The Gestapo found a number of ways to interrupt electrical service in areas where they thought wireless transmission was happening, and this was only truly remedied when operators were trained how to use car batteries for the purpose. The best defense against the German security services, however, was simply to use the set in different places all the time, never leaving a set at one permanent location.

It was also imperative not to send wireless transmissions of too lengthy a duration. The Germans monitored the radio waves constantly and could track any transmission that went on for 20 minutes or more. For example, some of the SOE's first agents in France and Belgium "insisted on sending messages so verbose that their operators had to remain at their Morse keys for hours at a time; and inevitably, they were caught."[37] Eventually the SOE passed a strict rule that no transmission should last longer than five minutes. Operatives also learned not to communicate by wireless between one another in enemy territory. All transmissions went to headquarters in London only.

With personnel recruited, safe houses established, and W/T sets in place, the group could go about its operations. Agents, when they got precise understanding of their geographical area, could recommend operations and, if approved, pursue them. They also would be given specific missions by SOE headquarters. The kinds of operations they pursued varied immensely, but the following are some examples. Particularly in coastal areas, ordinary people rode their bicycles to go to the grocery store or anything inconspicuous, passing by enemy military establishments. They would observe the layout of defenses, noting what ships, guards, and military units were in place in these particular locations. These observations would be transmitted back to headquarters, and after numerous such observations, large-scale maps could be drawn of enemy defenses. Such resistance information was key to providing Allied commanders their knowledge of what enemy armies were stationed where, and when they moved. Other types of missions included identifying vital war materials for the Axis military machine and finding the factories that produced them. Once a factory that made ball bearings or rubber vehicle tires (as examples) was located, its location was shared with headquarters. The SOE could then pass this on to bomber command, whose planes would try to demolish the factory by aerial bombing. It might also be decided that rather than an aerial bombing effort, the resistance team should attempt to get into the factory and place explosives. This could be done by infiltrating the workforce, or in a covert operation at night, but the object was to create an explosion destructive enough to shut down production for considerable time. Other missions involved identifying the key railroad routes that moved war materiel and actual troops. Having located the key railroad track locations, agents would work to blow up the tracks (although these could be repaired fairly quickly) or to actually blow up the train itself as it passed. The sabotaging of railroad operations was perhaps the most widespread of all the resistance projects. Other missions could involve actual attacks on military personnel, including large transports of troops, or sometimes individual attacks on key officers. These were confined to a very limited number, as the German reprisals after such attacks were always quite brutal.

The SOE also had to make sure that agents had the necessary materials to carry out their work. For the development of specialized gadgets and materials, the SOE established Station IX, a kind of "dirty tricks" laboratory in a mansion named the Frythe in the countryside north of London. Here they developed all manner of secret technologies for the art of sabotage and survival: sticky bombs, "time pencil" detonators, even the first working model of what would become the snowmobile (used for operations in Norway). Most often for sabotage operations, agents needed guns and plastic explosives. The SOE pioneered the use of plastic explosives, using a material known as Nobel 808 (created earlier by the Nobel Chemicals company), which could be stuck into important machinery and then detonated from a distance. Plastic explosives were also very useful as they could be molded into the shapes of ordinary things and painted to look real, such as squirrels, rats, or a doorstop. SOE agents became masters with plastic explosives.

There was also the matter of guns. Agents had to have the firearms they needed to protect their very lives in armed situations. But the SOE and the many other government organizations that often wrangled with them were concerned about dropping too many weapons into the hands of resistance organizations. Many of the resistance organizations longed to expand their operations and the ferocity of their attacks. They were often less concerned about reprisals than their governments-in-exile and were determined to launch guerilla-style warfare against the enemy. The SOE and the other branches of the British government, however, were not keen at all to see resistance armies provoke the Axis into intense reprisal attacks that might result in the blowing of networks, the exposure of SIS spies, or murderous reprisals. Beyond reprisals, there was also the simple fact that effective subversion had to be based on secretiveness and mobility. Foot explains why the SOE steadfastly refused to supply large-scale weaponry to resistance forces: "Guerillas who did not keep on the move lost their *raison d'etre*, might just as well not be there; their task was to harass the enemy, not to pin him down by set bombardments."[38] Resistance groups had the best chance of survival by guerilla tactics, and attempting to engage the Nazis in set battles would have been suicidal.

There was another important reason why the British government was reluctant to drop too many arms to resisters. As we shall see in the chapters to come, many of the most determined and effective resistance groups were formed from existing communist political groups. Many of these communist groups had been outlawed before the war, and so they were already functioning in underground cells, ready to operate when the war commenced. Also, after the summer of 1941 when the Nazis had invaded the Soviet Union, Stalin's message to the many communist groups around Europe was to carry the fight to the Nazis without quarter. Stalin's view of resistance was that it should be as widespread and vicious as possible, and that reprisals were no reason to hold back. As such, communist groups in places like France, Yugoslavia, Greece, and later Italy played leading roles in attacking the Nazis behind the lines. Often the most significant limitation on communist resistance groups was their lack of effective firearms. But the British and American governments, as well as the governments-in-exile, were in no hurry to provide unlimited arms to a group that might muscle their way into power when the war came to an end. This became a major political theme in the history of the resistance movements—the British and American governments trying to exploit the communist resistance movements to the maximum extent possible, while at the same time trying to ensure that they were not made powerful enough to have any political influence at war's end.

When arms were dropped to the various movements and resistance armies, they most often included Bren guns, Sten guns, rifles, bazookas, and mortars. These were generally reported to be the most effective arms for resistance.[39] The Bren gun was a light machine gun that could be stabilized with a two-pronged hinged mount on its barrel. It was difficult to fire without resting the barrel on a stable surface, and it was generally too large for concealment. The Sten gun, however, was far more practical for concealment and easy carriage. The Sten gun, manufactured by Enfield, was a very light submachine gun that could fold up into a smaller size quite easily. It was lightweight, small, and of quite simple design. For these reasons, this was the gun most employed in resistance behind enemy lines. From the point of view of the SOE, "the overwhelming advantage of the Sten was that it was cheap. Its designers took care to make it robust and simple."[40] Bazookas and mortars were obviously difficult to transport or conceal, but they provided the necessary power for attacking trucks, trains, and tanks.

In terms of key personnel, Hugh Dalton occupied the position of minister of economic warfare until a cabinet shakeup in February 1942. At that point, he was moved to the Board of Trade and was succeeded by Lord Selborne, a Conservative, who held that position until the end of the war. Sir Frank Nelson had been the initial director of the SOE, but he retired due to ill health in

Sten guns on the production line. The Sten gun was the most widely used weapon amongst the Resistance organizations of the war. (Library of Congress)

1942 and was succeeded by Charles Hambro. Hambro had proven himself in Norway and Denmark and had sat on the SOE's Executive Committee. But Hambro resigned his position in late summer 1943 over yet another dispute about command structure. The argument revolved around the military's insistence that SOE staff fall under the direct leadership of regular military commanders in non-occupied theaters. With Hambro's resignation, Gubbins was made director in September 1943 and would hold that position until the end of the war. He was generally acknowledged to be the most qualified and most energetic man to lead the organization. As Lord Selborne put it to Winston Churchill, "There is perhaps no officer . . . who is more vital to the continuance of the work of this organization than Brigadier Gubbins. He has seen the growth of SOE from its early beginnings, and . . . has acquired a technique, a knowledge and experience which are really irreplaceable."[41]

Certainly Gubbins was the leading character in the drama that was the SOE, but what about Churchill himself? He is often regarded as the man who created the SOE and championed its maverick agenda, which harmonized with his own embrace of the unconventional. There is another interesting historical debate surrounding Churchill's relationship to the organization. Was Churchill truly the "father" of the SOE? Linderman concludes that his role was certainly important, but it was others in government and the military that drove the process to create the SOE, and we should acknowledge their role. As he writes, "Credit where credit is due: SOE was not Churchill's brainchild."[42] Churchill's inspiring directive to Dalton—"And now, set Europe ablaze"—has become legend. But as we have seen in this chapter and will see throughout this book, that vision had to be tempered constantly. Churchill supported the SOE at times but was also critical at times, or even aloof. At other times he would become enthused about a certain strategy and suddenly demand action by the SOE, as with the project to supply the Maquis in France during 1943.[43] In the first years, there was certainly limited contact between Churchill and Dalton, as Churchill simply couldn't stand him. He had made Dalton the minister of economic warfare and given the SOE to that ministry in order to appease the Labour Party leadership as he was composing his coalition cabinet. But he had such a revulsion for Dalton that he is reported to have said, "Keep that man away from me!"[44] Churchill's personal intelligence advisor, Desmond Morton, was from the SIS and was openly hostile to the SOE, and so his influence could sometimes sway Churchill. But during difficult times, when other groups campaigned to have the SOE dismantled, Churchill stood by the organization and consistently supported the organization continuing its mission. So, while the SOE may not have been Churchill's own brainchild, scholar Mark Seaman writes, "On all the crucial issues vital to SOE's survival, he was the indispensable savior."[45]

With Churchill's help, the SOE stayed intact to make its greatest contributions during the Allied invasions of Europe in 1944 and during the long push into Germany itself. Along the way, of course, nations were gradually liberated, and the SOE's mission disappeared as this happened. As Europe was set free, the question now arose: Would the SOE or any kind of native resistance have a place in the postwar world? In the end, after the 1945 general election, the leaders of the new Labour government in Britain decided that it would not. The Attlee government made the decision to dissolve the SOE and terminated its operations during January 1946. Many of its staff went into branches of the military, others into the business world, and still others would move into MI6 and play a continued role in secret operations in the shadowy world of the Cold War.

But of all the resistance organizations, the SOE was the one most deeply involved in resistance all throughout Europe. In the pages that follow, the SOE will come up time and again, as we see how resistance groups were formed, supplied, and supported by the Allied powers. The SOE conceived, and its agents led, some of the most daring and sensational operations of the war. It was vital in helping widespread resistance play its role in the defeat of the Axis. But by 1942 there appeared another large-scale organization that would use its power and resources to expand the intelligence and subversion operations in Europe.

AMERICA'S OFFICE OF STRATEGIC SERVICES

Long before December 7, 1941, and the attack on Pearl Harbor, the United States government was busy preparing for the likelihood that it would somehow be brought directly into the war. While President Franklin D. Roosevelt had been careful to pledge continued neutrality in his campaigns, the growing level of U.S. assistance to the Allies, and steps like the Export Control Act (1940) and the oil embargo with Japan (July 1941), made it clear that the United States was already involved in the conflict— and unquestionably on the side of the Allies. As such, the Roosevelt administration took numerous, if quiet, steps to prepare the government apparatus for an eventual war. One of those preparatory steps was establishing an agency to manage the problem of secret information and intelligence gathering. In the wartime environment, Washington was awash in secret correspondence and clandestine information being gathered and guarded by multiple groups, such as the State Department and the various branches of the military. To centralize this, Roosevelt created the Office of the Coordinator of Information and selected William J. Donovan to occupy this post.

Donovan was born to Irish parents in upstate New York on New Year's Day, 1883. He attended Catholic schools and eventually went to Columbia

University, where he was a football star and earned his nickname, "Wild Bill." He would be known as "Wild Bill" Donovan for the rest of his life, though his temperament was generally cool and measured. He earned a law degree from Columbia and fought in World War I in France. After the war, he practiced law and emerged as a prominent Wall Street attorney, where he entered the heady company of America's professional and political elite. He served in the Department of Justice in the Coolidge administration and ran unsuccessfully for governor of New York in 1932. Despite being a dedicated Republican, he became friends with Franklin Roosevelt, and by the early 1940s he had become one of the president's close confidants. Roosevelt used Donovan informally as an emissary to Great Britain during the first years of the war. In Britain, Donovan's assignment was to assess that nation's chances to sustain the war effort against the Axis powers. In making that assessment, Donovan inspected most of the aspects of the British defense apparatus, including its intelligence agencies and the SOE. As a result, when Roosevelt asked a committee to recommend the best candidate for the coordinator of intelligence, Donovan was among the best informed on the subject in the country. Upon entering the position, Donovan had already put together a report that recommended that the United States establish a large agency for espionage, propaganda, and subversive operations. Roosevelt's committee, and eventually the president himself, approved this proposal.[46]

After the United States was brought into the war, the new agency went through some difficult periods as Donovan attempted to build a new infrastructure. Several configurations were discussed, and several different branches, particularly the military, disapproved of the new office and tried to have it shut down.[47] But Roosevelt eventually made the decision to divide the office into two separate entities: the Office of War Information (OWI),

William "Wild Bill" Donovan, Head of the Office of Strategic Services in World War II and later first Director of the CIA. (Library of Congress)

which would concentrate on propaganda, news, and information, and the Office of Strategic Services (OSS), which would be responsible for secret intelligence gathering and covert operations. The OSS was formally established on June 13, 1942, with Donovan at its head. Immediately Donovan and his staff traveled to London to discuss the details of cooperation between the OSS, the SOE, and the SIS. After lengthy discussions and negotiations with Sir Charles Hambro (deputy director of the SOE at the time), an agreement was reached that provided for extensive collaboration between the two agencies. This particularly included training in the early days, and OSS personnel immediately began using the training apparatus of the SOE in Canada at the training school known as "Camp X" near Toronto. As early as July 1942, an SOE document was prepared that outlined the training program for familiarizing American personnel with the realities of subversion behind enemy lines. The schedule for OSS trainees included "Para-military school, Industrial Sabotage School, Propaganda School, Radio School, Parachute School, and the Camouflage Station."[48] Over time the OSS would create its own network of eight separate training facilities spread mostly throughout Maryland and Virginia, known as "areas"—Area A for basic training, Area B (now Camp David) for paramilitary training, Area C for communications training, and so on.[49]

Donovan moved then to create the organizational infrastructure of the OSS, creating a number of distinct departments within the organization. They included the following:

Research & Analysis (R&A) for intelligence analysis

Research and Development (R&D) for weapons and equipment development

Morale Operations (MO) for subversive, disguised, "black" propaganda

Maritime Units (MU) for transporting agents and supplies to resistance groups

X-2 for Counterespionage

Secret Intelligence (SI) covered agents in the field covertly gathering intelligence

Special Operations (SO) for sabotage, subversion . . . and guerilla warfare

Operational Groups (OG) also for sabotage and guerrilla warfare, made up of highly trained foreign-language speaking commando teams.[50]

Most important to this study were the Special Operations and Operational Group teams, which recruited, trained, equipped, and inserted agents into occupied territory.

The OSS and the SOE worked out an agreement to coordinate their operations in terms of territory as well. The OSS ran operations in Greece,

Yugoslavia, Italy, Albania, and France alongside the SOE. But the OSS also engaged in serious work in Asia, particularly in China.[51] Perhaps the most famous or romanticized picture of OSS operations involves the spy networks established within Nazi Germany itself. Donovan selected Allen Welsh Dulles, one of his close associates and a fellow Wall Street attorney, to head up his espionage network in Europe. Dulles established himself in Bern, Switzerland at Number 23, Herrengstrasse. From here he ran spy networks into Germany and most of Northern Europe. Dulles was able to obtain extraordinary levels of secret German intelligence from German agents determined to undermine the Third Reich. Dulles made no secret of his presence in Bern, but remarkably the Gestapo paid him little attention. As Dulles's biographer Peter Grose writes, "Though well aware of his presence in Switzerland from the first, the Nazi chieftains evidently could not imagine that an enemy agent with political designs would present himself so blatantly. Until late in the war Berlin believed that Dulles, coming straight from Wall Street, was on a mission of economic espionage against the Nazi industrial war effort."[52] The most important of the German agents he cultivated was Fritz Kolbe, who by 1943 was employed as a diplomatic courier for the German government and traveled regularly to Bern. He secretly contacted the British to hand over documents, but he was dismissed as a probable plant. He then tried the Americans, and Dulles made the decision to accept his overtures and assess the information. Over time Kolbe proved to be the most prolific Nazi spy in the Allied network, turning over some 1,600 documents.[53] Dulles also was in contact with the members of the German underground who were involved in the plot to assassinate Adolf Hitler. He

Allen Welsh Dulles, Head of OSS espionage operations in Europe, stationed in Bern, Switzerland. Dulles went on to become the legendary Director of Operations in the CIA during the Cold War. (Prologue Magazine, spring 2002 [National Archives])

was prohibited from lending assistance, but he provided encouragement and monitored the progress of the plotters. After the war Dulles would become the OSS representative in Berlin, and he used that time to piece together the story of the German resistance movement. He published that information in the first comprehensive book on the subject, *The German Underground*, in 1947.

At its height, the OSS employed over 13,000 people and had an annual operating budget of $135 million.[54] When the war ended, the agency was disbanded by the Truman administration, but its remnants and many of its key personnel helped establish a new agency in the following year. In 1947, the Central Intelligence Agency (CIA) was born as a result of the passage of the National Security Act. Donovan, Dulles, and many others would renew their clandestine careers in the CIA during the years of the Cold War.

NOTES

1. A. R. B. Linderman, *Re-Discovering Irregular Warfare: Colin Gubbins and the Origins of Britain's Special Operations Executive* (Norman, OK: University of Oklahoma Press, 2016), p. 112.

2. Ibid., p. 112.

3. See David Lampe, *The Last Ditch: Britain's Secret Resistance and the Nazi Invasion Plans* (London: Frontline Books, 2007 [1968]), p. 5.

4. Ibid., pp. 91–103.

5. As an example, the SOE dropped some 470 agents into France, of which 118 did not return (all but one of them are known to have been killed). This is a death rate of approximately one in four. See M. R. D. Foot, *SOE: The Special Operations Executive 1940–46* (London: BBC, 1984), p. 59

6. See Mark D. Karau, *Germany's Defeat in the First World War: The Lost Battles and Reckless Gambles That Brought Down the Second Reich* (Santa Barbara, CA: Praeger, 2015), pp. 161–177.

7. David Stafford, *Britain and European Resistance 1940–1945* (Toronto: University of Toronto Press, 1980), p. 11.

8. Ibid., p. 12.

9. Ibid., p. 12.

10. Foot, *SOE: Special Operations Executive*, p. 11.

11. Stafford, *Britain and European Resistance*, p. 23.

12 "British Strategy in a Certain Eventuality," quoted in Stafford, *Britain and European Resistance*, p. 23.

13. From the war diaries of Hugh Dalton, quoted in Foot, *SOE: Special Operations Executive*, p. 19.

14. "Evaluation of SOE Activities in France," British National Archives, HS 8/422.

15. Foot, *SOE: Special Operations Executive*, p. 35.

16. Air Ministry file from Dept. of Plans, March 29, 1941, British National Archives, AIR 20/2901.

17. Stephen Phelps, *The Tizard Mission: The Top-Secret Operation That Changed the Course of World War II* (Yardley, PA: Westholme, 2010), pp. 243–244.

18. Foot, *SOE: Special Operations Executive*, p. 27.

19. Linderman, *Re-Discovering Irregular Warfare*, pp. 53–101.

20. Sir Colin Gubbins, address to the Danish/English Society in Copenhagen, April 29, 1966, quoted in ibid., p. 121.

21. Foot, *SOE: Special Operations Executive*, p. 23.

22. See ibid., p. 22.

23. Linderman, *Re-Discovering Irregular Warfare*, p. 125.

24. Foot, *SOE: Special Operations Executive*, p. 63.

25. Linderman, *Re-Discovering Irregular Warfare*, p. 126.

26. Ibid., p. 127. See also Foot, *SOE: Special Operations Executive*, p. 69.

27. Linderman, *Re-Discovering Irregular Warfare*, p. 127.

28. Ibid., p. 147.

29. Foot, *SOE: Special Operations Executive*, p. 57.

30. Sir Brooks Richards, "SOE and Sea Communications," in Mark Seaman, ed., *Special Operations Executive: A New Instrument of War* (London: Routledge, 2006), p. 35.

31. For the best account of this transport network, see David Howarth, *The Shetland Bus: A WWII Epic of Escape, Survival, and Adventure* (Guilford, CT: Lyons Press, 2001 [1951]).

32. See Foot, *SOE: Special Operations Executive*, p. 89.

33. Richards, "SOE and Sea Communications," p. 40.

34. "Evaluation of SOE Activities in France," British National Archives, HS/8/422, p. 3.

35. Ibid., p. 4.

36. "Method of Working—SO2," March 24, 1941, British National Archives, Cabinet Papers, CAB 119/43. Author's italics.

37. Foot, *SOE: Special Operations Executive*, p. 106.

38. Foot, *SOE: Special Operations Executive*, p. 79.

39. "Evaluation of SOE Activities in France," British National Archives, HS/8/422.

40. Foot, *SOE: Special Operations Executive*, p. 75.

41. Lord Selborne to Churchill, May 13, 1942, Gubbins Papers 3/1/8, quoted in Linderman, *Re-Discovering Irregular Warfare*, p. 6.

42. Linderman, *Re-Discovering Irregular Warfare*, p. 118.

43. Mark Seaman, "Churchill and SOE," in Seaman, ed., *Special Operations Executive: A New Instrument of War*, p. 56.

44. Quoted in ibid., p. 49.

45. Ibid., p. 56.

46. Linderman, *Re-Discovering Irregular Warfare*, p. 136.

47. Ibid., p. 137.

48. "Notice to War Office on OSS Formation," July 4, 1942, British National Archives, CAB/119/43.

49. See Patrick K. O'Donnell, *Operatives, Spies, and Saboteurs: The Unknown Story of WWII's OSS* (New York: Citadel, 2004), p. 3.

50. Ibid., p. xvi.

51. In China the OSS officers were a significant presence in Operation Dixie, which developed a relationship with the Chinese Communist Party of Mao Zedong.

52. Peter Grose, *Gentleman Spy: The Life of Allen Dulles* (Boston: Houghton Mifflin, 1994), pp. 154–155.

53. For a thorough discussion of Koble's contribution, see Lucas Delattre, *A Spy at the Heart of the Third Reich: The Extraordinary Story of Fritz Kolbe, America's Most Important Spy in World War II* (New York: Grove Press, 2006).

54. Linderman, *Re-Discovering Irregular Warfare*, p. 138.

3

"Vive la Résistance!"

The Story of the French Resistance
(June 1940–June 1944)

The largest and most complex of the European resistance movements was in France. The French resistance movement is also the most widely known and the best documented of the resistance movements of the war. When one thinks of the resistance against the Axis in World War II, it is the French resistance that most often comes to mind. While other movements were also quite complicated indeed, such as the Yugoslavian or the Greek resistance, the French national case stands out as the most complex of all, comprising nearly a hundred separate organizations and informal networks. As such, any attempt to write a history of the French resistance is a massive project. As an example, one of the finest of the surveys written on the subject is David Schoenbrun's *Soldiers of the Night: The Story of the French Resistance*, published in 1981. It runs to 500 pages. A more recent survey by Robert Gildea, *Fighters in the Shadows: A New History of the French Resistance*, runs to nearly 600 pages. The most thorough history of the movement is the masterwork produced between 1967 and 1981 by Henri Noguères and Marcel Degliame-Fouché, *Histoire de la Résistance en France*, which runs to an astonishing five volumes. The dizzying array of organizations and individuals, the extent of their missions and activities, and the extent to which France was a vital strategic battleground—all combined to make the story of the French resistance one of history's great epics. The constraints of a book of this size, however, require the author to condense the story into two chapters. This first chapter will discuss the beginnings of resistance in France, the basic structure of its organization, some of its prominent figures, and some of its important operations. The book's last chapter will discuss the vital work of the French resistance leading to the Normandy invasions in 1944, the uprising in Paris that year, and France's liberation.

One of the great questions regarding the French resistance is determining exactly how many people were actually involved in it. This is an extremely difficult matter to determine, as there were so many different shades of cooperation or resistance. If one lived in the southern zone, where there was a legitimate French government in place, one could be anti-Nazi and support the Vichy French government with true patriotism and only contempt for the Nazis. But given the level of cooperation between the Vichy government and the Nazis, others would consider that person to be a "collaborator." One might hate the Nazis and the Pétain regime with all one's heart but feel unable to join a resistance network without endangering their family. There were all kinds of ways to express "soft" or "passive" resistance without joining a formal resistance organization. Since 1945 there has been a kind of progression in the overall consideration of the resistant character of France during the war. First, there was the legend of the resistance fostered by Charles de Gaulle. This school of thought said that nearly all Frenchmen, though under the boot of the Nazis, resisted in any way they could—France had been a "nation of resisters." Historian Robert Gildea writes,

> To deal with the trauma of defeat, occupation and virtual civil war, the French developed a central myth of the French Resistance. This was not a fiction about something that never happened, but rather a story that served the purposes of France as it emerged from the war. It was a founding myth that allowed the French to reinvent themselves and hold their heads high in the post-war period.[1]

This "founding myth" was then reinforced with ceremonies, national holidays, naming of streets and squares, and the awarding of medals for the prominent heroes of the resistance.

The structure of this myth, however, was cracked in the 1970s by two major pieces of historical work. The first was a documentary film from filmmaker Marcel Ophüls titled "Le Chagrin et la Pitié" (in English, "The Sorrow and the Pity: Chronicle of a French City Under the Occupation"). Part two of this film concentrates on the experience of the French citizens who embraced the occupation for various reasons—the elimination of the leftists, anti-Semitism, or simple opportunism. It was a highly controversial film in France; although made for TV, it was banned from French television for ten years because it "undermined the official resistance story."[2] The other major work that chipped away at the Gaullist myth of the resistance was a book by the American scholar Robert O. Paxton, titled *Vichy France: Old Guard and New Order 1940–1944.* Paxton emphasized the very tiny numbers in the resistance, and that such activity appealed almost exclusively to those who were already outcasts. He explained that the lack of clarity as to the identity of the Vichy regime, and the lack of any real promise to do harm to the Germans, kept most Frenchmen out of resistance activities:

> Active opposition to an authoritarian and widely supported regime is a minority business at best. Resistance requires a clear target, and in the unoccupied part of France it was not altogether clear to a lot of anti-German Frenchmen whether Vichy was an enemy too. Resistance also requires some hope, and until late in the war, throwing the Germans back across the Rhine seemed beyond mortal strength. Resistance, finally, means accepting law-lessness on behalf of a higher good and the replacement of routine by a life of relentless improvisation. Only the young and the already outcast can adapt easily to a life of extended rebellion.[3]

Paxton suggested that France was certainly not a "nation of resisters," with only about 2 percent of the population involved in any real resistance activity. He also made the important point that nearly as many volunteered for Vichy's internal police, the Milice française, to stamp out the resistance. As he writes, "Some 45,000 volunteered for the infamous *Milice* in 1944, partly perhaps to escape labor service, partly for fanaticism, but at least in part to help defend 'law and order.'"[4]

But the view that grew during the 1970s, that France had been more col-laborationist than resistant, began to fade as well during the 1980s. David Schoenbrun's book *Soldiers of the Night* (mentioned above) suggested that while direct memberships in resistance networks may have been low, pas-sive resistance was quite common. He cites examples such as the death of Charles de Gaulle's mother during July 1940. With Vichy and the Nazis now declaring de Gaulle an outlaw, the information about his mother's death was suppressed from the newspapers. But word spread through underground networks, and French people "flocked to her funeral as a way to express support for de Gaulle . . . they came by the hundreds, bearing flowers and wreaths . . . And by doing so they were defying the Germans. It was in its way an early act of resistance, a spontaneous act of ordinary people."[5] Schoenbrun goes on to say that those actively involved "counted for about five percent of the population. But that is a very high figure if you understand what it means to give up everything, your job, your home, your family, your security, and live like a hunted animal . . . I also found that at the end of 1942 as many as . . . fifty-five percent (had the potential) for passive resistance."[6] Similarly, the work of Jonathan F. Sweets has been extremely important. In 1986 Sweets published an important monograph on the occupation in the city of Clermont-Ferrand, titled *Choices in Vichy France: The French under Nazi Occupation*. In it he also looks at the widespread potential in the French population for passive resistance. He cites the willingness of French people to assist active resisters, and he emphasizes the silent work of factory workers in sabotaging parts and materials for the Nazi war machine. These are all acts that can never be quantified, and as he asks, "Who knows how many, if any, airplane motors failed in flight or tanks broke down on the eastern front as a result of the sabotage of workers in factories at Clermont-Ferrand?"[7] Sweets ultimately concludes that the more pessimistic school of thought of the 1970s, which completely rejects the notion of a "nation of resisters," is too narrow. He writes, "The idea of a 'nation of resisters,' while unquestionably an exaggeration, cannot be dismissed out of hand."[8] While the number of resisters who were official members of established organizations was necessarily quite low (between 2 and 5 percent of the population), it is increasingly clear that the majority of the population was willing to resist in passive ways when the opportunity presented itself.

THE FALL OF FRANCE AND THE BIRTH OF THE RESISTANCE

The Nazi invasion of France and the Low Countries began on May 10, 1940, and progressed with astonishing speed, as summarized in an earlier chapter. The German thrust around France's Maginot Line and through the Ardennes Forest was swift and effective. By early June the British and French forces that had not been killed or taken prisoner were scrambling on the beaches of Dunkirk to board ships to escape to Britain. While estimates vary, it appears that about 140,000 French soldiers escaped to Britain out of Dunkirk, but that well over a million French prisoners of war were taken by the end of the fighting and deported to German POW camps.[9]

In the light of the Germans' overwhelming battlefield victories and the increasing reality that additional fighting would be pointless, the French government evacuated Paris and set up in makeshift fashion in Bordeaux, on the south Atlantic coast. A new government was thrown together, this time including one of the tank commanders who had achieved some limited success against the Germans. His name was Colonel Charles de Gaulle, and he was made undersecretary for war in the new cabinet formed on June 5. The young de Gaulle, who would soon be made a brigadier general, found himself in the middle of a fierce debate over the government's plan of action. Prime Minister Paul Reynaud and a few others believed that if the nation should collapse under the weight of the German attack, the government could move to French North Africa (Algeria and Tunisia) and carry on the fight with France's allies, and its empire. De Gaulle endorsed this course of action and gave such advice to Reynaud.[10] However, others in the government, most prominently Henri Philippe Pétain, a legendary figure from France's victory in the Great War, believed that further fighting was futile. France had no hope, said Pétain, and to continue sacrificing French lives in a pointless struggle was unforgiveable. Pétain, now deputy prime minister, had the support of France's top generals, like General Maxime Weygand, and many of the cabinet politicians. Despite visits by Winston Churchill and efforts by Reynaud to work with the British to form some kind of military alliance, Pétain's group won the day. Reynaud eventually gave up the fight, resigned his position, and recommended Pétain to take his place. Pétain became prime minister of France on June 16. He immediately went to work on the government's initiative to secure an armistice with the invading Germans. He was able to negotiate terms over a few days, and then he and some of his fellow ministers went to Compiègne in the north of France to sign the armistice agreement. This was especially humiliating for the French, and Adolf Hitler went to extraordinary lengths to make it so. Compiègne had been the site of the armistice signed in November 1918, when German commanders were forced to sign a humiliating armistice to end hostilities in the First World War. Hitler was able to find the actual railcar used for that meeting, and he had it removed from a French museum and brought to Compiègne. With the signature of the armistice, Hitler satisfied his deep, even pathological need for vengeance against the French who had humiliated his nation 22 years earlier.

The terms of the armistice established the basic structure of France going forward into the rest of the war. First, the Germans would formally occupy and govern the northern section of France and its Atlantic coastline—this would be called the "occupied zone." In the south, the French would retain a sovereign government in the section known as the "southern" or "unoccupied" zone. By leaving a sovereign French state in the south and no German occupation, Hitler saved troops that he planned to use in the coming invasion of Britain. Next, the French army was forced to demobilize, leaving only a force of 100,000 men for internal security. Third, the French naval fleet was to be disarmed and the ships docked in their French home ports. French prisoners of war (nearly one and a half million of them) would remain in captivity until a formal peace treaty was negotiated (though this never happened). The French government would be obliged to turn over all "anti-Nazi German refugees." Finally, the French would be forced to pay, in cash and produce, for the cost of German occupation troops in the northern zone.[11]

From here, Pétain assumed control of the French government; by July he was called premier and chief of the French state. He filled his government with reactionary, pro-fascist politicians like Pierre Laval, who was installed as prime minister, and Admiral François Darlan, who was made minister of marine affairs; this was a crucial position because of the question of the French fleet immediately after France's capitulation. In the event, Darlan ordered all French ships to sail to ports of France's overseas colonies, and he did not permit the Germans to take possession. Nonetheless, like Laval, Darlan would prove a dedicated member of the far right and a willing collaborator with the Nazis.[12] Government officials decided upon the spa town of Vichy to relocate the French administrative capital, and so the French state would become known as "Vichy France" until the country's liberation four years later. Pétain's government bore frightening similarities to the fascist dictatorships and offered cooperation with the Nazis in several areas. Vichy France would send enormous amounts of industrial produce, raw materials, and food to aid the German war effort. Particularly under Laval's leadership, the Vichy government would agree to send French laborers to work in German factories. The Vichy French government also passed laws against Jews and would work to round up thousands of them, who were ultimately sent to their deaths in the camps of the Holocaust.[13]

Certainly not all of France's politicians were pleased to accept the armistice; some were appalled but faced the reality of the situation and went along with it in order to continue to serve their nation. Others separated themselves from the government, refusing to be part of the capitulation, and simply went home to their families. Still others left France altogether. Some went to French possessions in North Africa to see if it was possible to carry on the fight. One figure, immediately after dismissal from Pétain's government, secured a flight to Great Britain on June 16. This was General Charles de Gaulle, and in Britain, one can only say, destiny awaited him.

De Gaulle was born in 1890 in the northern region of Lille to an aristocratic and traditional family. Steeped in the historical glory of France, he had become convinced early in life of a sense of destiny. He attended St. Cyr, France's military academy, and distinguished himself in the Great War, fighting under the command of Henri Philippe Pétain. Although he was a kind of protégé of Pétain, after the war the two had a serious parting of the ways regarding their different visions of future military tactics. Pétain was adamant about the importance of stationary defenses (lessons learned from the Great War), while de Gaulle became convinced of the power of mechanization and mobility. He would even write a famous tract, *Toward a Professional Army*, which argued for a new organization for the army based on mechanized divisions, and particularly emphasizing the role of the tank. The book was not influential among the French High Command and sold poorly in France; but it was read and studied closely by the German military in the interwar years. Now, in June 1940, de Gaulle had left France and taken refuge in Great Britain. He left with a few senior aides and a cache of 100,000 francs provided to him secretly by Paul Reynaud. As the only member of the pre-Pétain French government to go to Britain, he was given recognition and facilities by the British government. He was installed in offices at No. 4 Carlton Gardens in Westminster. Almost immediately after his arrival in Britain, he was given permission to make an urgent appeal to the French people via radio broadcast. On the evening of June 18 at 10:00 PM, only four days after the Nazi occupation of Paris, he made his now-legendary appeal over the BBC:

> The leaders who have been at the head of the French armies for many years have formed a government. This government, alleging the defeat of our armies, has entered into communication with the enemy to stop the fighting. To be sure, we have been submerged, we are submerged, by the enemy's mechanized forces, on land and in the air. It is the Germans' tanks, planes and tactics that have made us fall back, infinitely more than their numbers. It is the Germans' tanks, planes and tactics that have so taken our leaders by surprise as to bring them to the point they have reached today.
>
> But, has the last word been said? Must hope vanish? Is the defeat final? No! Believe me, for I know what I am talking about and I tell you that nothing is lost for France. The same men that beat us may one day bring victory. For France is not alone. She is not alone! She is not alone! She has an immense Empire behind her. She can unite with the British Empire, which commands the sea and which is carrying on with the struggle . . .
>
> I, General de Gaulle, now in London, call upon the French officers and soldiers who are on British soil or who may be on it, with their arms or without them, I call upon the engineers and the specialized workers in the armaments industry who are or who may be on British soil, to get into contact with me.
>
> Whatever happens, the flame of French resistance must not and shall not go out.[14]

That radio broadcast was never recorded, and so de Gaulle's own notes and a few written transcripts are all we have to document this landmark address. But the truth is that few heard it. It was unannounced and on an English-language radio station in the midst of a chaotic period. But those few who did hear it spread the word quickly. De Gaulle would make a second appeal by radio on June 22. It included much the same message as his first address and again called upon free Frenchmen, wherever they might be, to join him:

> It is therefore necessary to group the largest possible French force wherever this can be done. Everything which can be collected by way of French military elements and potentialities for armaments production must be organized wherever such elements exist.
>
> I, General de Gaulle, am undertaking this national task here in England.

I call upon all French servicemen of the land, sea, and air forces . . . I call upon the leaders, together with all soldiers, sailors, and airmen of the French land, sea, and air forces, wherever they may now be, to get in touch with me.

I call upon all Frenchmen who want to remain free to listen to my voice and follow me.

Long live Free France in honor and independence![15]

This time a wide audience in France huddled around their radios, took inspiration, and saw some glimmer of hope for the future of their country. The message in the two speeches, however, focused upon those who were able to leave France or who were already away from its shores. The central point was to assemble a fighting force to continue combat against the Nazis, alongside France's allies. But for those inside France, it suggested a course of action that was not explicit in his message—the pursuit of resistance against the enemy *within* occupied France. All over the country, those who had been disgusted by France's surrender—and even more disgusted with the government of Pétain—began to consider ways to undermine the collaborators of Vichy and the Nazi occupation forces.

Certainly the occupation process was brutal, humiliating and violent. Schoenbrun relates the story of one woman in the village of Luray named Madame Bourgeois. She was outraged when German soldiers came to requisition her home to use for military purposes. She screamed at the soldiers and shook her fists. The German soldiers then "grabbed her and tied her to a tree in her garden and assassinated her before the eyes of her horrified daughter. They told her daughter to leave the body tied to the tree for twenty-four hours, as a warning to all as to what would happen if anyone resisted German orders."[16] The local French government prefect, who heard about the incident, protested to the Nazi commanders and asked for the soldiers to be disciplined. Instead, he was jailed and beaten. The young prefect's name was Jean Moulin, and

Charles de Gaulle, Leader of Free France who called for the French to resist on June 18, 1940. (AP Photo)

we shall return to his story later in the chapter. With an occupying force so brutal, one might ask, "How could one fight back in any meaningful way?" Others asked, "How could one not?"

THE PEN IS MIGHTIER: EARLY RESISTANCE AND SPREADING THE WORD

The first recorded acts of resistance took place mostly in Paris just after June 14, when the Nazis occupied the city. There were some who scrawled graffiti with slogans like "Nazi Assassins!" and in the Jewish section of Paris, others painted six-pointed stars on the Nazi propaganda posters all over town.[17] These acts, brave as they were, did not undermine the Nazi occupation in any material way, but elsewhere some French men and women tried to take concrete action against the German military. Étienne Achavanne took it upon himself to find the telephone lines between the German command and the Luftwaffe stationed at the airfield at Boos, in Normandy. He was able to cut the lines himself. When an RAF raid appeared, the German air force had gotten no word of it, and so some 18 planes were destroyed on the ground and 20 Germans killed. Achavanne was caught, tried, and executed. Here was the first "martyr of the Resistance."[18]

For those who were burning with anger and a hunger to truly fight back, it would take something more effective. Clearly individual efforts would be futile, almost suicidal. The first method that several groups adopted to begin the process of resistance involved not bombs or assassinations or sabotage, but instead simple communication. In the months following the German occupation, not surprisingly, the conditions of censorship closed around the French press. Many French news organs were formally suppressed, though some were allowed to continue, but always subject to German censorship. Particularly, information about the war and discussion of the German occupation were strictly controlled. No Axis defeats were discussed openly, no open criticism of the dictatorships was allowed, and certainly no information about de Gaulle and his "Free France" was tolerated. In fact, in Vichy, Pétain's government had tried de Gaulle *in absentia*, found him guilty of high treason, and condemned him to death on July 13. For some enterprising souls, then, the first crucial job became apparent: the French people had to be alerted that there were others willing to resist, and to be given the truth about the course of the war and the viability of Free France.

The first documented effort in this direction came from a man named Edmond Michelet and the tiny group of supporters around him. They called their small group "Valmy" and began to run off a small mimeographed pamphlet that they distributed by hand to "safe" mailboxes in and around Paris. In their little paper, they called on the French people to take up resistance against the oppressors. Over the course of the war, this humble little pamphlet would grow into a full-fledged newspaper called *Résistance* that grew to a circulation of 120,000.[19] Michelet would ultimately be arrested in 1943 and sent to the Dachau concentration camp, where he miraculously survived until the end of the war. When the war was over, he would become a distinguished politician in the government of Charles de Gaulle.

Another of the early remarkable underground publications took shape in the basement of a famous Paris museum. Across the Seine from the Eiffel Tower is a complex of buildings and gardens called the Trocadéro, and world-famous museums flank this iconic landmark. One of those museums is the Musée de l'Homme, or the Museum of Man, dedicated to the study of the development of humankind from prehistory to the present. In 1940 it was staffed by a remarkable group of intellectuals who had been involved in anti-fascist politics before the war broke out.[20] Now, in 1940, they agreed that they must resist the Nazi regime. They already had printing equipment hidden in the basement of the museum, and now they put that equipment to work printing a small anti-Vichy, anti-Nazi newspaper. Slowly they developed a small network of friendly associates who volunteered to deliver the papers, including a young Christiane Boulloche, who recounted tales of delivering such papers in a false compartment in the basket of her bicycle. "Delivering some of these publications," says Boulloche's biographer was "one of Christaine Boulloche's earliest acts of resistance."[21] The Musée de l'Homme group was led by two of its top administrators, Anatole Lewitzky and Boris Vildé, who both worked to produce the newspaper and later to create a network of safe houses and contacts in order to build safe passages out of France. But the Gestapo found out about the network and began investigating. To infiltrate the group, they used an agent named Albert Gaveau (a native Frenchman, but unknown to the others, he had a German mother), who eventually betrayed the group and identified most of its key personnel. The Gestapo arrested them during 1941 and held them in prison until February 1942, when they went to trial. Five members were acquitted and released, but four were sentenced to multi-year terms in prison, and ten of the most important members were sentenced to death and executed.[22] The Musée de l'Homme group's work was finished by 1942, but by then a number of other groups had emerged to write anti-Axis tracts and to expand their work from circulating information to all-out action against the enemy. What follows is a brief overview of the five largest groups.

Libération

The first of the five largest "core" groups of the French resistance began with an individual, Emmanuel d'Astier de la Vigerie. D'Astier had been a prominent military and political figure before the war, having served in France's navy and eventually as the head of naval intelligence. But his anti-fascist political leanings got him dismissed from government service under Pétain. He was horrified at the Nazi occupation and appalled at the Vichy government's collaboration and swore to fight it. As head of naval intelligence, he had astonishing professional acumen; he knew how to run an espionage network and to conduct covert operations, and he was now free to do so. He set up his group in the city of Clermont-Ferrand, not far from Vichy, and was able to enlist the help of some remarkable people. The University of Strasbourg had been forced to evacuate the province of Alsace as it was absorbed into the German Reich at the capitulation. The university relocated to the city of Clermont-Ferrand and began to reestablish itself. As luck would have it, some of its highly intelligent, often anti-fascist faculty would move to Clermont-Ferrand. One such man was Jean Cavaillès, a mathematician and philosopher of science, who had been in the French army at its defeat. Cavaillès now returned to the university and was determined to find methods to resist the Nazis. He met d'Astier, and together they worked to form a small organization they called la Dernière Colonne, or the Last Column. They worked first to put together a network of associates, and here they met the remarkable married couple Raymond and Lucie Aubrac.

Raymond was a formidable engineer who had studied at both MIT and Harvard before the war, and he had been stationed on the Maginot Line when France surrendered. His wife, Lucie, was another powerful intellectual and a history professor on the faculty of the University of Strasbourg. Lucie was preparing to leave France to teach in America when the war broke out. As the French were clearly headed for defeat, she made the difficult decision to pull her bags off the ship headed for the United States— her husband was Jewish, and she knew that defeat might mean oblivion for him. Raymond was indeed taken prisoner and put in a POW camp immediately following the armistice. Lucie found the camp, and together they engineered an escape for Raymond: by faking illness, he managed to evade scrutiny long enough to get over the walls and into Lucie's car. They drove as fast as they could into the unoccupied zone, where Raymond got work as an engineer. Lucie went to Clermont-Ferrand to work at the University of Strasbourg. There they fell in with d'Astier; along with Cavaillès, this would form the core of the resistance group.

The entire group was left-leaning, dedicated to socialism and anti-fascism, and particularly concerned with the condition of ordinary working people. They worked to enlist the help of trade unions and industrial workers. They were not communists and were frankly opposed to Stalinist organizations, but they found fertile ground with the many left-leaning workers in the south whose trade unions had been outlawed by the Vichy regime. Their organization became "a place where Socialists and trade union types flocked, like the Aubracs . . . who were not Communists and did not want to work in Communist ranks."[23] After the prolonged process of putting together a string of trustworthy team members, the group began to attempt sabotage operations, which included raids on the key railroad stations at Perpignan and Cannes. Destroying railroad tracks and sabotaging locomotives was a common resistance activity, making it far more difficult for the Germans (or Vichy) to move troops about.

In February 1941 the group organized a mass distribution of propaganda leaflets, but this brought the attention of the Vichy police, and members of d'Astier's family were arrested, though he himself escaped arrest. The group ceased operations for a time but then reassembled and decided to expand their operations by producing a full newspaper. They called their paper *Libération*, and this would become the permanent name of their organization. A local newspaper agreed to secretly furnish the facilities and equipment, and local union workers provided the newsprint and other supplies to make it a large-scale operation.

While Libération was conducting its early raids and organizing its newspaper, Cavaillès had obtained a teaching position at the Sorbonne in Paris during 1941. In leaving the southern unoccupied zone to take up his position, he also took with him orders to begin creating a resistance organization in the northern occupied zone. He was able to get the network started, and soon the organizations became known as Libération-Nord and Libération-Sud. This network did engage in sabotage, but it focused much more on providing intelligence and circulating information through its underground newspaper. In fact, young Cavaillès made the decision to leave the Libération network to devote himself exclusively to sabotage operations, mostly upon the German naval bases and communications stations in Brittany. He was caught, tortured, and shot in February 1943. The Aubracs and d'Astier all survived the war and enjoyed distinguished academic and political careers in the postwar era.

The Alliance or "Noah's Ark"

The next major resistance network was also established by a former senior official of the French military. His name was General Georges Loustaunau-Lacau, but he would be forever known to the resistance by his code name, "Navarre." Loustaunau-Lacau had actually replaced Charles de Gaulle on the staff of Henri Pétain during the 1930s, but he was found to have extreme right-wing sympathies and to be working with a questionable political organization. He was removed from command but was recalled when the war broke out. French politicians were appalled to learn of his reinstatement into the army and to read his searing criticism of French defenses; he was dismissed and imprisoned before the German invasion of France ever began.[24] After the French surrender and the formation of Pétain's new Vichy government, Pétain released him from prison and appointed him chief of the army veterans' aid organization, the Légion Française des Combattants. Doubtless his far-right politics actually earned him some level of respect in a regime that was eager to obliterate the political left and to collaborate with the Nazis. But Pétain had misjudged Loustaunau-Lacau. Despite his extreme right politics, he was unable to accept a France under German domination, and he decided immediately to continue fighting the Nazis any way he could. Given an office in Vichy at the Hôtel des Sports and the position as head of a veterans' network, he used his job to recruit soldiers who also were furious about the German occupation. He interviewed hundreds of demobilizing soldiers and worked to create a network of associates who would cooperate in a number of resistance activities. These could be outright sabotage against the Germans, or these could be simply allowing escaping agents to hide in their houses, or escorting downed airmen out of the country and into Spain.

In a masterstroke, the man called Navarre would also recruit a remarkable young woman. She was Marie-Madeleine Fourcade, his secretary and political aide before the outbreak of war, who had helped the general (then out of the military) publish a political tract called *L'Ordre Nationale*, earning his trust and admiration. Now he turned to her to help him run the resistance network, which they called "the Alliance." Very early on he gave her the responsibility of managing the intelligence network, while he traveled about trying to make contact with the Free French and to galvanize commanders outside France. His efforts got him arrested in North Africa in May 1941, though he managed to escape and get back to France. Later on he would be captured again in France and deported to the concentration camp at Mauthausen. The result was that Marie-Madeleine was forced to run the majority of the network by herself for most of the war. What she accomplished has become legendary.

During the summer months of 1940, while Navarre and Marie-Madeleine were just beginning to cobble together their organization, Charles de Gaulle and his staff in London were putting together their organization for a formal government-in-exile, known simply as "Free France." As part of that state apparatus, de Gaulle created an intelligence service and put it under the leadership of Major André Dewavrin, who would from this point be known by his code name, "Colonel Passy." It was Passy who would run the Free French network of secret agents, training them, directing missions, and sending them into France. The organization went through several name changes but eventually was called the Bureau Central de Renseignements et d'Action (BCRA) as of January 1942. Passy also worked to utilize and command the internal resistance networks that had taken shape inside France. Some major networks were ready and willing to work under the command of de Gaulle's Free France; others preferred to remain independent. The Alliance organization was one of those that preferred to stay independent. Still, in the autumn of 1940, Navarre made contact with Charles de Gaulle in London to inform the general about the network that he and Marie-Madeleine were building. In his message, however, he made it clear that he was not submitting to the command of the Free French organization. He assured de Gaulle that he offered his "complete and warm co-operation in continuing the struggle," but said that "to start with, he would march with him 'in parallel,' for he considered it essential to maintain an underground command in France to take . . . on the spot, the decisions that changing circumstances dictated."[25] De Gaulle would eventually write back expressing his displeasure with Navarre's stance, and he ended the letter with the terse sentence, "Whoever is not with me is against me."[26] It became apparent that any material support such as weapons, supplies, and especially money that the group hoped to receive from Free France would not be forthcoming. As the group's leaders wondered what to do, they received notice from Britain's Special Operations Executive, and after a prolonged period of secret meetings in London and Lisbon, the SOE began formal support of the Alliance, which would become the largest and most important group working with the SOE in France.[27]

With money and supplies coming from Britain in semiregular parachute drops, Marie-Madeleine began to construct a more substantial network using businesses like grocery stores as fronts, and particularly focusing operations in Lyon and on the Mediterranean coast. By 1941 the group had six transmitters working from the cities of Pau, Marseille, Nice, Lyon, Paris, and one in Normandy. The group was almost entirely focused upon providing espionage and intelligence. They recruited agents who lived on the coasts and who would routinely monitor the German submarine bases and communications networks along the Atlantic and Mediterranean coasts. They tracked actual submarine vessels in and out of port; they provided maps of the docks and diagrams of the defenses. The Alliance was able to furnish so much of this information that a complete map could be drawn of Germany's coastal defenses. The greatest challenge, after an agent did the actual spying, was to get the information transmitted to London via radio or by couriers. This is where the danger often occurred, and in late 1941 Fourcade herself came to the attention of the Vichy police and had to make a harrowing escape. Her associates smuggled her inside a mailbag into the cargo section of a train, where she was forced to stay for nine painful hours but avoided detection. She briefly took refuge in Spain.[28] Upon returning to her operations after this scare, she had an inspiration—she would create a system of code names for her agents, using animal names. Navy types would be fishes, airmen would be birds, and others would be assigned names based upon their personal traits. Her organization became filled with agents with names like Tiger, Ermine, Petrel, Yak, and Zebra; she herself became known as "Hedgehog." Later, when the Gestapo became aware of the group and tried to monitor its agents, Gestapo officers gave her network the nickname "Noah's Ark."

She would later be arrested by the Vichy authorities but released. In a painfully ironic twist, it was found that her network had been initially betrayed by the first secret agent parachuted to her network by the SOE. The SOE had found a suitable agent with outstanding French language skills and knowledge of the country, trained him, and sent him to help Fourcade's network. He was set up as the radio transmitter in Normandy. But this man, code-named "Bla," was in fact a member of Oswald Mosley's British Union of Fascists (most of the BUF personnel had been arrested and imprisoned in Britain) and apparently was devoted to the Nazi cause. He made the decision to work for the Gestapo and infiltrated the SOE and then the Alliance. But Fourcade's agents discovered his true identity, trapped him and gave him a brief hearing, and then executed him. Having gained respect for Marie-Madeleine, he used his dying words were to inform her about the coming Nazi invasion of the southern zone, which would take place in November 1942.[29] She was arrested soon after the occupation, along with members of her staff, but managed to break out of prison by a narrow escape through a tiny window—she was forced to strip naked to make it through. From here she was able to get transport to Britain, where she spent most of the rest of the war directing her network from afar. After the war she enjoyed a distinguished career as an activist and author; most notably she wrote the memoir of her time in the resistance, titled *Noah's Ark*; published in 1974, it remains an essential source for the study of the resistance.

Henri Frenay and "Combat"

The next of the major resistance networks was established by the right-wing soldier and politician Henri Frenay. Frenay, who had been a captain in the French army before the war, rejoined the military when war broke out in 1939. He was captured by the Germans but was able to escape from his POW camp and make his way to Marseille. While at first encouraged with Pétain's government, he soon became disillusioned with Vichy's violation of the armistice terms, specifically letting German administrators into the southern zone, allowing German labor levies, and Pétain's open meetings with Hitler.[30] Despite his private disgust with Vichy, he received an appointment to the intelligence bureau of the French state, the Deuxième Bureau. He now made the decision to use his position to begin a resistance movement. He was able to collect volumes of important information in his position; with a few associates, he began to print up a small pamphlet that spoke "the truth" about Vichy and the brutal nature of the Nazi state. Its first mailing was sent to those he was reasonably confident hated the occupiers, and he watched how enthusiasm spread, turning up others who were eager for such information. The publication eventually grew, and Frenay and his staff gave it a new title, Vérités ("Truths").

In early 1941 Frenay had been delighted with Pétain's dismissal of Pierre Laval as prime minister. Laval was one of the most open and explicit collaborators. But within a few months, Pétain announced that their disagreement was resolved and that Laval would rejoin the government. Frenay took this to mean that Laval had gone to the Germans, who now insisted to Pétain that he take Laval back. Frenay was so disgusted that he resigned his post with the government (despite the advantages it could give his movement) and devoted himself fully to his group. He first called his group the Mouvement de Libération Nationale (MLN), but later it would change, along with the name of his newspaper, to "Combat."

Frenay was an experienced military and intelligence man, and he ran his movement with great care and caution. He learned to form cells that had no knowledge of one another, to constantly change code names, to master the art of false security papers, and continually to shift meeting places. Though certainly members of his group did get arrested, he "alone among Resistance leaders" was never arrested.[31]

The group achieved some remarkable things. First, Frenay's organization put all of its information together to create a master map of the administrative organization of France. This included Nazi authority, Vichy administrative districts, and resistance zones. The map and schematic organization chart came to be used by all the larger resistance groups and by Britain's military and SOE. Combat would also continue to release its newspaper and monitor radio traffic from Vichy and Paris, trolling for vital intelligence. The group armed a small force of soldiers, who would make attacks on collaborationist newspapers and on Vichy police and authorities.[32] This had to be done very selectively, as too forceful an attack could lead to terrible reprisals. In the southern zone, the French government was less likely to massacre its own citizens. In the northern zone, the Nazis would not hesitate.

When it came to cooperation with Charles de Gaulle and Free France, Frenay remained independent. As historian David Schoenbrun writes of Frenay, he "would come to have a better idea of what de Gaulle represented, but he never fully accepted de Gaulle's authority over the men fighting inside France. He came to view de Gaulle as a valuable source of financing

TEACHER
OF THE
MONTH

FACULTY MEM
OF THE
MONTH

and arms, even as a symbolic leader . . . but not as his superior officer or the overall leader of France."[33]

The Communist Francs-Tireurs et Partisans Français (FTPF)

One of the most furious of the fighting groups in the French resistance was the organization built around the French Communist Party, but this was not initially the case. When the war broke out, Stalin's Soviet Union, linked to the major communist parties around Europe, was an alliance partner with Nazi Germany. The Nazi–Soviet Non-Aggression Pact had been signed at the end of August 1939, and so the various affiliated communist parties were instructed to accept German expansion without any kind of resistance. Even written protest was discouraged. So, with only a few exceptions, communist organizations in France followed the "party line" and suppressed any attacks on the Nazi occupation force. But this would all change dramatically after the great German invasion of the Soviet Union, launched on June 22, 1941. As the war in the Soviet Union reached nightmarish dimensions, Stalin called on Soviet citizens to take up arms against the German aggressors, particularly those who found themselves behind the lines in German-occupied territory. These fighting groups became known as the Soviet "Partisans," and they attacked the German rear with the full force of combat troops. Joseph Stalin was not concerned about the potential loss of life, or about the savagery of German reprisals upon civilians. His policy was one based on ideology—that communist Russia must utterly destroy Nazism—and hence any loss of life in the process was irrelevant. The same instructions went out to the communist organizations around Europe, including the French Communist Party (PCF). The communists in France were some of the most effective fighters the nation had to offer, and the communist organizations were some of the best suited to resistance work. The PCF had already been a virtual underground organization before the start of the war, and had organized itself into covert cells, ready-made for resistance operations. The underground communist newspaper, *L'Humanité*, ran continuously through the occupation and had among the largest of any resistance paper's circulation. Many of its members had been members of the French army but also had gone to fight in the Spanish Civil War against the forces of Franco, and so were quite well trained. When the call went out from Stalin for all communists to take up arms against the Nazis, the French communists responded to the call without hesitation—but this struck others as extremely unwise. As Schoenbrun writes,

> The Communists were the first, the only *resistants*, to adopt a policy of execution of German soldiers and officers. The killings were senseless, for they did not substantially weaken the power of the German Army, while they

infuriated the Germans and brought more severe repression upon the French. For the first time the Germans announced that prisoners would be considered hostages and that for every German soldier killed, the French would pay with the lives of hostages. First it was five to one, then ten to one.[34]

General de Gaulle in London was horrified and condemned the communists' strategy of individual assassinations. He called for such efforts to be channeled into expanded factory slowdowns, sabotage of railways, or the bombing of electrical power stations. All of these would be "more effective than the shooting or knifing of an individual soldier."[35]

By February 1942 the PCF had condensed a group of organizations, including the Young Communists, into a more unified fighting organization called the Francs-Tireurs et Partisans Français, known as the FTPF or often shortened to the FTP. The group was commanded by the former metalworker turned trade union leader Charles Tillon, who would run military operations for the group until the end of the war. The FTPF was deliberately opened up to non-communists as well, and many left-leaning workers would join who had never been part of the Communist Party. Despite its theoretical independence, however, it remained in the control of the PCF. Different from the other major resistance groups, the FTPF focused less on intelligence gathering and almost entirely upon action. The group ran numerous sabotage operations of railroad and other transport infrastructures, and bombed numerous factories. Despite the general rejection of their policy of out-and-out combat against the Germans, the FTPF did continue to assault and kill German officers and French collaborators. The group reached its zenith of historical importance in 1944 when it played a leading role in the Paris uprising. That episode will be discussed in a subsequent chapter.

The Maquis

Finally, the last of the major resistance groups took shape later in the course of the war. It was not driven by any political program or organization, but instead by the rejection of Vichy and Nazi policies by masses of young Frenchmen. From the beginning of the war in 1939 through the surrender in 1940 and into 1941, the harsh realities of the occupation did not encroach aggressively into the rural lives of the French countryside. Particularly in the unoccupied zone, life in the rural towns went on much as before. But in the early months of 1942, this began to change. The Nazi war machine was becoming desperate for labor in German factories, and the Germans began to make demands on the Vichy government to supply French laborers. Hundreds of thousands of French POWs had been put to work, but the Germans needed many more. A deal was struck (imposed upon Vichy) between the Germans and Pierre Laval to return one French POW for every three laborers sent to Germany. A law passed on September 4, 1942, declared all males between ages 18 and 50 and all females between 21 and 35 eligible for conscription into the German labor program.[36] The demands for labor only increased as the months wore on, and conscription became quite ruthless. In addition, 1942 was the year when the anti-Jewish laws were ramped up and deportations began in earnest. As historian H. R. Kedward writes, "The savage round-up and deportation of immigrant Jews in August and September 1942 provoked impassioned objections from individuals, and gave a new moral urgency to Resistance."[37] The combination of labor conscription and the rising fear of imprisonment and deportation motivated large numbers of mostly young men to simply leave their homes and escape into the hills.

The result was pockets of roaming resisters, mostly male and of all nationalities and political backgrounds. They often gave their individual band a name, but collectively these groups became known as the "Maquis," and individuals as "maquisards." The word *maquis* derived from the Corsican language and meant an especially dense and prickly shrub. It carried the connotation of the wildest, most remote parts of the mountain territories. There were some bands that were mostly communist and led by communist leaders, but there were many others who were of different political makeup. More often bands were made of a number of individuals with varying political viewpoints, but who all shared a hatred of Nazism and an absolute unwillingness to labor for the German war machine. Women were particularly helpful, according to some of the maquisards themselves, in providing food and clothing and other supplies; sometimes these were brought into the hills by village women, or sometimes the Maquis came to the villages in secret. But certainly life in one of these mobile bands was extremely difficult; providing food and resources in that environment was nearly impossible, and ex-maquisards talk about routinely having gone two or three days with no food.[38]

The object of the Maquis was first and foremost to escape capture or conscription by the Nazis or Vichy. But the second priority was to fight the Nazis and the Vichy authorities. They were less concerned about the overall strategy of the resistance, which focused on providing vital information to the Allies in order to bring about a major Allied invasion into France. Intelligence and sabotage could turn to open combat once that invasion had begun, but in the meantime open combat would only mean vicious reprisals and lead to widespread arrests. The maquisards, however, were much less prone to any infiltration or rounds of arrests. They wanted to kill as many Germans and Vichy agents as possible. This was quite difficult at first, as they had very few arms available. As Joseph Nodari said in an interview, when his band first came together in November 1943, "We had no arms at the time, just a couple of revolvers from the First World War and a hunting gun."[39] But the story of the Maquis made its way to Britain, and Winston Churchill began to take a special interest in the phenomenon. He insisted that the SOE work with these bands and deliver to them arms and supplies. As a result, the maquisards were armed mostly by the British through parachute drops. They wanted heavy and powerful weapons to take on German troops, but the British were unwilling to go this far. As was mentioned in the previous chapter, virtually all in the Allied war leadership were reluctant to heavily arm any group over which they had no direct control. This meant that the maquisards were armed mostly with light weapons like revolvers and especially Sten guns (collapsible machine guns), and also with light explosive equipment for sabotage operations.

With these weapons, light though they were, the Maquis launched expanded sabotage on railroads, factories, and particularly against the Vichy secret police—the Milice. In the countryside it was rare to see regular Nazi troops, as they were stationed mostly in the cities. But the Milice were everywhere, and they were the agents responsible for arresting those in the resistance and rounding up laborers for conscription; the fact that they were Frenchmen made this all the more repulsive. As such, maquisards often targeted Milice agents, blowing up their vehicles and launching guerilla attacks to gun down entire groups of them when possible. As another ex-maquisard said in a personal account, "We made several punitive attacks on *Miliciens* before 6 June 1944. Most *Milice* came from outside the locality. We had to kill them: it was war. They were enemies."[40] As the great Allied invasion neared in the spring of 1944, the Maquis, like all the resistance groups, began to ramp up their sabotage and attacks, channeling their hits into actions most likely to impede the Nazi troop movements when the time came.

THE RESISTANCE FROM JULY 1940 TO 1943

Charles de Gaulle had made his legendary appeals to the French people to rally behind him in the middle of June 1940. From that point he began to construct a state apparatus to run a formal government-in-exile, creating departments and appointing ministers. But what was the actual response of those thousands of French men and women who were out of the country? The older, almost mythical story of the resistance painted the picture of a great rallying to de Gaulle and the quick formation of a valiant fighting force—the Free French—to carry on the fight. But such a picture is misleading. In fact, as historian Robert Gildea reminds us, the number of French who rallied to de Gaulle was at first quite small. As he writes, "Rallying to de Gaulle was . . . always a minority activity . . . De Gaulle's success was slightly greater with military personnel who found themselves in England, although even here only a minority came over."[41] Assembling a large-scale fighting force was a slow and painstaking process rather than a unified rush to de Gaulle's banner. Many French were at first unsure what to make of Pétain's government; others questioned the viability of continuing the fight; still others questioned the political motives of de Gaulle himself. Given his reputation and his persona, some wondered if de Gaulle had his own ambitions for some form of military dictatorship. According to Schoenbrun, de Gaulle was "obsessed with the idea of the grandeur of France, eternal France, and did not think of talking about the French Republic."[42] It was, in fact, one of the leaders of the resistance, d'Astier de la Vigerie, who conferred with de Gaulle on one of his brief journeys to Britain and explained to him the suspicions many French had concerning the general. "D'Astier explained that many resisters suspected him of Bonapartism and that it was necessary to refer frequently to Republican freedom for the French."[43] De Gaulle took the advice and soon made it clear that he stood for the reinstitution of the French Republic, and this made a significant difference in his support.

Churchill's government in Britain formally recognized de Gaulle and his fledgling organization as early as June 28, 1940, as "Leader of all the Free French, wherever they may be, who join him for the defense of the Allied cause."[44] But despite this, de Gaulle and Churchill had a very rocky relationship indeed. By all accounts de Gaulle was arrogant, demanding, and utterly inflexible. While Churchill never formally retracted his recognition, the British government was certainly willing to look for other figures who might make a more cooperative leader of Free France. The United States government was even less enthralled with de Gaulle, and Franklin Roosevelt and de Gaulle did not get on at all. The United States had recognized Vichy almost immediately and opened diplomatic relations, installing an ambassador at the new French capital. The Americans did this chiefly to have an open channel of information into the French state, rather than out of any meaningful support of the Pétain regime. But de Gaulle was infuriated, and this remained a wedge between the two men. By 1942 both the Americans and the British were looking around for a more suitable leader for Free France. They found a candidate in French North Africa. French North Africa had remained under the sovereignty of Pétain's Vichy France, though it was a gathering place for those who did not support the regime. One of those who did not support the regime and secretly was willing to lead an effort against it was General Henri Giraud. Numerous meetings took place, and several arrangements were made by the Allied leaders to make Giraud the head of Free France, outside the knowledge of de Gaulle.

This culminated with the Allied landings in North Africa, which began on November 8, 1942. "Operation Torch" was a British and American invasion of the Vichy-held territories. It was a mass of confusion for the French defenders—some fought, some surrendered, some simply watched. The end result was that the territory reverted to control by the Allied powers, and this would contribute greatly to the eventual expulsion of both the Nazis and the Italians from Africa altogether. De Gaulle had been informed of the invasion only just before it began, and American and British representatives tried to create a situation where Giraud was the figure left truly in charge of Free France. Predictably, this produced a bitter dispute, and eventually after a conference in Morocco, the Allied leaders agreed to a joint leadership situation with de Gaulle and Giraud as co-leaders of Free France. Over time, Giraud wanted to concentrate almost entirely upon military affairs, and so he stopped attending meetings on political matters. The result was that de Gaulle, over the course of about a year, emerged as the clear leader of Free France, and Giraud increasingly faded into obscurity.[45]

Inside France, there had been similar disputes regarding the ultimate leadership of the French resistance. There were groups who were clearly with de Gaulle, others who backed Giraud, and others who remained completely independent. One group, Henri Frenay's "Combat," had even made a deal with the American OSS and was delivering information to its representative, Allen Dulles, in Bern, Switzerland. Clearly some kind of unification and command structure was needed if the whole patchwork of resistance organizations was to be brought into line as a more efficient and effective organization. The man who would be charged with making this happen was named Jean Moulin.

Jean Moulin was born in June 1899 in Béziers, France, and was raised by his family with a strong political sensibility and sincere devotion to France's republic. After serving in the French army (he just missed the fighting in the Great War), he took a law degree and entered public service. By the time of World War II, he had served in the Foreign Affairs office and in the Air Ministry, and was serving as a prefect (appointed regional governor) in the department of the Eure-et-Loire. As mentioned earlier in the chapter, he irritated the invading Germans by demanding action regarding the murder of a protesting old lady in his district. Rather than discipline their soldiers, the Germans arrested Moulin and demanded he sign a document that claimed that black Senegalese soldiers had committed the murder. He refused and was severely beaten. Lying in his prison cell (with an actual Senegalese soldier who had also been beaten and tortured), Moulin believed that under any further torture he might give in and sign such documents for the Germans, or reveal crucial information. He decided to make sure that this did not happen by killing himself. He found shards of broken glass in the cell and used one to slit his own throat. The German guards found him lying in a pool of his own blood, near death.[46]

This was not uncommon later among devoted members of the resistance. The Germans were notorious for their brutal tortures, and former resistance members rarely talk about such agonizing memories, but a few have discussed the methods used. One woman, a student at the time involved in protests, said that the Gestapo agents "began beating me with their fists . . . then they lighted cigarettes and pressed the burning ends into my chest and my temples, just above the ears."[47] Others told of having their fingers put in the hinges of huge metal doors and then having the doors slammed shut, crushing their fingers to pulp. One SOE agent in France had his teeth knocked out with a mallet, one by one, and his ankles broken.[48] To avoid the horrors of torture, and particularly to avoid revealing crucial information, resisters would sometimes, like Moulin, try to kill themselves. One agent by the name of André Postel-Vinay, upon arriving at the prison facility, threw himself off a two-story balcony. The fall broke nearly every bone in his body, but he survived.[49] The agents knew well that Gestapo tortures could eventually break anyone, and so the resistance organizations established special procedures to deal with the arrest of a compatriot. Generally, the agent arrested had the responsibility to hold out for two days, in spite of the terror of Nazi interrogation. Immediately upon learning of the arrest, the resistance network would change contacts, change contact locations, change mailboxes, and so on.[50] By the time the agent finally divulged information, hopefully it would be useless.

Moulin, after his suicide attempt, was taken to a hospital where he recovered, but the cut left a vicious scar across his throat, and for the rest of his days, he would wear a silk scarf around his neck to hide it. He was released eventually and allowed to return to his post, but soon after this, the Germans demanded that he terminate a number of leftist mayors serving in his district. Again he refused, and this time he was simply removed from office. Out of office, Moulin moved to the Bouches-du-Rhône area, where he joined the resistance and soon became a highly respected member. He eventually escaped France and headed to Britain, where he would meet Charles de Gaulle in September 1941. He impressed de Gaulle immensely, and de Gaulle thought that he had found the kind of man who could somehow unify the multiple resistance organizations under de Gaulle's own leadership. Moulin agreed that this was certainly desirable, and so after some preparations during that autumn, he was secretly parachuted back into France on January 1, 1942. He went to work immediately meeting the heads of the largest networks, under the code name "Max," and he was remarkably successful in convincing some of the most prominent to accept unification. He was able to create a unified organization made up of the groups Combat, Libération-Sud, and Franc-Tireur (not to be confused with the communist FTPF). This group was established in January 1943 and agreed to submit to the orders of de Gaulle's government, through the head of de Gaulle's BCRA, "Colonel Passy." The organization was named the Mouvements Unis de la Résistance (MUR).

Moulin himself would act as the head of the MUR, serving as a direct delegate from Charles de Gaulle and the Free French government. Moulin worked to direct the continuation of the various newspapers and publications, improving their distribution networks, and crucially spreading the word that the resistance was now unifying under de Gaulle's leadership. The MUR coordinated and expanded its networks of safe houses and travel operations to improve its ability to move POWs and downed airmen out of the country. With a unified organization in place and a clearer chain of command, supply operations were improved and the various networks received greater levels of financial support. But Moulin's MUR created a subsidiary organization as well, which comprised the various units that were responsible for action. The soldiers who would plant bombs in factories, blow up railroad tracks, and attack Axis troops were brought together as a separate group. Together these armed military personnel were called the Armée Secrète, and command was given to General Charles Delestraint, code-named "Vidal." Delestraint had been a high-ranking tank commander in the French army before retiring after the fall of France. He had been recruited into the resistance by Henri Frenay and, while working for Combat, had visited London and gained the respect of de Gaulle. Now his organization would become the largest in France conducting active attacks on the Axis forces.

Moulin was seemingly a force of nature, highly persuasive and constantly on the move, meeting with the various other groups and always urging increased unification and coordination. Among his many innovative ideas, Moulin recommended that a special council of legal intellectuals be assembled to study and "draft a plan for the political, economic, and administrative structures of France immediately after liberation."[51] This was an extremely important idea, as some plan for the future structure of France would have to be in place immediately at the time of liberation to avoid a chaotic struggle between competing factions and maybe even civil war. The group of prominent judges and officials was assembled and became known as the Comité Général d'Etudes. Moulin played a vital role in another way. As a trusted confidant of de Gaulle, he was quite effective at convincing the hardheaded general to consider decisions that otherwise he might have dismissed out of hand. Moulin consistently urged including the radical leftist resistance groups within their unified coalition. There was hardly any stronger opponent of communism than Charles de Gaulle, but Moulin quite rightly explained that their operating groups were crucial to the cause, and that having them included would give de Gaulle's organization some measure of control over them.

Moulin's work in persuading de Gaulle and his constant negotiations inside France eventually produced a monumental achievement. The MUR had been established by January 1943. Now almost six months of work resulted in a vital meeting to take place in a quiet apartment on the Rue du Four in Paris. There, on May 27, 1943, Moulin convened with the leadership of the existing MUR groups and many more. In all, eight of the top resistance groups were present, leaders of two resisting trade unions, and representatives from the underground major political parties of the former French Republic. Included among the political groups was the Front National, the political face of the communist FTPF. The result was an agreement for all of these entities to work together under Moulin's direct leadership and ultimately to be part of de Gaulle's Free French government. The group called itself the Conseil National de la Résistance (CNR), and it was certainly, as historian H. R. Kedward calls it, "the crowning achievement of Jean Moulin's efforts to unite the Resistance within France under de Gaulle."[52] One of the prominent resisters of the time, Claude Serreulles, said in an interview, "Moulin's decision to bring the Communists into the fold prevented an outbreak of civil war in France at the liberation. 'We might have become another Greece.'"[53]

After bringing about this remarkable unification, Moulin's personal triumph would be very brief indeed. The CNR came into existence on May 27, 1943, and immediately work began to coordinate the new organization under new and old leaders, and to reconfigure its operations. That work had barely been started when disaster struck. On the afternoon of June 21, in Caluire, a suburb of Lyon, Moulin met with a group of southern resistance leaders in a private apartment. It was actually a suite used by a Dr. Dugoujon, and at the time of the meeting, it had a waiting room full of patients. Moulin and those accompanying him showed up some 45 minutes late. But before the meeting could even come to order, police and Gestapo agents closed in around the apartment; there was a brief gunfight with some members outside, and then the doors were bashed in. All of the resisters in the room were arrested. The raid had been masterminded by the head of the Gestapo in Lyon, Klaus Barbie, and Barbie had files on most of the suspected resistance leaders, especially Moulin. Moulin was brought in for interrogation and severely tortured. The Gestapo used what today is called "waterboarding," a kind of controlled drowning, and electrodes attached to his testicles. Moulin was subjected to unimaginable pain when hot needles were shoved underneath his fingernails. As David Schoenbrun writes, "There were whips and clubs and screw-levered handcuffs that could be tightened until they bit through the flesh and broke through the bones of the wrist. Barbie had all these means to make 'Max' talk. But he did not know the kind of man he had taken prisoner."[54] In fact there is no indication that Moulin ever divulged any information at all, an act of almost superhuman courage. The Gestapo decided to deport him Germany, presumably to a concentration camp for more brutal treatment. Moulin was last seen in Paris at the Gestapo headquarters on Avenue Foch, lying comatose.[55] From there he was put on a train for Germany, but he never made it to his final destination. He is believed to have died en route while his train waited at the Imperial Train Station at the city of Metz (at that time in German hands). Today there is a white marble plaque in that train station in memory of Moulin and honoring his death on July 8, 1943.

The debate about who betrayed Moulin still rages today. The figure most often cited was a member of Combat named René Hardy, who was a "specialist in railway sabotage."[56] His treatment at the time by the Gestapo raised major questions, and he was brought to trial twice after the war. But he was never found guilty of such a crime. Some have suggested that the socialist Raymond Aubrac betrayed him. Aubrac was arrested in March 1943, and, so the theory goes, he may have been released only on condition that he provided the Gestapo with key information that led to the arrest of others. According to historian Robert Gildea, however, "This accusation was shown to be completely unfounded."[57] Klaus Barbie himself was located in Bolivia in 1971 and was eventually extradited to France, where he stood trial for crimes against humanity. Barbie was found guilty and spent the rest of his life in prison, but even his trial did not clear up the question.

The CNR, however, was up and running and needed a new chief. The man de Gaulle appointed to take control was Claude Serreulles. Moulin had been quite concerned that the Gestapo was closing in. When the MUR's bulletin was released and distributed, it would be in the hands of the Gestapo in a matter of only three days.[58] Aware of this, he had been adamant that de Gaulle should send over new agents designated to succeed him in case of his arrest or death. Now Serreulles, having only been back in France for two weeks, found himself in that position. He and his successors would work to continue to expand and unify the resistance. But most of all, as the war moved into 1944, the resistance began to work closely with Allied command in preparation for the massive invasion that was to come—the D-Day landings of June 1944. When that expedition arrived, the resistance would have a key role to play in making sure that German troops could not move to reinforce the coast, that telecommunications would be impossible, and that German troops were tied down by local combat. The story of the Normandy landings, the Paris uprising, and the liberation of France will be discussed in a subsequent chapter.

NOTES

1. Robert Gildea, *Fighters in the Shadows: A New History of the French Resistance* (Cambridge, MA: Harvard University Press, 2015), p. 2.

2. Ibid., p. 5.

3. Robert O. Paxton, *Vichy France: Old Guard and New Order, 1940–1944* (New York: Columbia University Press, 1972), pp. 291–292.

4. Ibid., p. 294.

5. Schoenbrun, *Soldiers of the Night*, p. 44.

6. Ibid., p. 254.

7. Jonathan F. Sweets, *Choices in Vichy France: The French under Nazi Occupation* (New York: Oxford University Press, 1986), p. 227.

8. Ibid., p. 225.

9. Schoenbrun, *Soldiers of the Night*, p. 27.

10. Ibid., p. 28.

11. For the complete terms of the surrender, see William L. Shirer, *The Collapse of the Third Republic: An Inquiry into the Fall of France in 1940* (New York: Simon and Schuster, 1969), pp. 852–900.

12. See Paxton, *Vichy France.*

13. See Zander, *The Rise of Fascism*, p. 135. See also Peter Davies, *The Extreme Right in France, 1789 to the Present* (London: Routledge, 2002), pp. 109–111.

14. General Charles de Gaulle, June 18, BBC radio broadcast, quoted in Jean Lacouture, *DeGaulle: The Rebel 1890–1944*, trans. Patrick O'Brien (New York: Norton, 1990), pp. 224–225.

15. See "Charles de Gaulle Speech," BBC News, http://www.bbc.com/news/10339678, accessed July 28, 2016.

16. See Schoenbrun, *Soldiers of the Night*, p. 36.

17. Ibid., p. 32.

18. Ibid., p. 52.

19. Ibid., p. 51.

20. Their prewar organization was known as the Vigilance Committee of Anti-Fascist Intellectuals. See ibid., p. 71.

21. Henry Kaiser, *The Cost of Courage* (New York: Other Press, 2015), p. 58.

22. See Schoenbrun, *Soldiers of the Night*, pp. 118–121. Albert Gaveau, it was found, had a German mother. He left France for Germany after the liberation in 1944, but after the war, he moved back to France and settled in Normandy. He was eventually identified and brought to justice, and he was sentenced to life imprisonment in 1949.

23. Ibid., p. 154.

24. His analysis of France's defense suggested that the high command should be charged with high treason. The government was appalled and had him imprisoned in March 1940. He was released by the officials of Vichy. See Marie-Madeleine Fourcade, *Noah's Ark*, trans. Kenneth Morgan (New York: Dutton, 1974), p. 20.

25. Ibid., p. 31.

26. Ibid., p. 40.

27. Schoenbrun, *Soldiers of the Night*, p. 183.

28. Fourcade, *Noah's Ark*, pp. 80–81.

29. See Fourcade, *Noah's Ark*, pp. 146–153.

30. Schoenbrun, *Soldiers of the Night*, p. 132.

31. Ibid., p. 140.

32. Ibid., p. 141.

33. Ibid., p. 139.

34. Ibid., p. 119.

35. Ibid., p. 119.

36. H. R. Kedward, *In Search of the Maquis: Rural Resistance in Southern France 1942–1944* (Oxford: Clarendon, 1993), p. 2.

37. Ibid., p. 5.

38. Personal account of Joseph Nodari, March 28, 1991, in Kedward, *In Search of the Maquis*, p. 257.

39. Ibid., p. 257.

40. Michel Bancilhon interview July 5, 1982, in Kedward, *In Search of the Maquis*, p. 247.

41. Gildea, *Fighters in the Shadows*, pp. 24–25.

42. Schoenbrun, *Soldiers of the Night*, p. 180.

43. Ibid., p. 180.

44. Gildea, *Fighters in the Shadows*, p. 26.

45. Schoenbrun, *Soldiers of the Night*, pp. 221–233.

46. Ibid., p. 37.

47. Account of Edwige de Saint-Wexel as shared with David Schoenbrun in ibid., p. 93.

48. Ibid., p. 380.

49. Kaiser, *The Cost of Courage*, p. 79.

50. Ibid., p. 152.

51. Schoenbrun, *Soldiers of the Night*, p. 178.

52. Kedward, *In Search of the Maquis*, p. 291.

53. Claude Serreulles quoted in Schoenbrun, *Soldiers of the Night*, p. 286.

54. Schoenbrun, *Soldiers of the Night*, p. 290.

55. Ibid., p. 291.

56. Gildea, *Fighters in the Shadows*, p. 286.

57. Ibid., 286.

58. Schoenbrun, *Soldiers of the Night*, p. 283.

4

Resistance in Northern Europe

Norway, Holland, and Denmark

After the conquest of Poland during September 1939, the next great offensives launched by Nazi Germany were in northern continental Europe and Scandinavia. Early on the morning of April 9, 1940, Adolf Hitler simultaneously launched the invasions of Denmark and Norway. As has been described in a previous chapter, resistance in Denmark was insignificant and was finished within 24 hours. In Norway there was a series of tenacious land battles in the south, and particularly along the North Sea coastal regions. Both the British and the French sent military aid, but the campaign was lost by late May. On June 7 the Norwegian government and the royal family escaped Norway to Britain on a Royal Navy cruiser, where they would establish a government-in-exile. But on May 9, while the conflict in Norway was still being fought, the Nazis had launched another major operation invading France and the Low Countries. The Netherlands had proclaimed its neutrality at the commencement of the war in September 1939, but this meant nothing to the Nazi regime. The German army moved easily through Holland, and the planes of the Luftwaffe savagely bombed the crucial port city of Rotterdam on May 14. One day later, the Dutch government was forced to surrender, and its government and royal family also escaped to Britain. Denmark, Norway, and the Netherlands had been conquered in the span of just over a month.

These three nations, however, occupied a unique position in Hitler's vision of a Nazi-dominated European empire. None of these three nations had any lingering enmity with Germany from the First World War, and all three had ethnic populations that were considered to be racial kin to the "Aryan" German race. Their Nordic blood, according to Nazi racial theory, made these people a desirable part of the Nazi future. Their distinct national cultures, however, would have to be modified, and their people would have to be assimilated into Nazi German culture. This racial ideology guided the Nazi plans for these northern countries; they were not to be physically destroyed or their populations exterminated or enslaved, the fate that awaited most of the peoples of Eastern Europe. These nations were to be conquered and subdued but then to be reshaped into ideal Nazi states, with their current populations and future generations indoctrinated with Nazi ideology. But none of these three nations showed a larger inclination to go along with this twisted vision of a Nazified future. In all three cases significant resistance took place, despite intense obstacles and repression. Further, all of these three nations produced consequential resistance operations that hold an important place in the history of World War II.

THE RESISTANCE IN NORWAY

Even before Norway had formally surrendered, Nazi Germany sent its administrative governor to that nation on April 24, 1940, to take over its government operations. This *Reichskommissar*, Josef Terboven, was given supreme authority over all aspects of civilian administration and established his seat of government in the Stortinget (the former Norwegian parliament) in Oslo. While Terboven would rule over all civilian matters, another man, *Generaloberst* (Colonel-General) Nikolaus von Falkenhorst, was placed in command of the military aspects of the occupation. Falkenhorst had planned and commanded the military invasion of Norway; with his victory complete by June 7, he was assigned to remain in Norway, where he served until his dismissal in December 1944. Terboven administered the Norwegian police, while Falkenhorst commanded the *Abwehr* (military intelligence unit). But the most terrifying organizational threat to Norwegians was the notorious Gestapo, a division of the SS, which operated virtually independently in Norway, under the leadership of Heinrich Fehlis. Fehlis had some theoretical accountability to Terboven but was in reality accountable only to the head of the SD in Berlin, Reinhard Heydrich. It was a tangled and problematic organizational structure that was representative of the irrational and chaotic structure of the entire Nazi state. We shall see similar configurations throughout this book, with a number of competing commands all struggling against one another for supremacy and administrative responsibilities. Adolf Hitler seems to have intentionally designed the Nazi administrative apparatus in this fashion in every aspect of the state. He was convinced of the need for individuals to fight and struggle for supremacy in order to bring the best to the top. In reality he had created the most irrational and startlingly inefficient state structure imaginable; the Nazi state achieved its objectives by means of savage terror, not through any semblance of modern, efficient administration.

In Norway, however, there was a fourth organizational component intensifying the nightmare of occupation. This was the Norwegian political party known as Nasjonal Samling ("National Unity"), headed by its infamous founder, Vidkun Quisling. The party was a fascist organization and grew increasingly pro-Nazi through the 1930s. In the early days of the German invasion, Quisling had tried to elbow himself into power, taking to the airwaves and demanding that he be made prime minister. A fervent Nazi himself, he believed he could minimize the damage to Norway and that he could work with Hitler's government to create a Norwegian Nazi state. The existing government bluntly refused to give way to him, and even after the German victory, Quisling was not put into power by the Nazis. His party, however, was allowed to continue, while all other Norwegian political parties were outlawed and dismantled. Hitler finally agreed to put Quisling into power as the "minister president" of a "national government" in Norway on February 1, 1942, though the existing Nazi power structure remained in place. From this position, Quisling would attempt to work with the Germans to create a Nazified Norwegian state that would cooperate with Germany in Hitler's New Order. As such, patriotic Norwegians faced a multitude of challenges as they tried to live under the harsh conditions and privations of occupation. Those who tried actively to resist faced terror and repression from Nazi authorities, but also from their fellow citizens who supported Quisling's pro-Nazi government.

Despite all this, thousands of Norwegians did resist. Almost immediately after the Germans completed their victory and took control of the country, Norwegians began to find ways they could pass on information to Great Britain. Dozens of small, disparate groups of people, particularly in Oslo and in the coastal cities, began to form intelligence agencies to secretly observe Nazi operations and report on them. These groups popped up in places including Haugesund, Stavanger, and Trondheim.[1] Thousands of other Norwegians who were determined to continue the fight against the Germans decided they had to leave the country in order to do so. They found transport with departing British military craft, and especially with patriotic Norwegian fisherman and sailors willing to risk the dangers of sailing the North Sea to Britain. Once in Britain, Norwegian escapees found that they were first taken into custody by MI5 (Britain's security service in charge of counterespionage) and put through the interrogations at "Patriotic School," the nickname for MI5's screening facility. Once a Norwegian convinced MI5 authorities that he or she was not a German agent, they could contact the Norwegian government-in-exile and the British military authorities. Many Norwegians went back into uniformed fighting units of the British armed forces. Many others, however, were recruited for special work back in Norway. Britain's Secret Intelligence Service (SIS) was determined to build an infrastructure for intelligence gathering in Norway, and by the autumn of 1940, the Special Operations Executive (SOE) was intent upon launching sabotage operations.

By the summer of 1941, the rather haphazard bunch of sailing and fishing vessels moving between Britain and Norway was formalized into a special organization. Working with both the SOE and the SIS, the service became known as the "Shetland Bus," after its Scalloway base in the Shetland Islands north of the Scottish mainland. Both Norwegian and British crews worked these boats through intensely dangerous seas and the deadly risks of capture. By war's end they had transported some 192 agents into Norway and brought out 73 agents and 373 escapees. In addition the Shetland Bus crews transported vital supplies of food and weapons, estimated at 400 tons.[2]

Those who remained in Norway resisted the Nazis in various ways. From the early days of the occupation, Norwegians tried to display their defiance by wearing pins or spraying graffiti with the "H-7" symbol, which cryptically symbolized their support of the Norwegian King, Haakon VII, in exile in Britain. Other forms of nonviolent defiance included student demonstrations with the wearing of paper clips through the lapel.[3] This simple gesture symbolized the binding together of the Norwegian people against the Nazis. Norwegian groups, like resistance groups elsewhere, printed a number of underground newssheets to keep Norwegians informed with accurate news about the war and to constantly urge Norwegians to be vigilant in their support of the Allies. These saw distribution as early as late September 1940.[4] There was also significant resistance from a group of Norwegian professional organizations. The Nazi government (and later Quisling's "national government") were determined to force Norwegian industries and civil service functions to reorganize under Nazi-based professional groups; this was to facilitate the transition of all of Norway to Nazism. But organizations like the shipowners steadfastly refused to change their organization and leadership. The teachers of Norway openly refused to give in to demands for a Nazi-based curriculum in their classrooms, despite over 1,100 of them being arrested and sent to concentration camps. Nor would the leadership of Norway's Protestant churches agree to support the occupation or Nazism. In fact, the church pastors sent a defiant message to the Quisling government, and some ministers read this statement aloud to their congregations:

> When those in authority in the community tolerate violence and injustice and oppress the souls of men, then the Church is the guardian of men's consciences . . . On that account the bishops of the Church have laid before the Minister some of the facts and official announcements concerning the administration of the community . . . which the Church finds to be in conflict with the law of God.[5]

That message was later broadcast to the people of Norway on the BBC's Norwegian service. The firm resistance by professional industrial leaders, labor union leaders, teachers, and religious leaders eventually forced Quisling to abandon his cherished desire to reorganize Norway along "corporative" lines—that is, to reorganize the country's economy and professions into boards that managed entire industries, as had been pioneered in fascist Italy and Nazi Germany. The Norwegian people's refusal to cooperate made it unworkable, and this was a quiet but truly important victory for nonviolent resistance in Norway.[6]

There was also a good deal of active and violent resistance in Norway, including gun battles with Nazi troops and particularly industrial sabotage. By May 1941 the many various resistance and intelligence groups were able to consolidate into a single coherent military organization, or "Milorg." Controlled by a civilian committee, this group was not well coordinated with either the Norwegian government in Britain or the SOE. The result was a series of botched and unsuccessful operations. But by the end of 1942, Milorg had come under the command of the Norwegian high command in Britain and was working directly with the SOE. Its primary work involved two principal functions. The first was establishing a series of safe houses and contacts for the escape route to neutral Sweden across the eastern border. The second was in recruiting larger numbers of "Joessings" or "true Norwegians" to serve in an eventual army that would rise up against the Nazis whenever the Allied forces arrived. Part of that activity was receiving and hiding stashes of weapons sent by the SOE. Milorg policy (strongly supported by the Norwegian government-in-exile) was to keep actual combat and sabotage actions to a minimum in order to avoid Nazi reprisals on innocent Norwegians. All the same, some notable raids did take place, even before the formation of Milorg.

Two of the most important of such raids were "Operation Claymore" and "Operation Archery." These two operations were launched as cooperative efforts by Britain's SOE, the British armed forces, and the Norwegian resistance. Claymore was a seaborne attack raid on the Lofoten Islands, which extend like a crooked finger off the northern Norwegian coast. Those islands were centers for factories producing fish oil and glycerin that the Germans used for their own production of military explosives. Two British commando regiments from the Royal Engineers and over 50 Norwegian sailors landed on the islands on March 4, 1941. Ships fired on the factories from the sea, and the commandos stormed the factories, disabling most of the production on the island and destroying 3,600 tons of oil and glycerin, while sinking some 18,000 tons of German shipping. The raid also took 228 enemy prisoners. Operation Archery was launched in December 1941 with a similar mission: to engage the German troops in the coastal island town of Måløy and to destroy the fish oil and glycerin production facilities there. Once again the raid was successful in terms of disabling industrial production, but the greatest accomplishment of these raids was to convince Hitler to deploy an extra 30,000 troops for coastal defense in Norway. Hitler became convinced that an Allied offensive would eventually be launched in Norway, and this kept over 300,000 German troops there that would have been vital to defenses elsewhere.

One of the costliest casualties in the raid on Måløy was a Norwegian officer working with the SOE, Captain Martin Jensen Linge. Linge had been a Norwegian liaison officer to the British as those armies fought together against the Germans in the spring of 1940. He was wounded and evacuated to Britain, where, after his recovery, he helped organize a Norwegian resistance force, formally named the Norwegian Independent Company One. They worked closely with the SOE to train soldiers for secret work and transport operations to Norway. The organization was proficient and gained the nickname of the "Linge Company," and some of its members would perform daring and heroic operations. Linge was killed in the raid on Måløy on December 27, 1941, though his unit continued under his name.

Such raids and resistance activity produced deadly reprisals by the Nazis. The Gestapo was diligent in infiltrating and destroying the resistance organizations and was quite successful, for a time completely disabling Milorg operations in the south. Those arrested were subject to fearsome torture and execution. But the Nazis could also take collective vengeance upon innocent Norwegians for resistance work. The most infamous of these examples was the assault now remembered as the "Telavåg Tragedy" of April 26, 1942. The town of Telavåg sits among the coastal fjords on the southern coast of Norway, and it was a vital point for sea traffic to and from Britain. Nazi authorities discovered that locals were hiding two Norwegian soldiers from the Linge Company, and the Gestapo was called in to arrest them. The Norwegians were able to resist, and there was a brief gun battle that killed one of the Norwegians and two Gestapo men. The remaining Norwegian agents were taken and arrested, but the Nazis took a frightful revenge on the entire town for the death of the Gestapo agents. Personally overseen by Terboven, Nazi troops dynamited the harbor and all buildings in the town. Every boat in the harbor was sunk, and all agricultural products were taken, including all livestock. Most of the men in town were rounded up and executed on the spot, while the rest of the survivors were sent to the Sachsenhausen concentration camp, where most would perish before the end of the war. The Nazis had their revenge. But already by this time, another operation was in the planning stages in Britain that would involve members of the famed Linge Company. It would live in Norwegian history as one of the most vital operations of the war, and it is just possible that it saved humanity.

THE HEROES OF VEMORK: THE RAIDS ON GERMAN HEAVY WATER PRODUCTION

An obscure factory tucked away in a deep and barely accessible valley over 100 miles north of Oslo emerged by 1941 as a key strategic point in the outcome of the war. The factory was a hydroelectric and chemicals plant built by Norsk Hydro, a Norwegian company, and had been in operation since 1905. Producing a number of chemicals like ammonia, chiefly for fertilizer production, one of the by-products generated from its systems was collected and stored; and it had come to be a prized commodity for the German weapons scientists. Astoundingly, you can pour this chemical by-product over ice in a glass and take a refreshing drink—it is a rare variant of water called deuterium oxide, or "heavy water." Containing a larger proportion of the hydrogen isotope deuterium, the substance was found to be an essential component in creating the necessary chain reactions to produce an atomic bomb.

The atom was first split in the 1930s by German scientists Otto Hahn, Lise Meitner, and Fritz Strassmann, whose research later evolved into the full discovery of the process of nuclear fission. Ironically, Lise Meitner would not be present to fully participate in the expansion of their discoveries, as she was forced to escape (with secret help from Otto Hahn) to the Netherlands and then to Sweden. Lise Meitner was Jewish. Hahn and others, however, joined together to advance the science and worked to produce a weapon based on the energy released in the division of a uranium or plutonium atom. Heavy water was a necessary ingredient as a "slowing agent" to regulate the process. In order for the German atomic weapons program to achieve its objective, it needed a large and regular supply of heavy water. At that time, heavy water in such amounts was produced by only one factory in the world—the Norsk Hydro plant in the town of Vemork in the Rjukan valley in Norway.[7]

In the scientific community outside Germany, top physicists had some idea of the potential of the German nuclear program; particularly those who had escaped the fascist dictatorships, like Albert Einstein and Enrico Fermi, issued warnings about that potential. The eventual result of such warnings was the creation of the Manhattan Project in the United States, which would, by 1945, succeed in producing the world's first atomic weapons. But back in May 1941, British intelligence sources passed information indicating that the German program was requesting a "tenfold increase" of heavy water at Vemork to 3,000 pounds per year, and later that figure was upped to 10,000 pounds per year. "There could be no doubt that Hitler was exerting the greatest pressure on his scientists to beat the Allies in the race to build an atomic weapon."[8] Winston Churchill's personal scientific advisor, Lord Cherwell (nicknamed "the Prof") presented a report to the prime minister on the subject, which persuaded the War Cabinet to consider some kind of operation to stop the supply of heavy water. Planning for the operation involved collaboration between the SOE and the War Office. The easiest option seemed to be bombing the nearby concrete dam that held back an enormous lake, thereby flooding the entire Rjukan valley. Naturally, the Norwegian government-in-exile strongly rejected this, as the loss of innocent life would have been catastrophic. The planners also decided that direct aerial bombing of the plant was too risky to Norwegians in the area and (as the Norwegian government reminded them) could cripple the local economy after the war. Instead, the operation would use a combination of Norwegian secret agents and British commandos from the Royal Engineers to pull off a daring sabotage raid.

The SOE immediately went to work recruiting suitable Norwegian agents, mostly from the existing Linge Company. They selected 10 men based upon outstanding physical condition, familiarity with the natural environment, and mental ability. All 10 went into the SOE's special training schools and spent much of their time in the Scottish highlands, learning to use specialized weapons, how to use wireless, and especially how to navigate the harsh terrain they would encounter. While the Norwegians trained, the SOE and War Office planners received two miraculous gifts from Norway. The first was in the person of Dr. Leif Tronstad, a first-rate scientist whose work in nuclear chemistry had led him to a pioneering role in heavy-water research. He, in fact, had been the top consultant in the design of the heavy-water containment systems at the Norsk Hydro plant. He had fought against the Germans in 1940 and then turned to intelligence work for the British after the surrender; upon his group's exposure, he fled to London in September 1941. Now he worked directly with the SOE in providing detailed information about the plant and how to disable it. The second godsend arrived on a humble fishing vessel, in the form of Einar Skinnarland. The 23-year-old Skinnarland was a young engineer from Rjukan who actually worked at the Norsk Hydro plant. He had left his job and home during a vacation break and found passage on a Norwegian fishing boat to Scotland, and upon his arrival, the interviewers couldn't believe their good fortune. He was passed along to the SOE, which used his intimate knowledge of the factory—and particularly of the German defenses there—to help plan the operation. He was given an abbreviated training course and then parachuted back into Norway, where he would help facilitate the operation. He reported back to work at the end of his vacation period, and no one had any inkling that he had ever left.[9] He informed the SOE that the Germans had approximately 100 troops in the town of Rjukan and about 20 in the actual factory complex; there was a guard station at the road entering the plant, and the Germans had stretched steel cables across the open valley to prohibit any low-flying aerial attacks.[10]

Four Norwegians were selected for the initial drop into Norway and were prepared to begin the operation, which was code-named "Operation Grouse." But the notorious Norwegian weather resulted in a few aborted attempts and weeks of anxious waiting. Finally on October 18, 1942, they were successfully parachuted into Norway. They were dropped into one of the most hostile environments in all of Europe. Adjacent to the Rjukan valley is a massive mountain plateau that covers some 2,500 square miles in all directions; it is known as the Hardangervidda. Its elevation is 3,500 feet, and it is mostly flat plains with a few lakes scattered in hill valleys. By October it was covered in snow, and the white emptiness stretched before the Norwegian agents with few indications of any areas for refuge. After collecting their equipment and burying their parachutes, the group took off south on their skis, but they had to sleep in dugouts in the snow to stay alive. Eventually the group found a few of the hunter's shacks built in the wilderness for the few hunters and adventurers who visited the area. In one of these huts, the four would settle down and create a base camp, waiting for orders for the next stage of the operation. It was severely challenging, as their food rations were limited and there was precious little wood for fire; the wireless set was problematic but eventually provided adequate communication.

Finally on November 17, word arrived that the second part of the operation was on, and the Norwegians made their preparations to greet the British commandos who were on their way and scheduled to land on the night of November 19. This much larger landing party was code-named "Operation Freshman." It would turn out to be one of the most tragic failures of the "secret war." Two Halifax bombers took off from Scotland, each towing a glider full of men secured by cable. Fighting terrible weather, the two planes finally arrived over Norway and prepared to release the gliders, which sought to land on the Hardangervidda close to the waiting Norwegians. Because of severe icing, though, the first Halifax turned around and began to head home, aborting its mission. But the ice on the towing cable became so heavy that the cable snapped, and the glider spun out of control toward the earth, eventually crashing atop a small mountain over Lysef-jord. A local farmer found the horrific crash site and went to get help. Seventeen men were on board, of which eight were killed immediately in the crash, with four others having catastrophic injuries; five men were uninjured. When help arrived, it was in the form of Nazi SS troops. The men were taken for intense interrogation and torture with their hands bound by barbed wire. After their interrogations they were all summarily executed and tossed into a mass grave.

The other Halifax had fared no better. It released its glider at a high altitude and, turning for home, went into severe clouds. With no visibility to speak of, the bomber crashed into the side of a mountain, killing all its crew. The glider, meanwhile, crash-landed on a plain near the town of Egersund. Seven of its men were killed in the crash, and all survivors were injured. Two men limped off to seek help, but again German SS troops arrived at the crash site and arrested all of the surviving men. Like their other comrades, they were taken into custody in a German camp, faced interrogation with the torturers exploiting their wounds for maximum pain, and then shot. They were executed despite their military uniforms, which normally would have gotten them placed in a German prisoner-of-war camp. But Adolf Hitler had only just issued a new order regarding airborne saboteurs that read, "Caused by the growing number of cases, where planes are used for the landing of saboteurs, and as through this great damage has been done, I hereby order that crews of sabotage planes are to be shot at once by the troops isolating them."[11] His orders were carried out to the letter. Operation Freshman was a terrible human tragedy, but it was a serious strategic one as well. All 34 of the Royal Engineers' commandos were dead, along with their flight crews. But now the Germans were well aware that the British were targeting the heavy-water facility at Vemork. They immediately began to redouble their defenses in the area, and planners in Britain went back to work to figure a way to sabotage the plant before it was too late.

The four Norwegians stuck on Hardangervidda were left on their own to survive until some decision was made about what to do. This was a serious and life-threatening situation, as on the plateau there was virtually nothing to eat, and the food rations were running out. They also faced the harshest conditions of winter. It is fitting that one of the finest accounts of this mission, *The Real Heroes of Telemark: The True Story of the Secret Mission to Stop Hitler's Bomb* (2003), was written by author Ray Mears, who specializes in adventure and survival writing rather than military history. It was truly a remarkable trial of the human will to survive. But through the months, as their food was nearly exhausted, the men finally encountered a herd of reindeer and were able to kill enough to provide sustenance. They ate and dried the meat, of course, but they also found that they needed carbohydrates desperately. Trained outdoorsmen as they were, they knew that in such a situation, the moss inside a reindeer's stomach could be used for nutrition, and so they mixed blood, meat, and moss in a kind of stew. It saved their lives.[12]

During this period the men came to a decision and wired Britain to say that they would be willing to carry out the mission themselves. The SOE, now in complete control of the operation, began to plan such a raid. Planners decided to send over the remaining crew of six trained Norwegians. This second party would be code-named "Operation Gunnerside" and was scheduled for February 1943. The SOE, meanwhile, changed the code name for the "Grouse" mission to "Swallow," in case the Germans had come across the original name in any radio traffic. It appears that the Germans never did. On February 16, 1943, the Gunnerside men dropped safely into Norway, buried their equipment, and found the nearest hunting lodge. From there they would work to find the Swallow team. This was an immense challenge in such an enormous and forbidding wilderness; one could go weeks or months without ever seeing another person or even an animal. But the teams did find each other, and they began planning the details of a raid on the Vemork factory. The Gunnerside men were shocked at the appearance of the four Swallow men, who looked extremely gaunt and malnourished, and that night they all shared a feast including raisins and chocolate.[13] They also discussed a strange development. Despite the odds, the party *had* encountered another person on the Hardanger plain who turned out to be a local reindeer hunter. The party had been ordered to kill anyone who might jeopardize the mission in any way. The men interrogated the hunter to find if he was a Quisling supporter or not—he answered that he was "known to be a supporter, but had not gotten round to joining."[14] It was not entirely clear whether this man, one Kristian Kristiansen, was terrified that they were German agents, or if he truly was a Quisling supporter. The party eventually decided to let him go, believing he was a loyal Norwegian who was lying to save his life, but there was dispute about this move. Some said he should have been shot to ensure the secrecy of the mission.

The group took only a short period of time to plan out their attack on the factory, and they carried out the mission on the night of February 27–28. They skied to the very edge of the Hardanger plateau, which dropped off directly into the great Rjukan valley. They were forced to climb down one sheer side of the valley, cross the river at the bottom, and climb back up a sheer cliff face to get near the factory. Once up the other side, they approached on the side of the motor road that ran along the cliff side leading into the factory complex. They carried chloroform with them to take out any guards, but thankfully this proved unnecessary.[15] Once inside the factory complex, they split into groups, with one group standing guard and two groups trying to enter the heavy-water facility. One group of two men was able to get into the facility through doors, while another was forced to smash windowpanes to enter, but they were never confronted by German guards. Inside the heavy-water area, they did encounter a stunned and terrified Norwegian guard. He was forced to face the wall at gunpoint and wisely did not cry out for help. The men then attached plastic explosives to the key machines and to the existing stores of heavy water. Then the footsteps of a second guard echoed and the man appeared—not a German guard, but another Norwegian civilian. The group then fled the facility as fast as they could, leaving the guards to their own devices. The timed detonator gave them only two minutes. When all the men were rushing out of the factory complex under cover of darkness, they heard the explosion, but they were surprised to find that it was a fairly small, dull thud. The Germans were not at first alarmed, and only after a period of several minutes did an investigation reveal what had happened. This fortuitous delay gave the Norwegian agents the time they needed to flee the complex and then make their way through the valley. Going into the operation, they had expected a gun battle and had agreed that anyone wounded must take their cyanide capsule to avoid any possibility of talking under torture. But no firefight took place. They escaped without losing a man and without detection. They were further aided by a deep snowfall later that night, which covered up any footsteps and ski tracks. In the hours and days that followed, the Germans had no idea where to even begin looking.

In response to the raid, several local Norwegians were taken hostage by the Germans, and unless locals revealed what had happened, the Germans threatened to execute these people. But eventually the head of the German military, General Falkenhorst, determined (from artifacts intentionally left behind by the saboteurs) that the raid had been carried out by British commandos, and thus no reprisals against civilians were carried out. Instead they launched a massive manhunt for the commandos, which would include searching Hardangervidda. The Norwegian agents now split up, with several taking the escape routes to Sweden, and two others, Arne Kjelstrup and Knut Haukelid, staying behind in Norway to continue working with the resistance. The two traveled to Oslo, and while there, in the home of a resistance friend, in an unbelievable twist of fate, Knut Haukelid's own father showed up at the flat. Knut had to hide until his father left, as it was imperative that no one outside the resistance knew of his presence, not even his own father. This was the last time he would see his father alive. At war's end, he got the agonizing news that his father had been deported and had died in the concentration camps.[16]

In the aftermath of the raid, the Germans immediately set to work repairing the facility and renewing the production of heavy water. Within six months the factory was again producing heavy water in significant amounts for transport to Germany. In Britain, military planners were urged that this must stop at all costs, and a new strategy was adopted for assaulting the factory at Vemork. Now the U.S. Air Force would take on the job with its supposedly super-accurate bombing sights. On November 16, 1943, 154 American Flying Fortresses bombed the Rjukan valley, dropping nearly 1,000 bombs. Only 18 bombs hit their mark in the Vemork factory, and tragically a bomb hit a nearby bomb shelter, killing 21 innocent Norwegians.[17] Maddeningly, the heavy-water facility was not severely damaged, and German production could continue, but the German High Command was now convinced that the site of heavy-water production should be moved to a safer location. On January 29, 1944, Knut Haukelid got word from the SOE over the wireless about the German plans: "It is reported that the heavy water apparatus at Vemork and Rjukan is to be dismantled and transported to Germany. Can you get this confirmed? Can this transport be prevented?"[18]

In the days to come, Knut Haukelid emerged as the leader of a new raid that would attempt to destroy all the existing stores of heavy water as they were transported to Germany. According to Haukelid's personal account, the belief was that if all existing stores could be eliminated, "we could stop them for a year or two, perhaps for the rest of the war."[19] So Haukelid went to work, using resistance contacts who actually worked at the factory and who knew the logistical plan of moving the water. The course to be taken began at the Vemork factory, where the barrels of water would be loaded onto railcars and shipped by train out of the Rjukan valley. The train stopped at the edge of a very long and deep body of water known as Tinnsjå (Lake Tinn). The train would stop at the northern end of the long lake, where the cargo would be transferred and taken by ferry to the southern end of the lake, where it would be loaded onto a railcar and taken by train the rest of the way to Norway's southern coast. There it would be loaded onto a German transport ship. As Haukelid examined the route and the best possible strategies, he decided that bombing the ferry in Lake Tinn would be the most effective solution. If the ferry were blown up at the deepest point in the lake, the drums would sink to a depth of some 1,200 feet.

To make this operation effective, though, Haukelid would need timing devices for the explosives and specific kinds of detonators. He was able to secure both, by working with local Norwegian machine shops and an SOE agent in the area.[20] They spent several days scouting the planned route and examining the ferry. Then on February 18, 1944, he and another agent observed the shipping of the barrels and boarded the ferry. While the other agent stood guard, Haukelid went below decks to place the explosives and set the timers; then the two quietly exited the craft and waited. The knowledge that innocent people would die preyed heavily upon their minds. As Haukelid wrote just after the war, "What would happen now at Rjukan?

How many Norwegian lives would be lost through this piece of devilry? The explosion on board the ferry must cost lives, and the reprisals at Rjukan certainly no fewer. The English had sacrificed 43 men with the gliders. . . . The bombing had cost 22 lives. How many would it be this time?"[21]

The explosives detonated in a tremendous blast that tore a huge hole in the bottom of the ferry. The boat and its cargo went down within minutes, including 3,600 gallons of heavy water never to be recovered by the Germans. Haukelid had been right: fourteen innocent Norwegian lives were lost, along with four German lives. But Germany's nuclear program had been significantly undermined by the lack of the crucial heavy water needed to bring its research to fruition. As Mears writes, "Clearly Hitler's atomic program had not been terminated, but the wider intelligence indicated that they were so off the pace established by the American scientists that the threat was no longer considered significant."[22] There remains a great deal of debate about whether or not the German program was ever truly likely to have produced a bomb. There were many obstacles, not least of which was Hitler's neglect of the program in the early years of the war. Additionally, the heavy bombing of German industry and the flight of key scientific minds from the Nazi regime hindered the program. But, says Mears, the Germans' failure to get their hands on Vemork's heavy water "was undoubtedly a major blow to the program."[23]

The 10 Norwegians who had worked for the SOE in the various sabotage operations, along with the handful of resident Norwegians who played a role, live on as national heroes in Norway. They all survived the war, and many went on to establish notable careers in politics, the military, and broadcasting. Their exploits are memorialized today at monuments in Vemork and in the Norwegian resistance museums in Oslo and Bergen.

THE DUTCH RESISTANCE AND THE DISASTER OF THE *ENGLANDSPIEL*

The German invasion of the Netherlands commenced on May 10, 1940, despite that country's acknowledged neutrality and without any declaration of war. The Dutch did deploy their military troops and planes to fight the Germans, but they were overwhelmed very quickly. On May 14 the Nazis savagely bombed the crucial and historic seaport of Rotterdam, killing nearly 800 people and leaving large parts of the city in ruins. The Dutch government was informed that unless it surrendered immediately, a similar fate would befall the other major Dutch cities. The Dutch government capitulated, and its queen, Wilhelmina, and her key ministers escaped to Britain to establish a government-in-exile. The Nazis then set about establishing a permanent occupation.

Almost immediately there were Dutch citizens who wanted to translate their outrage into resistance action, but it was clear from the outset that this would be extremely difficult in the Netherlands. Any Dutch resistance faced almost insurmountable obstacles. The Netherlands, quite simply, was not geographically suited to sustain an active resistance movement. It has no prominent mountain ranges or great forests; it is generally a flat plain. Nor does it have vast expanses of wilderness into which a resistance group might disappear. The land is characterized by large industrial cities, suburbs, and acres of flat land under cultivation. Over the centuries, virtually all of that land has been connected by an efficient system of roads and canals. In other words, for a resistance group, there was nowhere to hide. There was also the problem of borders. Holland was bordered by occupied Belgium to the south, and after that occupied France. Its northern and eastern borders were with Germany itself. It did have a long coast along the North Sea, but this was heavily guarded and developed by the German military, with naval bases and a constant coastal patrol. Recognizing the vulnerability of the coastal region to resistance activity, the Germans restricted the entire coastal zone, and Dutch citizens were forbidden to enter.[24] One of the central functions of resistance groups all over occupied Europe was helping others to escape to free territories. But in the Dutch case, with the coast hermetically sealed, one had only one way out, and that was south over three different borders—Belgium, Nazi-occupied France, and Vichy France—in order to get to either Spain or Switzerland. The likelihood of surviving such an escape route riddled with Nazi authorities was very small indeed. As a result, the Dutch resistance case was unique. It was less focused on escapes, sabotage, and outright fighting (although a minimal number of these acts were carried out) than upon nonviolent defiance within its own borders. It was focused primarily on helping the Dutch population to survive a brutal occupation.

That brutal occupation began with Adolf Hitler's appointment of Arthur Seyss-Inquart as *Reichskommissar* over the occupied Dutch territories. Seyss-Inquart was a lawyer and politician from Austria who had been deeply involved in the Austrian Nazi party. Emerging as the leader of that party, he had been forced into the position of chancellor of Austria during the tensions that led to the eventual absorption of Austria into the German Reich (the Anschluss) and was responsible for drafting the legislation that ended Austrian independence. In 1939 he served briefly in Hitler's cabinet without portfolio and then in occupied Poland. He began his administration of Holland with calls for Dutch and Nazi collaboration and a constructive incorporation of Holland into the new Nazi world order. In his inaugural address, he said he "saw it as his most important task to persuade (not to force) the Dutch people—after all a people of Germanic brothers—to embrace National Socialism."[25] He worked with the small

Dutch Nazi party, the Nationaal-Socialistische Beweging (NSB), to allow them some role in the government, and he used their uniformed private army of thugs (the Landwacht) to help enforce Nazi policy on the streets.

He was unsuccessful in his efforts to gradually mold the Dutch nation into a "good Nazi state." In a hundred ways, the Dutch people refused to accept Nazi ideology, and so the policies of Seyss-Inquart grew increasingly forceful and eventually moved into all-out terror. As a Dutch psychologist wrote just after the war, "The Germans used two weapons to persuade the Dutch to accept their regime. The first was propaganda, the second terror, and as the first was shown to have little effect, they resorted more and more to the second."[26] The Dutch scholar Louis de Jong, the most eminent historian of Holland's war experience, elaborates upon the goals of the Nazis in occupied Holland. He asserts that the first goal of the Nazis was indeed to persuade the Dutch to accept Nazi ideology and to "transform the Netherlands into a National Socialist state." But here, he says, the Nazis failed miserably and never approached the accomplishment of this goal. However, the Nazis also had three other principal objectives in Holland:

— To exploit fully the Dutch economic potential, including the Dutch labor force
— To purge the Netherlands of Jews
— To prevent all aid to Germany's enemies.[27]

In the pursuit of these three objectives, says de Jong, despite heroic efforts by the Dutch resistance, the Nazis were largely successful. The Nazis were able to force Dutch industry into war production for the German war machine. As de Jong writes, "Broadly speaking, half of Dutch industry worked exclusively for the German war effort," and by 1943, "two to three percent of all the weapons the German armed forces acquired were produced in the Netherlands."[28] This also included the Germans rounding up nearly 500,000 Dutch workers to be forcefully deported to work in factories in Germany.[29] By 1941 the Nazis began to impose their murderous policies concerning the Jews in Holland. There existed in the Netherlands a population of approximately 140,000 Jews (according to the definition of "true Jews" within the German "Reich Citizenship Law" of 1935),[30] of which the Nazis would eventually arrest and deport some 107,000, or about 76 percent.[31] The Nazis were also greatly successful at restricting intelligence from leaving the country and suppressing armed resistance. We will discuss this further in the sections below. But by sealing its borders and sealing its coasts, in a nation of 9 million people, only about 1,700 Dutch citizens were ever able to escape. The levels of success by the Nazis in these four areas may at first seem like a total victory for the Nazis in

Holland. But de Jong reminds us that "every act that opposed any of those four German goals was an act of resistance."[32]

The first acts of resistance in the Netherlands were similar to nonviolent resistance in other nations, mostly gestures and nonviolent acts of subtle protest. These included graffiti and refusal to follow rationing procedures; and in a unique gesture, they used the left side of their envelopes for Nazi-issued stamps when posting a letter—they said the right side was reserved only for stamps with Queen Wilhelmina's image. The Dutch also were able to run a prolific series of underground publications with calls for resistance, and with accurate news of the war, especially Allied victories. In the beginning these publications were merely mimeographed sheets, but over time a huge number of pamphlets and papers evolved into formal publications, and the most prominent of them were released in editions of tens of thousands of copies. De Jong estimates that there were some 1,200 different publications circulating by the end of the war.[33]

These milder expressions of resistance turned into more active expressions by February 1941. By that time, the Nazis were ramping up their efforts to round up the Jewish population of Amsterdam. The Communist Party and other labor groups worked to coordinate a large-scale general strike in protest, and untold numbers of ordinary Dutch citizens joined in, demonstrating in the large squares of the city. The Nazis intervened violently, firing on crowds and killing nine people. But this did not stop the Dutch permanently. In April 1943 the Germans announced that they intended to "re-arrest" all the members of the Dutch army who had been released from prisoner-of-war camps in the spring of 1940. Once again the Dutch conducted mass strikes all over the country, lasting about a week. The Germans again cracked down with violence and arrests. In the end the Germans executed some 80 people, 95 had died in the streets, and over 400 people had been wounded in shootings and street fighting. Nine hundred were deported to concentration camps. The Germans forced young workers to sign oaths of loyalty, and if workers would not sign, they were deported to work in German factories. As a final blow, the Germans forced all Dutch citizens (except resident Nazis) to turn over their radios. In September 1944, with parts of Belgium being liberated by the Allies, the Dutch railroad workers struck again, playing a tangible role in hampering any Nazi troop movements. The strike was ordered by the Dutch government in Britain as the famous "Operation Market Garden" was moving forward. The rail strike hampered German efforts to defend against this massive attack, but they quickly brought in German rail workers to get the trains moving again. The strike once more prompted vicious reprisals, with some 50,000 men arrested and taken to Germany.[34]

So resistance in the Netherlands was largely characterized by its people's refusal to accept Nazi initiatives and by large-scale strikes. But the

Dutch would also create the "hidden armies" that are the focus of this book. There was certainly a secret Dutch underground, though its activities were necessarily quiet and mostly nonviolent. The largest and most important of these underground networks was called the National Organization of Help, or in the Dutch abbreviation, LO. The LO was primarily concerned with assisting those under threat by the Nazis—mostly Jews and the workers in hiding known as *onderduikers* (or "under-divers" in English). Rather than assassinations and railroad sabotage, the LO worked to build a network of willing helpers who would open their homes to shelter those on the run. Henry Paape estimates that there were about 15,000 helpers who provided safety for those in danger. The numbers of those who were actually in hiding are much less certain, with estimates between 150,000 and 300,000.[35] The vast majority of these were workers and elites avoiding deportation or detention. De Jong estimates the number of Jews in hiding at around 25,000, with only around 16,000 avoiding detection through the end of the war.[36] Though the LO was primarily concerned with arranging safe hiding for these victims of Nazi repression, the need to supply and feed these people meant a pressing financial burden. To help with this, there developed two separate groups. First was the National Support Fund, which created a network of donors and international contacts to supply money to the LO. The second group was much less elegant: the National Assault Group (LKP), which was made up of toughs in a "strong-arm squad" that was generally armed. This group carried out strategic attacks and robberies of food supplies, bureaucratic offices for official papers, police stations for weapons, and money wherever it could be found. This was also the group called upon to eliminate those who had been identified as Dutch traitors and informers.[37]

The reader might ask by this point, "What about assistance to the Dutch resistance from groups like the SOE? Wouldn't this have helped expand their operations?" Certainly the SOE went to work in Holland along with its other initial efforts of assistance and development. But its operations were woefully unsuccessful and nearly resulted in the closing down of the SOE. The most notorious failure of the SOE happened within its Dutch operations, and it is known as the saga of the *Englandspiel* (or "England Game"). To the Germans at the time it was known as "Operation *Nordpol*" ("North Pole"). It remains a controversial subject, with vigorous debate eventually leading to a significant question: Who was to blame? There have been interpretations emphasizing the failure of the SOE's coding staff, who simply missed clues in the codes they received that should have notified SOE leadership immediately. But there have also been arguments, chiefly by Leo Marks, the head of SOE's cryptography section at the time, that suggest that the coders knew the situation early, but because of interdepartmental rivalries, they could not convince SOE leadership to investigate or reveal the failure. Marks died in 2001, but he has left a book about his time in SOE, *Between Silk and Cyanide* (1998), pressing this interpretation. Historians are also fortunate to have a personal memoir from the German perspective written by Major H. J. Giskes, the head of German military counterespionage in Holland at the time. His book, *London Calling North Pole* was published in 1953. While Marks's and Giskes's books go into minute detail, the brief résumé of the *Englandspiel* episode in this chapter cannot. Nor does it seek to offer any new insights. It will merely provide the reader an overview of the calamity and its effects on the Dutch resistance.

By May 1942 the SOE had dropped three two-man groups of specially trained agents into Holland, each with a wireless set, though only one set proved operational. The groups then all would physically meet to pass their messages home through the one functional wireless set. Those messages were detected by the German *Abwehr* under the leadership of Major Giskes. Giskes and his group were able to arrest and seize the wireless operators and their set, and they found its coding materials in the raid. From this point the Dutch operators were forced to send messages back to Britain indicating that all was well, and that further drops of agents and equipment could proceed. Over time, the agents that were sent to parachute into Holland were seized immediately and their wireless kits set up and operated by the German police. The Nazis were able to send false information to London, and they continued to monitor and foil all attempts to send agents into the Netherlands. The captured agents who were forced to transmit messages back to Britain (under threat of death) did so without making any obvious mistakes or sending any obvious warnings. But there are quite subtle ways to signal trouble, and these were employed. The speed of the transmissions, the language used, key phrases, and other nuances can all be recognized as an agent's "handwriting" in their coded messages. But any attempts to use subtle changes in these transmissions did not alert the coding staff at the SOE. Giskes wrote in 1953 that he eventually had German policemen (ORPO men) study the coding and take over as the transmitters. Even then the SOE staff did not seem to notice a problem:

> We were now in a position to bring an ORPO man on to the key in place of either operator without London suspecting anything. . . . In this procedure we ran the risk that the "handwriting" might have been recorded in London and that a comparison might easily give rise to suspicion. By means of touch, speed of operating and other individual characteristics of a transmission technique an experienced ear can detect the difference between different operators . . . (but) our experience hitherto had not disclosed any special degree of watchfulness on their part . . . The carelessness of the enemy is illustrated by the fact that more than fourteen different radio links were established with London . . . during the Nordpol operation, and these fourteen were operated by six ORPO men![38]

It is a damning assessment of the SOE coding staff. Later, in 1943, two prisoners in Holland escaped German captivity and made for Britain. Giskes alertly sent messages over the wireless saying that the Germans had sent two secret agents to Britain posing as Dutch escapees; the two men were interrogated by British intelligence and then arrested. They were trying to tell the British that their operation in Holland was compromised, but the Allied determination to protect absolute security for the upcoming Overlord invasions trumped all else, and they were interned as suspected agents spreading disinformation.[39]

Whether or not the SOE recognized the problem, other departments began to suspect problems. In a remarkable document in Britain's National Archives, a junior officer of the RAF, L. G. S. Payne, discusses his work in identifying the causes of the steep operational losses in Holland. He wrote to Group Captain J. A. Easton, "I have been trying to piece together the various bits of information we have concerning recent unsuccessful air operations over Holland." He goes on to discuss the numerous times that RAF aircraft were attacked by German night fighters *after* they had dropped agents. He complains of the difficulty in untangling the problem because of the top-secret nature of SOE operations and the lack of any shared information. Scratching his head, he admits, "To the best of our knowledge we have not lost any of our agents in Holland."[40] But of course what he did not know was that they had all been arrested by the Germans upon arrival, and their wireless communications run by German operators. The concerns of the RAF eventually led to investigations revealing the reality of the Dutch disaster. By December 1943 the testimony of the two escaped agents was being taken seriously and the War Cabinet was discussing the extent of the debacle. A secret memorandum to the deputy prime minister admitted that "the whole of SOE organization in Holland has been penetrated by the Germans and has been run by the Germans for at least a year . . . If this information is accurate, it means that for over a year every man and container of material sent to Holland has fallen directly into the hands the Germans and that the Germans have been operating wireless sets in Holland which communicate with SOE in England."[41] That assessment proved correct. SOE operations in Holland were temporarily suspended, and a follow-up memo to Winston Churchill recommended a full reorganization of the SOE, bringing it under the defense minister.[42] The SOE eventually survived the *Englandspiel* disaster intact and kept its independence from the SIS, but unquestionably with significant damage to its reputation.

In assessing how much the Germans actually gained from the *Englandspiel*, M. R. D. Foot has concluded that the gains were minimal. The Germans never obtained key information about the upcoming D-Day expedition (Operation Overlord), which was their most urgent objective.

This was because the Allied command had done a superb job of keeping its details secret. It did, of course, severely disrupt and delay the construction of resistance operations in Holland, says Foot, but we should also remember that afterward the SOE sent in another 56 agents.[43] As events played out, Holland did not emerge as a key battlefield for the liberation of Europe, and so the great necessity for a large and lethal resistance army did not materialize. But, as Foot asserts, the most damaging result of the *England-spiel* was that "it helped to implant deep suspicion of the Dutch Resistance in the minds of the highest British commanders . . . with some distressing consequences at Arnhem."[44] The city of Arnhem was the focus in the large-scale offensive known as "Operation Market Garden" launched in September 1944. The dismissal of Dutch resistance reports of German troop positions was one of the many factors that led to the ultimate failure of that operation, with terrible loss of life.[45]

The Dutch resistance used agents and the weapons and equipment from the SOE to build the largest fighting force it could by the later stages of the war. The Allied path into Germany generally bypassed Holland, but resistance fighters did accelerate their attempts at sabotage and direct attacks on German staff. One such operation took place on the night of September 30, 1944, when a group of Dutch resistance men ambushed a car carrying two German officers and two corporals. After they fired into the car, one officer was captured and later died of his wounds. The others escaped and reported the attack. The result was characteristic of German reprisals. The small town of Putten, where the attack had taken place, was burned down, several of its citizens were executed, and over 600 of the town's men were deported to camps as slave laborers. Only 48 of them would survive the war.

Despite the many serious obstacles to an effective Dutch resistance—geography, restricted coastlines, key airfields for defense, and SOE mismanagement (whoever is ultimately to blame)—the Dutch resisted the Germans heroically in never accepting Nazi ideology, in providing intelligence, in protecting hundreds of thousands from deportation, slave labor, and death, and in eventually creating a fighting force. As Foot concludes, "It was far from useless, and deserves its place on the battle honors of successful resistance against Nazism."[46]

RESISTANCE IN DENMARK

Denmark was invaded by the Germans on the early morning of April 9, 1940, as the first phase of the operation that included the assault on Norway. Resistance by the Danish armed forces was tiny and was soon halted by the government. The Danish king, Christian X, protested, but his government reached an agreement with the Nazis whereby they would remain in place, working with Nazi civil and military authorities. Given the perceived racial affinity between the two peoples, it was important to the Nazis to make Denmark a "model protectorate" and convert its population to the Nazi ideology. Thus Denmark's status was officially as an independent state, though it was occupied by German troops. But as in the other occupied nations of northern Europe, the vast majority of people in Denmark rejected Nazism in numerous ways. One difference from nations like France or Norway was that Denmark did not have any significant number of pro-Nazi supporters before the invasion. There was no large "Quisling group" waiting to seize power and lead the Danish people into a Nazified future. But the Danish government's token defense, and its willingness now to work within the Nazi imperial system, initially earned it serious criticism for weakness and collaboration. The Danish government also signed on to the revised version of Germany's Anti-Comintern Pact, which created the appearance that the Danes were openly declaring themselves German allies. In fact the Danes had demanded to have no military obligations, and to remain a technically neutral nation. The Germans had been outraged by this, but they agreed to allow it, under the condition that it would be a secret protocol of the treaty. With this information unknown, then, the Danish government had created the appearance of open collaboration.

Despite this, resistance to Nazi occupation, however restrained, took shape almost immediately, and like other nations, this first took the form of printed communication. Early on, groups began to publish underground pamphlets and news sheets. These were begun by military types, student groups, and underground political groups like the Danish communists. From tiny releases, these publications gradually grew into large-scale papers, such as the "Student Enlightenment Service" established in July 1942. Beginning with just a very small issue, it would grow to a peak of 120,000 copies per issue by 1944.[47] The Danish also developed a taste for selling and buying books that were banned by the Nazi party in an underground network of book shops. Perhaps the most important contribution to the dissemination of underground news was the creation of the *Information* service by the newspaper writer Børge Outze. He worked to develop a news bureau that could smuggle accurate news about Nazi activities to Sweden, and that could smuggle in accurate news from the outside world and spread it to the various publications within Denmark. He was eventually captured, but he talked his way out of execution and survived the war. Like Outze, those who distributed such underground publications were subject to arrest, torture, and death. The Nazi *Reichskommissar* over Denmark, Dr. Werner Best, said in a speech, "Every editor will be answerable with his life for further attempts to poison the popular mind."[48] But despite Nazi threats, the circulation of illegal news continued to expand. The chief

SOE agent in Denmark wrote that in November 1943 there were 23 known papers with a total circulation of around 250,000.[49]

There were at first only small and disparate groups intent on providing intelligence to the Allies and perhaps even actively fighting against the enemy. They were initially aided in this task by a Danish journalist named Ebbe Munck, who made his way to Stockholm and made contact with the British. After a series of negotiations, the steps were put into place to form an intelligence network. The intelligence was gathered in Denmark and moved to Munck through a group of Danish military intelligence officers who got the code name of "the Princes."[50] With a Swedish base, it was far easier to pass intelligence to Britain and also to help the SOE begin its work in building resistance organizations inside Denmark. The SOE began its operations in Denmark during 1941, sending in arms, supplies, and trained agents to help build the organizations. They developed an ingenious method for secretly bringing in supplies, using metal supply canisters that would be dropped into the sea just off the Danish coasts. The canisters had anchors attached that would take them straight to the bottom but, in the process, released a buoy marker that would float to the surface. Resistance members would sail to the buoy markers and release them, which in turn released the canister from its anchor and allowed it to float up to the surface. Parachuting agents and equipment into Denmark, with its numerous airfields controlled by the Luftwaffe, was an extremely dangerous proposition; but "sea-drops," as they came to be called, were a far safer means of getting equipment to the resistance.[51]

Eventually two principal organizations developed for resistance within Denmark, both based in Copenhagen. The first was established by members of the Danish Communist Party and was initially called KOPA (for "Communist Partisans"), but it soon opened its membership to non-communists and changed its name to BOPA (for "Civil Partisans"). BOPA produced a communist newspaper but was particularly focused on violent resistance, particularly industrial sabotage. With connections to workers in key factories, it was able to secure vital knowledge of production and factory layouts to help with its raids. Despite its record of effectiveness, the SOE was reluctant to arm the group and withheld any explosives until late 1944.[52] The other major group was known as Holger Danske; it was established mostly by Danish ex-soldiers who had fought against the Soviets in Finland during 1939. Like BOPA, Holger Danske concentrated on sabotage, though it also included a small "liquidation cell," which carried out the killing of nearly 200 known Danish traitors and informers.

Through the early years of occupation, the Danish resistance was generally quiet, carrying out only a minimal number of small-scale sabotage operations. This changed during the crucial year of 1943. By that year, the character of World War II had visibly changed, with Allied victories in

North Africa, the Pacific, and the Soviet Union; Danes became increasingly aware that an eventual Allied victory—and their liberation—was now a likely possibility. The year 1943 also marked the point by which organizations like BOPA, Holger Danske, and the groups established by the SOE were emerging as viable organizations with the personnel, networks, and weapons needed to move into serious operations. Fairly reliable statistics are available for this period for the groups being run by SOE agents, as the SOE's chief agent in Denmark, Captain Flemming Muus, prepared a lengthy and detailed report for the SOE leadership. In that thorough report, he discusses his initial challenges in establishing a base of operations, but, he says, by 1943 he had established groups in Randers, Aalborg, Aarhus, Odense, and Copenhagen. He also stresses that his groups had established excellent relations with the Danish police—who, though directed by the Germans to crack down on saboteurs, were in fact aiding the resistance significantly. Before August 29, says Muus, "I used to be furnished daily with a copy of all the reports that came into the Danish Police HQ by tele-printer."[53] The direct aid from the Danish police reflected the more general reality of the failure of the Nazis to win over the Danish public. Muus says of the general populace of Denmark, "Without the assistance of the greater part of the population we should never have been able to achieve the results now actually reached. 98% of the Danes are pro-British . . . any parachutist may walk into almost any house in Denmark and be housed in greatest safety."[54]

Having established the organizations, built the networks for information, created the wireless transmission stations, and armed his personnel, Muus's groups now embarked upon what Lord Selborne would call an "orgy of sabotage that has spread throughout the country."[55] Muus describes in his report how he and his groups approached the destruction of factories. With connections in the key government offices, they could obtain virtually any blueprints they wanted of any industrial facility, get them photographed, and then return the papers to their files within about two hours. With the schematics in hand, they would put the factory under observation to check its defenses and the basic geography. With this information, they could form the best plan. Muus emphasizes that his groups "make a point of always using incendiary bombs in connection with as much petrol as possible."[56] Their priority targets were those doing work directly for the Wehrmacht, and particularly those working on "radiolocation," which would aid the production of the V-1 and V-2 rocket programs. But another favorite target, he said, was factories producing ice; the ice was essential for the storage of food products like fish, eggs, and butter and for their shipment out of Denmark to Germany. The report goes on to list the statistics for sabotage operations during 1943:

Major Acts:	400
Minor Acts:	500
Cutting of Railway Lines:	500
Ships Sunk:	9[57]

Among the factories attacked were ironworks, ice factories, shoe factories, uniform factories, oxygen-producing factories, oil and petroleum refineries, electrical plants, and many more.

The extraordinary burst of sabotage attacks often resulted in local German reprisals, which in turn often produced strikes by local workers. This chaotic cycle reached such a level that by the end of August 1943, the Germans had had enough. They demanded that the Danish government declare a state of emergency (meaning martial law) and immediately execute all captured Danish saboteurs. The Danish government quite simply refused to do this, and resigned. On August 29 the Germans declared Denmark no longer an independent state, and formally under German occupation. With this development, there was a question as to what the next political step would be for patriotic Danes. Should the Danish simply continue with no governing body? Should Danish politicians escape to Britain and form a government-in-exile? The decision made was not to create an exile government, but instead to create a special ruling council, secret and underground, that would act as the coordinating and commanding body for the various groups of the resistance. The group became known as the Freedom Council and came into being during September 1943.

Very soon after the Freedom Council was established, the Danes were dealt another indignity by the Nazi regime. Up to this point, the Germans had not actively attacked the Jews of Denmark, given its supposedly independent status and Nazi efforts to maintain positive relations with the Danes. But after August 29, such treatment was abandoned, and on October 1 the Nazis launched an all-out effort to round up and deport all of Denmark's Jews, nearly all of whom lived in Copenhagen. Once again the Danish population would prove itself adamantly anti-Nazi, as all over Copenhagen groups of resistance members and ordinary civilians worked to smuggle nearly the whole Jewish population out of Denmark to safety in Sweden. One of the many resistance cells involved was a small student group, of which a young Jørgen Kieler was a member. In his memoir, *Resistance Fighter: A Personal History of the Danish Resistance Movement, 1940–1945*, he tells the story of his group's swift work to round up and move out the Jews. Moving immediately, with the limited money they had accumulated, the group arranged transport with multiple fishing vessels at the docks. Then they worked to coordinate the movement of Jews in the downtown neighborhoods, using taxis and bicycles to move them to the harbor areas without notice. At the docks they would pay the shipowners and get the Jewish passengers hidden aboard. Out at sea, sometimes the fishing boats actually had to stop and do a little fishing to convince any German patrol boats that nothing unusual was happening. When out of view of the German patrols, they steamed for Swedish harbors.[58]

Another group that worked to save Denmark's Jews was ordinary citizens in the medical profession. When the notification went out that the Nazis intended to deport the nation's Jews, one doctor, K. H. Koster, wanted badly to help but wondered how. How could the Jewish community be contacted quickly, secretly, and in time? He had the brilliant idea that family doctors would know their Jewish patients and would have their contact information, and so Koster and any helpers he could find began calling every family doctor they knew. Those doctors in turn contacted their Jewish patients and urged them to get to Bispebjerg Hospital, where Dr. Koster was working with other members of staff to try to coordinate some way to get the Jews to safety. Jewish families began to show up at the hospital in quite large numbers, larger than the staff was prepared for. But they managed eventually to house them all in the nurses' living quarters, which were located within the hospital complex. The Jews were fed with hospital food, and Dr. Koster told the administrators that they could bill him for all the food. The administrators then realized what was happening and said nothing, and no bill was ever issued. Late at night, taxis were called again to transport the Jews to the harbors, where negotiations took place with dozens of shipowners to load their boats with the Jewish passengers.[59] There were around 8,000 Jews in Denmark by October 1943, and of these the Germans succeeded in arresting and deporting a total of 481. About 100 Jews went into hiding in Denmark and survived the war. But the vast majority, some 7,056 people, were helped to safety by the resistance, doctors, students, and sailors who together, over the course of a few weeks, pulled off a mass operation that came to be called "Little Dunkirk."[60] The Danish people managed to save the lives of about 91 percent of the Jewish population, and all while under the boot of direct Nazi occupation—a unique feat in the war.

In 1944 the level of sabotage continued and increased. Particularly in the late months of that year and into 1945, the large peninsula known as Jutland erupted into almost constant resistance attacks. In the late days of 1944, the Allies were on the move toward Germany, making their way through northern France and Belgium, headed for German territory. In December 1944 the Germans launched a final great offensive in the west, known as the Battle of the Bulge (also known as the Battle of the Ardennes, December 16, 1944, through January 25, 1945), which caught the Allies by surprise and produced two months of slaughter. Though the Allies overcame the German offensive, the casualties on the western front were horrifying, with nearly 8,500 American troops killed and over 80,000 wounded in less than two months. The Nazis were able to mobilize around 450,000 troops for this offensive, but they certainly could have used many more. In these months, Danish sabotage was at its peak in the Jutland area, as the resistance worked with Danish rail workers to devastate the railway system. When members of the resistance saw German troops board trains for the south, they would notify Danish railway workers and other resistance cells by calling the railway stations down the line. They would use the code phrase "Ferdinand will send you a packet of cigarettes in three days," which meant that the train would hit their station in around three hours.[61] A resistance squad would be notified, and it would head to the area to destroy the switches or, more often, to simply blow up the tracks. The Germans began to keep repair crews with their troops for such emergencies, and when the tracks were repaired, the train would continue on its way—only to be sabotaged again miles down the line. This got to be such a problem for the Germans that they took to carrying hostages with them—Danish workers and captured saboteurs rode along with the military troops. When the train was stopped due to sabotage, the hostages would be taken off the train and gunned down on the spot. Still it went on, at one point stopping all rail traffic in Jutland for a period of two weeks. The Germans could only manage to get a token amount of troops out of Denmark to aid in the campaign on the western front, and then to defend Germany itself. Like the bottling up of German troops in Norway, the trapping of troops in Denmark was extremely important in keeping them away from the western front. As historian David Lampe writes,

> The Jutland railway sabotage operations—which numbered thousands— may have been Denmark's strongest direct contribution to the victory in Europe. Certainly the Danes did nothing that had a greater strategic effect in the war. General Montgomery . . . said it had changed the entire tide of the Battle of the Ardennes.[62]

In the early years of the war, there was mounting criticism of Denmark among the Allies for its inability to mount resistance to the German invasion, and then for its governmental collaboration. But as the years wore on, the Danish resistance movement developed into a highly efficient force and one of the most active of the war. Denmark's population at the time was around four million, and of this population about 30,000 are believed to have been involved in the resistance in some way. Of these, about 3,000 made the ultimate sacrifice—being caught, tortured, and executed. But this resistance saved Denmark's reputation (some might say its very soul) and made genuinely significant contributions. Beyond destroying industry, food, weapons, uniforms, and the like, the Danes trapped tens of thousands of German troops and kept them away from the defense of Germany. At the liberation of Copenhagen, there were still 40,000 now-useless German troops in the country, simply waiting to surrender.[63]

NOTES

1. Tore Gjelsvik, *Norwegian Resistance, 1940–1945* (London: C. Hurst, 1979), p. 10.

2. David Howarth, *The Shetland Bus* (Guilford, CT: Lyons Press, 2001 [1951]), p. 228.

3. Gjelsvik, *Norwegian Resistance*, p. 7.

4. Ibid., p. 15.

5. Ibid., p. 35.

6. Ibid., p. 65–70.

7. Knut Haukleid, *Skis Against the Atom* (Minot, ND: North American Heritage Press, 1989 [1954]), p. 69.

8. Ray Mears, *The Real Heroes of Telemark: The True Story of the Secret Mission to Stop Hitler's Bomb* (London: Hodder & Stoughton, 2003), p. 9.

9. Ibid., p. 23.

10. Ibid., p. 42.

11. Haukleid, *Skis Against the Atom*, p. 64.

12. Mears, *Heroes of Telemark*, p. 103.

13. Thomas Gallagher, *Assault in Norway* (New York: Harcourt Brace Jovanovich, 1975), p. 99.

14. Ibid., p. 93

15. Mears, *Heroes of Telemark*, p. 159.

16. Ibid., p. 201.

17. Haukelid, *Skis Against the Atom*, p. 178. This inefficiency in bombing accuracy was consistent with bombing in general during the war. The famous "Butt Report" (August 1941), for example, proved that British bombers only achieved a 33 percent accuracy rate for their bombs—and the criteria for "accuracy" was hitting within five miles of the target!

18. Ibid., p. 181.

19. Ibid., p. 181.

20. Mears, *Heroes of Telemark*, p. 219.

21. Haukelid, *Skis Against the Atom*, p. 195.

22. Mears, *Heroes of Telemark*, p. 228.

23. Ibid., p. 228–229.

24. Harry Paape, "How Dutch Resistance Was Organized," in M. R. D. Foot, ed., *Holland at War against Hitler: Anglo-Dutch Relations 1940–1945* (Portland: Frank Cass & Co., 1990), p. 70.

25. Ibid., p. 73.

26. A. M. Meerloo, *Total War and the Human Mind: A Psychologist's Experiences in Occupied Holland* (New York: International University Press, 1945), p. 21.

27. Louis de Jong, *The Netherlands and Nazi Germany* (Cambridge, MA: Harvard University Press, 1990), p. 33. This book is a condensed group of three important essays based on his much larger masterwork, *The Kingdom of the Netherlands during World War II*.

28. Ibid., p. 37.

29. Ibid., p. 38.

30. Zander, *The Rise of Fascism*, p. 159.

31. De Jong, *The Netherlands and Nazi Germany*, p. 40.

32. Ibid., p. 33.

33. Ibid., p. 46.

34. See Paape, *Holland at War against Hitler*, pp. 75–83.

35. Ibid., p. 90.

36. De Jong, *The Netherlands and Nazi Germany*, p. 41.

37. Paape, *Holland at War against Hitler*, pp. 89–90.

38. H. J. Giskes, *London Calling North Pole* (London: British Book Centre, 1953), p. 94.

39. M. R. D. Foot, "The Englandspiel," in M. R. D. Foot, ed., *Holland at War against Hitler*, pp. 128–129.

40. Memo from L. G. S. Payne to Group Captain J. A. Easton, British National Archives, CAB 102/648.

41. Memo from Minister of Defense to the Deputy Prime Minister, December 1, 1943, British National Archives, CAB 102/648.

42. Memo to the Prime Minister, January 5, 1944, British National Archives, FO/954/24A.

43. Foot, *Holland at War against Hitler*, pp. 129–130.

44. Ibid., p. 130.

45. See Cornelius Ryan, *A Bridge Too Far: The Classic History of the Greatest Battle of World War II* (New York: Touchstone, 1974), pp. 159–160.

46. Ibid., p. 130.

47. David Lampe, *Hitler's Savage Canary: A History of the Danish Resistance in World War II* (New York: Skyhorse, 2011), p. 3.

48. Dr. Werner Best, speech quoted in Lampe, *Hitler's Savage Canary*, p. 6.

49. Report by Captain F. B. Muus, British National Archives, SOE/43/12, p. 12.

50. Foot, *SOE*, pp. 208–209.

51. Lampe, *Hitler's Savage Canary*, p. 32.

52. Ibid., p. 37.

53. Report from Captain F. B. Muus, British National Archives, SOE/43/12, p. 10.

54. Ibid., p. 10.

55. Letter form Lord Selborne to the Foreign Minister, December 23, 1943, British National Archives, SOE/43/12, p. 1.

56. F. B. Muus, SOE/43/12, p. 12.

57. Ibid., pp. 19–22.

58. Jorgen Kieler, *Resistance Fighter: A Personal History of the Danish Resistance Movement, 1940–1945* (New York: Gefen, 2007), pp. 101–108.

59. For the story of the Bispebjerg Hospital operation, see Lampe, *Hitler's Savage Canary*, pp. 69–77.

60. Kieler, *Resistance Fighter*, p. 108.

61. Lampe, *Hitler's Savage Canary*, p. 170.

62. Ibid., p. 176.

63. Ibid., pp. 226–227.

5

Anthropoid

The Czech Resistance and the Mission to Kill Reinhard Heydrich

---

After the Nazi absorption of the Republic of Austria during March 1938, known as the Anschluss, the next nation to come under German attack was Czechoslovakia. During the summer of 1938 and through September, Hitler made numerous threats that he would intervene in that nation in defense of the German-speaking minority living there. That German-speaking minority, mostly in the western borderlands of Czechoslovakia, was known as the Sudeten Germans, and the territory they occupied was known as the Sudetenland. The crisis over the question of Sudeten German "self-determination" provided Hitler with the pretense he needed for an eventual invasion and seizure of Czechoslovakia. As has been described in chapter 1, the diplomatic crisis that ensued saw France and Britain refuse to honor their existing diplomatic agreements that bound them to protect Czech sovereignty. France and Britain agreed to allow Hitler to take possession of the Sudetenland with no military intervention. The agreement was signed on September 30, 1938, and during early November, German military forces moved into the border regions and began the process of absorbing these areas into the German Reich. For Czechoslovakia this was a devastating development, as all of the nation's defensive fortifications were in the borderlands, and now with these in German possession, the country's new western borders were virtually undefended. Over

100,000 of the Czech population of the Sudetenland began a panicked rush to escape into the remaining rump territories of Czechoslovakia. The vast majority of the Sudeten Germans, on the other hand, rejoiced and embraced their new status as citizens of Hitler's Reich.

Hitler had always intended to secure the whole of Czechoslovakia as a means to realizing his ultimate aims. Its strategic position was valuable for his plan of dominating Eastern Europe and for a massive invasion of the Soviet Union. Hitler was also determined to get his hands on the considerable industrial production of the Czech armaments makers, particularly the factory complexes of the Škoda Works, which produced guns, armor, and explosives of all kinds. The so-called Munich Agreement with Britain, France, and Italy gave him a temporary status of legality but actually delayed his ultimate objectives.

On March 19, 1939, Hitler moved to complete his conquest of Czechoslovakia. While his troops were on the move, he summoned the Czech president, Emil Hácha, to Berlin for a conference. There he revealed that his troops were already moving into Czechoslovakian territory and threatened to level Prague with aerial bombing if Hácha did not accept German occupation. Hácha suffered a heart attack in the conference under the strain and was treated by Hitler's doctor. Struggling to recover in his terribly weakened condition, Hácha agreed to sign the documents permitting German occupation. Thus the invasion of the rest of Czechoslovakia continued, but Prague was saved from devastation. The eastern half of the country, Slovakia, had already seceded from Czechoslovakia and declared itself an independent, pro-Nazi state. The new Slovakian Republic would go on to be a German ally during the Second World War, with a nominally independent government that was in reality a German satellite state. The western half of the country was made up of two large regions, Moravia and Bohemia, which included the capital city of Prague. The Germans converted these regions into the "Protectorate of Bohemia and Moravia," under German colonial government. The Czech people would suffer terribly under German domination.

The German occupiers were forceful, but they restrained the extremes of terror that characterized their rule in Poland or the Ukraine. They did this for one important reason. The Germans were constantly concerned with keeping the Czech population nourished enough and complacent enough to carry on with the vital work of arms production in the factories, now essential to the German military. It was certainly not the case that the Nazis saw the Czechs as fellow racial equals—Nazi discourse was rife with denigration of the Slavs and discussions about how to manage such inferiors. Reinhard Heydrich said, for example, "The Czech . . . is more dangerous and must be handled differently from Aryan peoples . . . Slavic man is very difficult to convince . . . And the consequence of this is that we must constantly keep our thumb on him so that he always remains bent, so that he will obey us and cooperate."[1] Hitler later complimented Heydrich's "management" of the Czechs, making clear the ultimate goal:

> The fear of being compelled to evacuate their homes as the result of the transfer of population we are undertaking will persuade them that it will be in their best interests to emerge as zealous cooperators with the Reich. It is this fear which besets them that explains why the Czechs at the moment— and particularly at the war factories—are working to our complete satisfaction.[2]

The Nazis saw the Slavs as a racially inferior people to be dominated and enslaved, but they tempered their viciousness and did not exterminate them for the moment; the necessities of war demanded their productive capacities. Once a German victory had been achieved, however, along with complete control of Eastern Europe, it seems highly likely that the Czech population would have been slated for extermination.[3]

In the first phase of Nazi rule in the Czech protectorate, Hitler appointed his former foreign minister Baron Konstantin von Neurath as *Reichsprotektor* in charge of all civil administration. Neurath was not a fervent Nazi but a conservative aristocrat of the pre-Nazi era. He had distinguished himself as Germany's leading diplomat during the years of the Weimar Republic and in the early years of Hitler's Nazi government. Hitler named him foreign minister in 1933, and Neurath served him well in handling many diplomatic crises, such as the German reoccupation of the Rhineland in 1936. But Neurath's lack of enthusiasm for radical Nazi ideology eventually doomed him, and he was replaced as foreign minister by a very radical Nazi, Joachim von Ribbentrop, in 1938. At that point Neurath's tendency toward finesse rather than terror was seen as potentially useful in a nation where cooperation was needed from the people for war production. Neurath certainly was not easy on the Czech people. He worked to quash protests among the population, censored the press, and implemented the German policies against Jews in the territory, ending their right to emigrate, and enforcing the wearing of the Star of David.[4] But during his tenure, there were growing student protests, a number of workers' strikes, and an emerging resistance movement. For these reasons, and above all because of the reduction in worker productivity, Hitler decided to remove Neurath and replace him with a man with steely and merciless resolve—a man Hitler nicknamed "the Iron Heart." During September 1941 it was announced that Neurath was taking an indefinite sick leave, and that his position was to be filled by the terrifying leader of the Nazi SD, Reinhard Heydrich.

Heydrich was born in 1904 to aristocratic parents in Halle, in Saxony. His father was a noted composer and operatic performer, and he instilled in his son a passionate nationalism. Reinhard was tall and slender with a rather unusual face with flattened features and small, cold eyes. He was also a gifted musician and athlete, talents he would develop into his adulthood. He was too young to fight in World War I, but in 1922 at the age of 18, he entered the German navy, where he thrived and worked his way into the officer ranks. But he was dismissed from the navy in 1931 for conduct "unbecoming an officer and gentleman" when he broke an engagement with one woman to marry his future wife. The woman he married, Lina von Osten, was a fervent Nazi with many connections in the party. Heydrich, devastated by his ejection from the navy and with no firm plans for the future, was eager to meet with members of the Nazi party. His wife made arrangements for Heydrich to meet with Heinrich Himmler, who was at the time in the planning stages for creating an intelligence division of the notorious SS. Famously, in his interview Heydrich discussed his approach for creating an intelligence division, and this so impressed Himmler that he was hired forthwith. Over the years Heydrich would rise in the SS to become in reality its second-in-command behind Himmler, and he was considered to be Himmler's own protégé. He established and ran the SD, in charge of counterintelligence, and he would later assume the leadership of the notorious Gestapo. When he was made *Reichsprotektor* of Bohemia and Moravia he gave up no position, but merely added colonial governor to the list of his existing responsibilities.

His initial measures in the protectorate were chilling. He immediately declared martial law and moved to smash student organizations, workers' groups, communists, and underground resistance organizations. Martial law gave him the legal authority to establish special courts that could ignore the due process of standard trial law. In his first three days, 92 people were sentenced to death; in two months over 6,000 people were arrested, of which 404 were executed. Most of the rest were sent to concentration camps.[5] The resistance was especially hard hit, and within a few months it was virtually dismantled. Such were the methods that earned Heydrich the nickname "the Butcher of Prague."

It was during these initial months that he took part in a conference in the Berlin suburb of Wannsee. On January 20, 1942, this conference got under way with Heydrich himself as chair. He helped organize the meeting to finalize a large-scale logistical project that had been in the planning stages for some time. The project was the "enhancement" of the process for the liquidation of the Jews of Europe. The early phases of exterminating Jews in Eastern Europe had involved specially formed police squads known as the Einsatzgruppen, who rounded up Jews in newly conquered territory and either shipped them to ghettos in places like Warsaw or Łódź or, more often, executed them *en masse*. Jews were typically herded into trucks, taken into the countryside, gunned down, and finally tossed into mass graves. By the end of 1941, however, it was hoped that this process could be accelerated, made more efficient, and made less emotionally taxing for those performing the mass murders. An enhanced, coordinated process would help bring about what Hitler had termed the "final solution to the Jewish question." A key designer of the new system was Reinhard Heydrich, who worked with others to develop the plans for a network of specially designed death camps (some converted from existing concentration camps) connected by railway lines to the ghettos and equipped with mass killing apparatus. At the Wannsee conference Heydrich was joined by numerous figures from the Foreign Ministry, Gauleiters (Nazi regional administrators) from several districts, and the heads of many other ministries including Justice, the Interior, and the various states. Here they would be briefed on the structure of the new death camp system and receive an explanation as to how it would work. Remarkably, minutes from the meeting still exist, and they make clear Heydrich's insistence that Jews be killed with industrial efficiency, but also that many should be used as slave laborers until they were worked to death. He was quite firm that these Jews should be worked and starved to death, because if the healthier and stronger Jews were to survive, he said, "they would, as a natural selection of the fittest, form a germ cell from which the Jewish race could build itself up again."[6] Heydrich was not only the "Butcher of Prague"; for his leading role in the construction of the Holocaust, he is considered one of the most hateful and destructive human beings ever to have lived.

Meanwhile, back in Prague, Heydrich had all but disabled the Czech resistance network. The underground in Czechoslovakia was never particularly extensive, though early in the war it could be quite effective. After the Munich Agreement was signed in the fall of 1938, the Czech president, Edvard Beneš, was forced to resign. He fled to America, but he was soon convinced to come to Britain to establish a Czech government-in-exile. In Britain he was reunited with his former head of intelligence in Prague, František Moravec. Moravec had been able to escape from Prague in March 1939, just before the Nazis moved into Bohemia and Moravia, and he was able to smuggle out volumes of key intelligence files of the Czech government. Now in Britain, Moravec would serve Beneš again as head of Czech intelligence and coordinator of the resistance. Initially the efforts of the Czech resistance were focused almost exclusively upon intelligence gathering. It was clear that violent resistance would produce vicious reprisals by the Nazis, and Beneš and his government wanted to preserve the safety of the Czech people as much as possible. But over time, this strategy would have to change.

In Czechoslovakia there had developed four principal resistance groups: Political Center (PU), the "We Remain Faithful" Committee (PVVZ), the Nation's Defense (ON), and the Communist Party of Czechoslovakia

(KSC). By 1941 the three non-communist groups had been unified, with the help of Moravec's organization, into a single controlling organization known as the Central Leadership of Home Resistance (or UVOD). The UVOD was committed to a future republic with democratic socialist elements, but after the German invasion of the Soviet Union, the UVOD also worked closely with the KSC. The UVOD acted as the primary communication link with the government in Britain and provided routine reports on German troop movements and arms production.

In Britain, though, there was increasing pressure upon Beneš and his government to expand the operations of the underground. Before the British and the Soviets were allied, the British government seemed satisfied with Czech resistance being primarily concerned with intelligence gathering. But the Soviets had a quite different view of the role of resistance. Stalin believed that resistance should be active and violent and should create the maximum level of chaos and casualties to Nazi troops. If this produced savage reprisals and high civilian death rates, so be it. Stalin had little regard for the preservation of human life at the best of times; at this most desperate of times, it was utterly irrelevant to him. He began to press for control of the resistance movements in Eastern Europe, and this threatened the position of Beneš and his democratic government. If Stalin and the communists took over the resistance in Czechoslovakia, it could mean communist control of the nation at war's end. Czechoslovakia could quite possibly move into the future as a communist nation, with Beneš and his democrats rendered powerless. To prevent such a development, Beneš needed the support and commitment of the western democracies, and those nations increasingly wanted a larger contribution from the Czech resistance. Beneš and Moravec began to contemplate a larger role for their agents in order to increase their credibility in the eyes of Britain and later the United Sates. As historian Callum MacDonald puts it, "If Czechoslovakia was to be supported by the Allies, it must make a contribution to winning the war."[7] The Allies, including the leadership of the SOE, supported an increased role by the Czech resistance as part of an overall effort to reduce German strength on the Russian front.

The appointment of Reinhard Heydrich as *Reichsprotektor* of the Czech protectorate provided a tempting new possibility for just such a contribution. Heydrich was considered one of the top figures of the Nazi inner circle. The decision appears to have been taken in late October 1941 by the Czech government in London, in conjunction with the SOE, to mount an expedition to assassinate Heydrich. This would make an unmistakable statement about Czech courage, reliability, and the value of Beneš's government as an ally. All involved must have understood, though, that this would mean brutal reprisals by the Nazis. Despite this, the necessities of war and political intricacies pushed the plan forward. It was codenamed "Operation Anthropoid."

To carry out such a mission, the plan called for a team of two specially trained Czech agents to parachute into the protectorate and establish themselves in hiding. From a series of safe houses provided by the underground, the two would then observe Heydrich and make their own plans for the best method of killing him. Then they would carry out their mission and go immediately back into hiding. SOE recruiters observed numerous Czech soldiers and selected two very talented and experienced men for the mission. They were Jozef Gabčik and Jan Kubiš. Gabčik, born in 1912 in Slovakia, had been a blacksmith and a locksmith in his early years, but he entered the Czech army in 1932 and served until 1938. He was released from duty after the signing of the Munich Agreement and was working in a chemicals factory when the Nazis moved into the country. During March 1939 he escaped the country and made his way to Britain, where he trained as a soldier in a Czech division. He served with distinction in the Battle of France during the spring of 1940, winning the French Croix de Guerre, and the Czech War Cross. He was 29 years old when he was selected for the mission.

His compatriot Jan Kubiš was born in 1913 to a peasant farming family in the Třebíč region of Moravia. He entered the Czech army in 1935, where he reached the rank of platoon sergeant. He was discharged in 1938 after the Munich Agreement and went to work in a brick factory. Upon the German invasion in March 1939, he escaped to Great Britain, where, like Gabčik, he fought bravely in France during 1940, also winning the Czech War Cross.

According to MacDonald,

> Both men were highly professional soldiers, nationalists who had endured the shame of demobilization after Munich and had seen their country fall to the Nazis without firing a shot. It was a burning desire to reverse this verdict which had carried them across the frontier and preserved their spirit during the military debacle in France. Both were anxious to seize the first available opportunity to hit back at the Nazis.[8]

After France, Gabčik had applied to join the RAF as a better way to get at the Nazis in combat. But now, selected by the SOE for special assignment, they would both "have an opportunity to fight the enemy in a far more direct and personal way than by serving in the RAF."[9]

They went to work in an intensive six-week course of training in the SOE manor houses in the Scottish highlands. They were trained in the use of multiple weapons, explosives, underground skills, and specialized tasks. They also, of course, took parachute training, as they would be reinserted into the protectorate by airdrop. Their mission took off on December 28, 1941, and was very nearly ended before it started, as the RAF Halifax was twice attacked by German fighters. The pilot, a Lieutenant Hockey, artfully evaded disaster and dropped them in a wooded area outside the city of

Prague. This was actually a mistake, as they had planned to start their journey in the city of Pilsen, but the new-fallen snow made navigating by landmark nearly impossible. The men adjusted and found their way to their intended contacts near Pilsen. This was made much more difficult because Gabčik had seriously injured his leg in the landing. But he was treated by a doctor, and his condition began to improve.

The resistance was in a desperate condition by the time the men dropped into the protectorate. Heydrich and his SD (Sicherheitsdienst—the intelligence and internal security branch of the SS) had cracked down on the resistance with great success during the autumn of 1941, arresting hundreds of people and, significantly, seizing the vast majority of the wireless sets that linked the movement with London. Communications with London were severed before Anthropoid, and the number of safe contacts in Pilsen and Prague was down to a precious few. To reestablish radio contact, weeks before the Anthropoid drop, the SOE had dropped two other groups of agents, the first code-named "Silver A" and the second "Silver B." The Silver B group damaged its wireless set and had to abandon its mission and go into hiding. The Silver A group, however, was successful in setting up a communication link. As such, the Czechs had gotten word of the Anthropoid drop and now secured the two men in a series of safe houses they had prepared. They were moved around regularly to avoid detection, but they spent most of their time with a particular family in the town of Žižkov, just on the outskirts of Prague. This was the home of the Moravec family. The father was a railway worker, but he seems not to have been involved at all in the resistance, and he was completely unaware of his wife's involvement. Mrs. Moravec used her work for the Red Cross and other charities as a clever cover for courier work for the local branch of the UVOD. Their 21-year-old son Ata, a young musician, was eager to help, though he was kept out of any serious resistance work. In all the homes they stayed in and through the time with the Moravec family, they "kept their distance in one important respect—they never let slip the nature of their mission."[10]

Despite their discipline, the nature of their mission eventually revealed itself. The two agents used the months ahead to begin scouting Heydrich—his home, his offices in the Ćernín Palace, the local train system, the roads. They watched and charted his routines, as well as his schedule of visits to Berlin. The two eventually decided that the best way to assassinate the man would be during his departure by car. The road from his suburban castle home into Prague ran down a hill on a winding track that eventually came to a hairpin turn at the bottom of the hill. This forced any car to slow down to a crawl to manage the turn. In that very area, there was a tram stop that would provide cover for the agents to wait without drawing attention to themselves. Finally, there were no German police stations or security facilities in the area. The two would use a third man to act as look-out while they waited at either end of the tram stop. When Heydrich's car slowed down for the turn, they would run up to it, one firing with a Sten gun, the other tossing a grenade. One rather remarkable decision on Hey-drich's part made this plan quite feasible. Heydrich insisted on riding in an open convertible Mercedes limousine, despite the security regulations for German administrative staff in foreign environments—which he himself had issued. This insistence on displaying his courage and superiority over the Czechs may well have cost him his life.

The constant work by Gabčik and Kubiš in scouting Heydrich led ulti-mately to the resistance members figuring out the nature of their mission. In late April the leading resistance officials held a meeting with the agents, including one of the Silver A agents, Lt. Alfréd Bartoš. When confronted, the two agents confirmed their target. Bartoš and the others were appalled at the prospect, insisting that Nazi retribution would be beyond imagina-tion. The Nazis would, of course, target the resistance and likely eliminate the last traces of the remaining organization; but on top of that, they would surely take vengeance upon innocent Czechs. Could the life of one man possibly be worth this potential bloodbath? In the personal account of one of the members present, Ladislav Vaněk, he states that the two agents remained steadfast in their commitment to the mission. As he says, "The young men asserted that their mission was perfectly clear: they were to organize and carry out the killing. They were soldiers, so they could not find fault with the killing or discuss its point or lack of point . . . they could do nothing against the order they were given."[11] Vaněk eventually con-tacted London himself and requested that the mission be called off. The Czech government in London met to discuss this possibility, and there are conflicting accounts about whether Moravec or Beneš endorsed its cancel-lation and about the stance of Britain's SIS (the SOE was never informed of the discussion). But whatever the arguments, the decision was made to move ahead with the mission, and the order was not revoked.[12]

On the morning of May 27, 1942, Gabčik and Kubiš awoke to a beautiful spring day and fortunately no precipitation (which could have affected their plans). They set off for their tram stop and took with them a third team member named Josef Valčík, one of the initial parachutists from group Silver A. He filled the need of "spotter" to keep an eye on the sur-rounding area while they prepared their assault. Heydrich was planning to travel to Berlin later that day and to be away for some time. It was crucial, therefore, for the agents to succeed in their attempt, or another opportu-nity might never present itself. Because he would be leaving his family for a time, Heydrich took extra time to play with his children that morning before he left his chateau home to drive along the route into Prague. The wait was absolutely agonizing for the agents, who wondered why Heydrich was deviating from his regular schedule. They had earlier recovered the equipment they brought with them from Britain in the parachute drop. Once they had landed, they hid the equipment in cabins in the woods, and the guns and explosives sat through months of cold winter weather. Now the question was, would these guns and grenades work when the time came? At around 10:30 AM, they finally saw the black Mercedes 320-C working its way down the road; Heydrich sat in the front, exposed and unprotected, next to his guard and chauffeur, *Oberscharführer* Klein.[13] As the car slowed to a creeping pace to handle the sharp curve, Gabčik ran out into the road in front of the car, threw aside his overcoat, and fired his Sten gun into the Nazis in the front. But, horrifyingly for Gabčik, his gun simply didn't work, producing only a dull click with no firing. Heydrich and his security men could have then accelerated and swiftly driven away to safety, but they made another choice. Heydrich demanded that the car be stopped and that Gabčik be picked up for arrest. With the car stopped and the guard moving out of the car, Kubiš now rushed the car and lobbed his grenade. It was not a particularly good throw, and it rattled underneath the car rather than inside it. It exploded against the rear tire, blowing the car into small shards of metal and even shattering the windows of the nearby tram that had pulled up and stopped. Kubiš took a number of fragments, which bloodied his forehead. Heydrich was also hit, but he was initially unaware that he had been badly injured in the blast. Kubiš made a run for it and got out of the area quickly, reaching a bicycle and pedaling for all he was worth. Gabčik was forced to take cover behind a telephone pole, and he engaged in a brief gun battle with the Nazis. Heydrich got out of the car and tried to fire at Gabčik, but he eventually stopped firing and collapsed in pain over the car's hood. Heydrich had been hit in the back by pieces of shrapnel that had lodged in his vital organs, particularly damaging his spleen.

Gabčik now fled the scene; he turned down a street and dove inside a butcher's shop to hide. The hulking Nazi guard Klein was on his tail and suddenly saw a butcher in his apron running down the street, screaming that there was a man with a gun in his shop. Gabčik had made a very unlucky choice, as this particular "butcher of Prague" was a Nazi sympathizer. Now Klein approached the shop, but Gabčik fired shots into his legs with a pistol. Klein fell to the ground in agony, and Gabčik lunged over him and sprinted away. When Klein limped back to the scene, he found Heydrich in agony; Klein swiftly commandeered a delivery van nearby, and the *Reichsprotektor* was taken to Bulovka Hospital in Prague. When examined by Czech doctors, Heydrich initially rejected surgery, but after German doctors arrived at the hospital and insisted that surgery was essential, he agreed. His ethnic and racial prejudices persisted even with his life in the balance.[14]

The surgery was an awkward affair with the chief surgeon, Dr. Josef Hohlbaum, unable to control his nerves and trembling. He eventually had to turn over the surgery to another surgeon present, who completed the surgery successfully. The operation revealed that shrapnel from the blast had torn the spleen apart and left a three-inch piece of grenade casing lodged in the organ. There was also a considerable clump of horsehair matted inside, which had been blown from the stuffing of the car seat. The spleen had to be removed, but the surgery was completed without complications. Heydrich would show regular progress in his recovery over the course of about a week but then develop a severe fever. The fever broke on June 3, and it appeared that he was now on his way to full recovery. He took a full meal, but while eating he suddenly pitched over and lapsed into a coma. He would not last the night. Early on the morning of June 4, the Butcher of Prague—the architect of the Holocaust, and the man Hitler called "the Iron Heart"—expired. He received a magnificent state funeral in Berlin, with Himmler and even Hitler delivering eulogies. His body was interred to the strains of Wagner's "Twilight of the Gods."

There is a controversy regarding the ultimate cause of Heydrich's death. There is a question as to whether the horsehair caused a particularly serious infection. This seems unlikely, given Heydrich's subsequent recovery and rise in strength. Another theory has been put forward by the British pathologist and microbiologist Paul Fildes, who worked at the secret medical research facility at Porton Down during the war. Fildes worked with the SOE and claimed to have modified the grenades for the Anthropoid mission by filling them with botulinum toxin. That this killed Heydrich seems highly unlikely, as Kubiš was hit by fragments of the same grenade and never suffered any symptoms of the kind. Also the grenades had been stored for five months in very cold winter weather, which would have destroyed the toxin if it were present. The sudden nature of the death of Heydrich and the subsequent results of an autopsy suggest that he most likely died from a cerebral embolism.[15]

The Nazis had lost one of their most beloved figures, one who represented the ideal of Nazi masculinity and ideological commitment. Now those who had killed him would pay a hundred times over. Already on June 9 Hitler was giving specific orders about the brutal retribution he demanded.[16] The Czech village of Lidice in the district of Kladno to the northwest of Prague had been rumored to be a hotbed of resistance activity, wrongly as it turned out. But based on this false assumption, the Nazis decided upon the complete destruction of the town. The Nazis arrived on June 10 and immediately rounded up all men of 14 years or older. All 172 of them were executed on the spot. The women (184) and children (88) were bundled into trucks and shipped to the Ravensbruck concentration camp. The children were screened, and those few (there were nine) deemed racially fit were given new German identities and sent to live with German families. All the other children were killed in the death camps.[17] Less well known is the Nazi destruction of a Czech village at Ležáky, again near Prague. In the intense manhunt for the killers of Heydrich, a wireless set was discovered in Ležáky that had been parachuted into the country by the Silver A team. The Nazis sent an SS death squad to the village on June 24 and killed all 33 adults in the village and leveled every building, wiping the village off the face of the earth.[18]

Agents Gabčik and Kubiš meanwhile had returned to their underground existence in Prague. But their presence in the homes of resistance-connected families was now becoming too much to ask. The Nazis issued a proclamation demanding that the Czechs turn over the culprits by June 18 or there would be a great profusion of blood. What remained of the resistance was able to arrange for the two to take refuge in the underground crypt of the Greek Orthodox Karel Boromejsky Church in Prague. There they might have stayed long enough to see Nazi vengeance subside and to later escape in quieter conditions. But it was not to be. In the terrifying atmosphere of the manhunt, one Czech SOE agent decided to try to save his own life and profit from the betrayal of his colleagues. He walked into the Gestapo headquarters in Prague at the Peček Palace and identified himself. His name was Karel Čurda, and he voluntarily talked to the interrogators, revealing that although he had no idea where the two agents were, he did know where they had hidden out in the homes of resistance members. Perhaps these people could lead the Nazis to their hidden prey. Čurda would accept a one-million-Reichsmark reward for his cooperation, and he spent the rest of the war working for the Gestapo. After the war he was tracked down, tried for treason, and hanged by the Czechoslovakian government in 1947.

Now the Nazis targeted the family homes revealed to them by Čurda. The most important of these was the Moravec home. When they arrived, the father was bewildered but began to realize that his wife had been involved in the resistance. After being beaten, his wife excused herself for a moment and quickly went to the washroom, where she took a cyanide pill, killing herself. She knew of the terrors to come. The father and the 21-year-old son, Ata, were taken to Gestapo headquarters and down into the basements of the Peček Palace. These were the torture rooms, and young Ata was savagely beaten but revealed nothing. With Ata inches from unconsciousness, the torturers changed tack and began to force brandy down his throat to the point of extreme intoxication. He still did not talk, and so the Nazis tried the technique of extreme shock. They brought into the room a large fish aquarium with his mother's head floating in it. They informed him that if he did not talk immediately, the same would happen to his father. At this point the hysterical Ata revealed the location of the church. The Nazis showed their gratitude by sending Ata, his father, and the other surviving members of his family to the Mauthausen concentration camp, where they were all murdered.[19]

The next day, June 18, in the early morning hours, SS security forces quietly surrounded the church with men and vehicles. Inside, Gabčik and Kubiš had taken refuge with a few other SOE agents who were split into two groups. Kubiš and two other parachutists, Adolf Opálka and Jaroslav Švarc, were established in the upper-floor choir stalls. They had weapons including Sten guns, pistols, and some grenades from their SOE drops. Gabčik was in the basement crypt with Josef Valčik, Josef Bublik, and Jan Hruby. The SS stormed into the church at around 5:00 AM, and a thunderous firefight broke out as the agents fired into the SS squads. Their superior position and their arms allowed them to hold off the SS for nearly two hours, but eventually the SS men were able to fight their way upstairs using grenades and gunfire. Eventually the Czechs were killed. Kubiš was seriously wounded and brought out while still alive, but he died in medical treatment without ever regaining consciousness. The priest who oversaw the church, Father Vladimír Petřek, was put under extreme pressure, and he revealed that there were more men in the crypt. The SS quietly searched the church until they found the trapdoor. They burst into the stairwell, and again there was a savage gun battle. To save their own numbers, the SS retreated and pursued another strategy. They found small windows to the crypt and began to use firehoses to pump water into the chamber. The SS also found adjacent underground tunnels and began hammering at the walls. Finally, realizing their time was up, the Czechs committed suicide, and the battle of Karel Boromejsky Church was finally over. Today the church still stands, and visitors can see its walls, deeply scarred by bullet holes, which remain as a memorial to the tragic events there in June 1942.

In the months that followed, the Nazis redoubled their attacks on the resistance and effectively dismantled it. As Heydrich biographer Robert Gerwarth says of the effects of the Nazi terror,

> The Czech underground was almost completely wiped out and was never to recover from the blows it suffered in the weeks after Heydrich's death . . . Up to 4,000 people . . . were rounded up and placed in concentration camps or ordinary prisons. The terrifying memory of the *Heydrichiada*, as the wave of terror . . . was soon to be known . . . served as a powerful deterrent to a revival of active resistance. Contrary to Benes' intentions, the War Office in London noted a "dying enthusiasm" for further resistance with the Czech population.[20]

In hindsight, historians must struggle with the question as to whether this operation was worth its consequences. One of the most notorious figures in world history had been killed, and the Czech people could take pride that they had made this happen. It is difficult not to argue that the world was a better place without Reinhard Heydrich in it. But in terms of the human cost and the cost to the war effort, it was surely a mistake. The Holocaust was not slowed in the least. Heydrich's contributions to its planning were already in place, and the death camps would move on to do their nightmarish work with or without him. After the killing of Heydrich, the other principal objective of the mission was to inspire the Czech people to greater levels of rebellion and sabotage—to increase the harassment of German troops, and to bring chaos to the transport network behind the Eastern Front. As we have seen, this certainly did not happen, as the Czech resistance was all but eliminated. If anything, any potential aid it could have brought later in the war was lost. Finally, there is the question as to whether it boosted the position of Beneš and the forces of democracy in Czechoslovakia. It certainly elevated Beneš's government-in-exile for the duration of the war, but events would eventually overwhelm any hope he may have had to lead a liberated Czechoslovakia into a democratic future. The occupation of the area by Soviet troops eventually led to a communist government there, and domination by Soviet Union. The benefits were few, and so one is left to ponder the disturbing costs of the mission—the individual deaths of the agents, the resistance workers and their families, the people of Lidice and Ležáky, and the thousands who were arrested and interned. In all, something like 5,000 people were destroyed as a result of Operation Anthropoid and the killing of the man with the "Iron Heart."

NOTES

1. Robert Gerwarth, *Hitler's Hangman: The Life of Heydrich* (New Haven: Yale University Press, 2011), p. 230.

2. *Hitler's Table Talk 1941–1944* (London: 1953), p. 494. Quoted in Gerwarth, *Hitler's Hangman*, p. 242.

3. Gerwarth, *Hitler's Hangman*, p. 288.

4. For a full discussion of Neurath's administration, see John L. Heineman, *Hitler's First Foreign Minister: Constantin Freiherr von Neurath, Diplomat and Statesman* (Berkeley: University of California Press, 1979), pp. 186–212.

5. Gerwarth, *Hitler's Hangman*, p. 227.

6. "Notes from the Wannsee Conference," in Zander, *The Rise of Fascism*, p. 170.

7. Callum MacDonald, *The Killing of SS Obergruppenfuhrer Reinhard Heydrich* (New York: Free Press, 1989), p. 92.

8. Ibid., p. 101.

9. Ibid., p. 101.

10. Ibid., p. 144.

11. Ladislav Vaněk, quoted in MacDonald, *The Killing of Reinhard Heydrich*, p. 156.

12. Ibid., pp. 157–158.

13. Ibid., p. 170.

14. Charles Rivers, ed., *The Assassination of Reinhard Heydrich*, p. 19.

15. Ibid., p. 22. See also Robert P. Harris, *A Higher Form of Killing: The Secret History of Chemical and Biological Warfare* (London: Chatto and Windus, 1982), pp. 70–108.

16. Gerwarth, *Hitler's Hangman*, p. 280.

17. Ibid., pp. 280–281.

18. MacDonald, *The Killing of Reinhard Heydrich*, p. 196.

19. Gerwarth, *Hitler's Hangman*, p. 284.

20. Ibid., p. 285.

6

Tragedy in Warsaw

The Polish Resistance and the Tragedy of the Warsaw Uprisings

Establishing the exact commencement of the Second World War is a contested subject. Japan's invasion of the Chinese mainland in 1931, which resulted in the establishment of Manchukuo (the state of Manchuria), is sometimes cited as the real beginning of the war, as is the full-scale invasion of China by Japan in 1937. The Sino-Japanese conflict was certainly already years in progress when the European conflicts merged with those of Asia to create a larger, more global conflagration. Despite this, the date that is most generally accepted is September 1, 1939, the date of the massive Nazi invasion launched into Poland. This invasion resulted in the declarations of war of both France and Great Britain, and the Soviet Union soon joined the attack on Poland as a quasi-partner of the Nazis. While the Axis powers (Germany and Italy) had been fighting in the Spanish Civil War and conquering and bullying neighboring nations during the 1930s, it is the German invasion of Poland that is most often identified as the key starting point of the most destructive war in history. The Polish people would arguably sustain the most destructive military assaults and endure the most savage occupation of any of the victimized nations . . . from the opening day of the war to its last.

As described in chapter 1, the military conquest of Poland lasted a relatively short time: only about one month. In the middle of the German assault, on September 17, while bombs rained down on Polish cities and the Polish army attempted to retreat to safer ground in the east of the country, Poland was hit by a second major invasion across its eastern border. The Soviet Union sent its forces into eastern Poland and within a matter of weeks claimed that half of the country for itself. This, of course, had all been agreed upon by Hitler and Stalin beforehand as part of the Nazi–Soviet Non-Aggression Pact of August 1939. With the Polish army overwhelmed and any meaningful resistance extinguished by October 2, the Polish government escaped to France, where a government-in-exile was established. Germany's subsequent attacks in Western Europe forced the Poles to reestablish their government in London in June 1940. The president of this government was Władysław Raczkiewicz, and while the government was just arriving in France, he appointed Władysław Sikorski as its prime minister. Sikorski would be the most important of the Polish wartime politicians, and he took direct charge of the government-in-exile and supreme command of the Polish armed forces. He was a famous soldier who had served the Polish independence cause in the war with the Soviet Union from 1919 to 1921. He later emerged as a prominent politician, even serving as prime minister during the 1920s. He had opposed the Piłsudksi coup d'état in 1926 and gradually withdrawn from politics in the 1930s, separating himself from the semi-dictatorship of the far-right Sanacja regime. Now that Poland was part of the fight against right-wing dictatorship, he would be a prime minister that the leaders of the democratic West could accept. Sikorski was also a distinguished military man, having held key positions in the armed forces and written a number of important books on the theory of warfare. He was an ideal candidate to lead the Polish government-in-exile during wartime.

Sikorski and his government rapidly went to work assembling a cabinet and organizing its various functions, while also beginning the process of managing the Polish military effort. During and immediately after the German invasion, thousands of Poles escaped their country, mostly through Romania, and made their way to France and Britain. These Free Poles fought in the Battle of France, with many dying in combat or being taken prisoner. Sikorski was able to evacuate over 20,000 of these men to Britain, where they would form their own "Polish Armed Force of the West." These units fought with distinction in a number of engagements, including as flyers in the Battle of Britain and as ground troops in the North African and Italian campaigns. While Sikorski and his government managed the day-to-day requirements of their government and the Free Polish armed forces, another vast part of their responsibility was working with the Polish people at home under occupation. This was extremely difficult for many reasons, but the Polish resistance organization would produce miracles.

THE GERMAN OCCUPATION OF POLAND

Adolf Hitler's plans for Poland were part of his larger vision for a massive, German-dominated state that included virtually all of Eastern Europe and the Soviet Union. The natural resources of this vast area would belong to Germany, and with those resources, the living space, and a growing German population, Hitler's "Thousand-Year Reich" could become a reality. Germany would be large enough, wealthy enough, and powerful enough to dominate the planet for the foreseeable future. The conquest of Austria and Czechoslovakia had been the territorial first steps on the way to this twisted dream. The Austrians, being German-speaking people, were incorporated into Germany proper, and they would (with the exception of the Jews) enjoy the fruits of German expansionism. The Czechs, however, as a branch of the Slavs, were considered ethnically inferior and would not be part of the Thousand-Year Reich. Like all the Slavic peoples, they were ultimately slated for extermination and enslavement by the Germanic race. But in the near term, Czech laborers were needed to produce the armaments necessary to conquer the rest of Eastern Europe. Thus, the Czechs were ruled repressively by the Nazis but not destroyed, oppressed, or starved to the point where their industrial production would be dramatically affected. In Poland there would be no such restraint.

When Poland was entirely defeated, the Nazis imposed a new organization on the country. The Soviets controlled the eastern portion of the country, but in the new Nazi-controlled middle and western portions, three districts were established. In the north, there was East Prussia, already German, and administered as a territory of the Reich; it was slated to have its large ethnic Polish population evicted. The westernmost region of Poland was also established as a group of territories: Upper and Lower Silesia and the districts of Wartheland and Danzig. Together this group was administered as one large administrative territory and, like East Prussia, was slated for "Germanization." In the middle of occupied Poland was a large territory that included its two largest cities, Warsaw in the north and Kraków on the southwest border. This area was named the Polish "General Government." Poles identified and rounded up in the other areas occupied by the Nazis would be shipped here for the near future. The process of "Germanization" was quite simply the process by which ethnic Poles would be forcibly moved out of German-annexed territories and shipped to the General Government, while ethnic Germans were shipped in for colonization. The process was extremely brutal and degrading. Families were forced from their homes, businesses and farms were confiscated, and property of all kinds was simply taken and held for incoming Germans. Over the years the German provinces were emptied of Poles, with the exception of small groups retained for forced agricultural and industrial labor.

Inside the General Government, Poles arrived in trains and trucks run by the German SS, but refugees also arrived, pushing wagonloads of whatever property they could carry. They then did the best they could to find shelter and work. Many went to the cities, but there the occupation would be at its most terrifying. In major cities, such as Łódź and (most importantly) Warsaw, the Nazis established bizarre, fenced-off districts in the city centers. These were special areas designated for the Jews that came to be known as the Jewish ghettos. In the effort to ethnically "cleanse" the German territories, Jews were identified and herded out of their homes and into the ghettos in the cities. Inside the ghettos they were packed by the thousands into tiny neighborhoods. There were efforts to buy food, but soon there was no food to buy, and none coming in. Some non-Jewish Poles would come to the chain-link fence and sell bits of food to the Jews for their money, or jewelry, in a mix of charity and opportunistic greed. The Nazis brought in food but deliberately made sure that the Jews did not get enough food to survive—it was a calculated plan of slow starvation. But Jews from all over Poland and Eastern Europe were now segregated into one place, where the Germans could decide where and how to exterminate them at some later date. By 1941 German efforts to clean out Polish towns and villages became even more savage, particularly for Jews. The German SS had developed groups known as the Einsatzgruppen, or police squads, whose job it was to identify and round up Jews in any area selected for ethnic cleansing. While many Jews continued to be sent to the urban ghettos, the Einsatzgruppen now began exterminating Jews in mass executions. Hundreds of Jews might be taken to the center of a town to be beaten and tortured in public. Then they would be herded into trucks and taken to the countryside, where they would be gunned down in mass shootings. The Einsatzgruppen generally used mass graves, often dug by the terrified Jews themselves, to bury their victims.

Non-Jewish Poles that were residents of the cities now tried as best they could to continue their lives under occupation. It was imperative to keep out of sight and avoid attracting attention, as German patrols routinely rounded up Poles for forced labor, or simply shot them at random. Thousands of Poles found themselves lined up against walls and shot for doing nothing other than taking a particular public bus, or walking in a large group on the sidewalk. Basic institutions like the arts, public associations, and the education system were all shut down by the Nazi head of government, Hans Frank, who once remarked, "The Poles may have access only to such possibilities of education that show them the hopelessness of their national existence."[1] The horrors of the occupation and "Germanization" immediately inspired great numbers of Poles to take up the challenge of resistance.

THE POLISH RESISTANCE AND ITS CHALLENGES

In the days during the close of the fighting in late September 1939, and in the subsequent weeks and months, thousands of Poles left the country. Most left over the southern border of Romania and then made their way to Spain, France, Britain, or any nation where they may have had connections. Those Poles who could continued the fight, forming the Free Polish forces in Great Britain. But the masses that were left behind to deal with the occupation now attempted to create their own functioning networks of resistance. As early as November 1939, the germs of resistance were sprouting all over Poland and particularly in its cities. There was no central organization to coordinate this at first. Rather, it was initially formed by tiny groups of individuals who knew they could trust one another, and who were determined to actually do something about the nightmare in which they found themselves. As the Polish historian Włodzimierz Borodziej wrote, "Hundreds of underground organizations—not only in Warsaw—were established 'from below' in conjunction with existing ties to family, job, friendship, and neighbors. Protective associations and other paramilitary groups, scouts and athletic federations, simply all social bonds, proved to be rallying points."[2] The prominent chemist Jan Rosinski, who has recently written his own memoir of the resistance, was able to join a network of student resisters based at the Warsaw Polytechnic Institute where he was studying.[3]

Over the months, the various groups began to make contact and merge into larger, more organized groups. There was a group led by the remnants of the defeated Polish armed forces that remained loyal to their own Sanacja leaders, who had been in power before the war. This group was "nationalist, anti-Semitic, and xenophobic, but anti-Nazi," and by 1942 it called itself the Narodowe Siły Zbrojne (NSZ), or "National Armed Forces."[4] A corps of around 70,000 members, the NSZ fought the Nazis and the Soviets but would also on occasion fight against Polish communists. On the left were two prominent groups: the "peasant-socialists" and the communist resistance whose armed forces were known as Armia Ludowa, or "People's Army." The peasant-socialists were independent for the most part, but the communists remained tied to the Soviet government in Moscow and worked for a Soviet-style communist state for Poland after the war.

The largest and most famous of the resistance groups in Poland developed around loyalty to Sikorski's government-in-exile. This group supported the dream of liberating Poland and returning it to an independent and democratic state. Gradually, dozens of independent groups merged into this umbrella organization, which formalized itself into the Armia

Krajowa (AK), or "Home Army." The AK was intended to be just that—a fighting force for the occupied peoples against both the Nazis and the Soviets. From 1940 it began to organize, recruit, train members, and prepare for a mass action to liberate the country.

The resistance in Poland was not, however, limited to a military arm. The government-in-exile also worked to create a kind of shadow government that operated in Warsaw and carried out functions out of sight of the Nazi overseers. This shadow government, representing the London government's principals, became known as the "Underground State" but was formally named the Delagatura. It developed into a remarkably sophisticated organization, given the intensity of Nazi oppression. It was organized into five principal branches. First was the Department of the Interior, which worked to develop a new Polish administration and which acted as the symbolic and visible delegation from the London government. It worked to appoint administrators to run transport, communications, and finances but also worked to design the future government after liberation. Next there was the Department of Press and Information, which worked to collect news from overseas and distribute it through a group of underground newspapers and pamphlets. It also recruited numerous agents to act as couriers to secretly deliver these publications. Its presses would also distribute a number of books on politically important subjects. Third was the Department of Education and Culture, which worked to reestablish schools for children, often in apartment blocks or basements. University teachers carried on teaching their courses underground as well, and any who had knowledge that was directly relevant to the combat branch of the resistance provided training; for example, medical training for nurses and physicians, or chemistry for those building bombs and arms. A judicial apparatus was also established, with judges and juries who tried cases of local criminals but particularly known collaborators. According to Borodziej, there were "hundreds of sentences against individual collaborators . . . making treason even more risky."[5] Finally, there was the military arm of the Delagatura, the Home Army or AK. The AK would eventually reach a membership of between 300,000 and 350,000 nationwide, though only a small number were armed.[6]

The AK was headed up by Stefan Rowecki, a veteran of the Polish–Soviet War and a tank commander during the defense of Poland in September 1939. He managed to escape capture and leave Poland, he but returned to Warsaw to head up the fledgling Union for Armed Struggle, the core group that would evolve into the Home Army. The AK was formally established in February 1942, and Rowecki was made its commander. He oversaw four principal areas of activity: (1) sabotage of German communications and transport; (2) providing intelligence to the Allies,; (3) capture and execution of key Nazi personnel and prominent collaborators; and (4) preparations and stocking for an eventual mass rising.

Despite its large size, its sophisticated organization, and its willingness to act, the AK received very little help from the Allies. When the AK was in its formative stages, Britain's SOE was also in the process of establishing itself. Aid to the Polish resistance would seem to be a natural place to start for the new SOE, but it had very little means during 1940 and 1941 and was mostly busy with establishing its own infrastructures, particularly recruiting and training. Nevertheless, the SOE did attempt to send help. According to A. R. B. Linderman, the British made 485 airdrops into Poland, sending some 600 tons of supplies, weapons, and food to the resistance. Linderman explains, though, that 40 percent of that material was dropped during the Warsaw Uprising of 1944. The SOE also trained some 318 agents and dropped them into Poland to aid in the building and operating of the AK, and who were under the authority of the government-in-exile.[7] Geography and interdepartmental tensions were immense obstacles here. To fly missions to Poland and back tested the range capacity of RAF aircraft to the extreme, and there was no safe territory nearby for any kind of emergency landing. During 1940 and 1941, the entire flight would have been through dangerous enemy territory. The RAF leadership was doubly reluctant to send its planes and pilots on such terribly risky missions, given what they saw as the questionable value of supplying resistance movements. Thus, Poland received only a very small level of assistance from Britain during 1940 and the first half of 1941.

On June 22, 1941, the Polish situation changed dramatically. On that day, the Nazis launched Operation Barbarossa, and the German armies poured into the Soviet Union. They also poured into Soviet-occupied Poland and displaced the Russians there, taking over that territory for themselves. For ordinary Poles, life was still oppressive and tenuous, the only real difference being that one group of oppressors had replaced another. But politically and militarily, the Nazi betrayal of their Soviet ally had momentous consequences for the Polish war effort. Negotiations were soon under way that saw the Polish government-in-exile forced to accept the Soviets as allies. The Poles really had no choice but to accept the situation, given that the Soviets had joined the British as the core of the anti-Axis force. But the Poles were all too aware that the Soviets had just eagerly and opportunistically invaded their nation and conducted a brutal and terrifying occupation. Polish prisoners taken in the war were missing by the tens of thousands, and certainly the Poles suspected the Soviets of a variety of war crimes. As Borodziej writes, there were some 700,000 Poles "who had disappeared since the autumn of 1939 into the Gulag, the Far East, and Kazakhstan, in prisons, camps, and construction battalions of the Red Army. The fact that most of the captured officers had already been murdered by the Soviet Secret Police in mass shootings in the spring of 1940 was not yet known."[8] The horror of those Soviet mass executions would eventually be revealed by the Nazis in March 1943, when they announced their discovery of enormous mass graves in Katyn Forest. When confronted by the Polish government-in-exile, Stalin denied any Soviet involvement and insisted that these mass killings had been carried out by the Nazis in their advance during the summer of 1941. But subsequent research has confirmed that the Soviets killed nearly 22,000 Polish soldiers and civilians in these mass executions. They were mostly Polish intellectuals and elites, about 8,000 of whom were military officers.[9] But this atrocity remained unknown in 1941.

In terms of the Polish resistance, the new alliance with the Soviets had three principal consequences. First, for those in the eastern region, the enemy target (i.e., all Soviet personnel, supplies, transport, etc.) had become an ally, and completely new targets were to be established. Secondly, at the request of the Polish government-in-exile, the Soviets began to develop a fighting army from the tiny number of Polish captives who had not yet been liquidated. The army's formal name was the "Polish Armed Forces in the East," but it became known as the "Anders Army," after its commander, Władysław Anders. This army would aid the Soviets in their fight against the Nazis during 1941 and into 1942. The Soviets, however, were unable to feed and equip the army, and eventually they allowed it to leave the Soviet Union, passing south through Palestine and eventually under British command. These Polish troops were united with their cohorts in the "Polish Armed Forces in the West," and many fought together during the Italian campaign. The third major consequence was also the most damaging for the Polish resistance. With the partnership of the British, the Soviets, and later the Americans, Allied planners agreed that Poland now passed into the Soviet "sphere of influence." What this meant in practical terms was that Britain's SOE and the American OSS diminished any existing direct aid to the Poles. Historian David Stafford writes that the SOE concluded that "British responsibility for arming them (the Poles) was both unnecessary and undesirable for larger political reasons . . . on the grounds that they would inevitably enter a Soviet sphere of influence . . . [F]rom this moment on the idea of arming Polish or Czechoslovak resistance for 'secret army' purposes was abandoned."[10] Flights did continue from Britain, but they were few and far between, as the great distance was a constant problem. "Indeed," says Linderman, "so long were the flights that they could not be done under cover of darkness during the summer because the night was too short."[11] Thus, with the Soviets now directly involved in the Polish resistance situation, the British (and later the Americans) could justify a serious reduction in their extremely risky Polish aid operations.

The Soviets, meanwhile, would not contribute a great deal to the Polish resistance effort, because of their own precarious military situation. Stalin was certainly interested in harassing and undermining the Nazi ability to make war, but he had his own Soviet partisan groups to do this, so aid to the Poles was quite scarce. As a result of these circumstances, the Polish resistance, particularly the AK, adopted a fairly clear two-phase mission. Both the London government and the leadership of the AK, says Borodziej, were "in complete agreement on the precise separation of the tasks of the resistance for 'now' and 'later.' The country was now to provide espionage work for the Allies, sabotage German armament and transportation, and be ready for reprisals against especially brutal actions of the occupier; but the real goal—the Uprising—was still in the unforeseeable future."[12] The AK worked to secure weapons and ammunition—from Allied airdrops, but also from thefts, capture from German supplies, and anywhere else they could be found. These were stored in secret caches while soldiers were recruited and trained for an eventual mass attack on the Nazi occupiers. Soldiers learned how to use various guns, explosives, and ammunition, and how to move about by stealth. There were also personnel trained for transportation and medical care. The great question would be *when* to launch such a rising. The precise moment should be when the Nazis were on their heels and ready to retreat in a weakened condition, but it should also be done far enough in advance that Soviet troops would not be on hand to seize Polish territory. It would prove to be an extremely difficult question.

The Home Army was well organized and was divided into the following "sections":

1. Section I—Organization, which saw to matters of personnel and political relations

2. Section II—Intelligence, which managed intelligence networks, passing information to the Allies, and counterintelligence (the ferreting out of infiltrators)

3. Section III—Operations and Training, which prepared plans and training for an eventual large-scale uprising

4. Section IV—Logistics, which managed food and supplies for members

5. Section V—Communication, which managed the radio networks and airdrops between the Allied agencies, the government-in-exile, and the Poles

6. Section VI—the Bureau of Information and Propaganda, which ran the underground press and disseminated the declarations of the government-in-exile and the "Underground State"

7. Section VII—the Bureau of Finance, which worked to secure and manage the funding for the entire operation

The eighth group in the AK's organization was known as Kierownictwo Dywersji, or the "Directorate for Subversion." This group included men and women who conducted the armed and violent operations for the AK. The vast majority of the AK's soldiers were not armed, but they trained in hopes of an eventual large-scale uprising. Those in the Kedyw, as the Kierownictwo Dywersji was known, were involved in armed conflict on a daily basis. Kedyw soldiers conducted raids for arms and food; they carried out hundreds of raids on the German transport network, particularly during the Russian campaign, to wreck the German troop flows east. This was also the group that took action against local informers and collaborators, usually capturing them for a court trial, or sometimes executing them outright. It also occasionally took direct action against Nazi officials deemed especially despicable.

Despite the decision to defer a major combat challenge until the appropriate moment, the AK and the other, smaller groups did engage in some important operations from 1941 to 1944. To review several of such operations is beyond the scope of detail of this book, but the distinguished historian István Deák has recently published some important cumulative statistics from this period. He includes data from the "non-Communist, non-right wing Polish resistance," which means predominantly the work of the AK and its affiliates. He lists some rather staggering statistics from the Polish records: 6,930 locomotives destroyed or temporarily put out of commission, 732 German military transports derailed, and 19,058 railway wagons damaged; and he says Polish workers built some 92,000 faults into German artillery missiles.[13] Though precisely calculating the military effects of such work is probably an impossible task, "there can be no doubt," according to Deák, "that the German war industry had to spend millions of man-hours to replace machinery destroyed by the Polish guerillas. Nor should we forget the thousands of German soldiers in partisan-infected areas of Poland and the Soviet Union who had to guard transports instead of joining those on the front line."[14]

ANNUS HORRIBILIS: THE CHALLENGES OF 1943

Nineteen forty-three proved to be a momentous and tragic year for the Polish people and the resistance. First, on April 16, the Nazis announced their discovery of the mass graves in Katyn Forest and made the (quite correct) assertion that this atrocity had been committed by the Soviets. Sikorski's government in London demanded an explanation from the Soviets but got only firm denials from Moscow and claims that the killings had in fact been carried out by the Nazis. Not satisfied, Sikorski demanded an investigation, and with this, Stalin severed relations with the Polish government-in-exile on August 25. The strained relations between the two governments, and armies, would have repercussions until the end of the war.

The second major development of 1943 was the heroic but tragic uprising in the Warsaw Ghetto during April and May of that year. In the middle of Warsaw, a large district of the city had been cordoned off and secured with chain-link fences, barricades, and barbed wire. Inside this large area, the Jews from Warsaw and from the "Germanized" lands were dumped to make a life as best they could. Inside this ghetto there was little security, and Jews were able to live their lives inside apartments, stores, restaurants, libraries, and so on. But there were practically no material supplies left on which to live. The food ran out in the homes and restaurants almost immediately, and the Nazis supplied only enough food for a starvation diet. No food, clothing, medical supplies, or any other essentials could come into the ghetto, unless desperate Jews sold their jewelry through the chain-link fences to Poles who had a spare loaf of bread or a potato. There they suffered and tried to survive in a makeshift life, using whatever materials were left in the various homes and businesses. A special Jewish council, the Judenrat, conducted relations with the German authorities and tried to work with them to improve life however this could be done. The leaders of the Judenrat were also tasked with disseminating the details of German policy and orders, and ensuring that the Jewish population acted as it was ordered. In mid-1942, orders came from the Germans to round up several thousand of the ghetto residents for "resettlement" in other areas. Most Jews, including the Judenrat leader, Adam Czerniaków, believed that this would mean relocation to German-annexed areas of Poland and forced labor in German factories. Thus, the Jews cooperated. Later, reports made their way into the ghetto, probably from resistance members outside, that the thousands had been deported to the death camp at Treblinka. Czerniaków committed suicide, and the other Jews now faced a terrifying dilemma. If the Germans demanded further roundups for resettlement, the Jews decided, they would not go quietly, but instead rise up in a mass action. Among the Jews stuck in the Warsaw Ghetto were members of two specifically Jewish resistance groups: the "Jewish Combat Organization" (ZOB), and the "Jewish Military Union" (ZZW). Each of the groups had been formed in the earliest days of the German occupation and had small cells in towns all over Poland, but their leadership stayed in the ghetto. In view of the program of mass murder now being launched into action by the Nazis, these two organizations resolved to fight to the death. Each group had only tiny core units of armed soldiers. There were precious few arms in the ghetto, and between the two groups, there were only about 1,000 armed fighters. But they worked day and night to create handmade weapons and makeshift guns. They had a few land mines, stolen from the Germans, a few guns, some machine guns (again stolen from the Germans), and a number of Molotov cocktails they made themselves.

On January 18, the Germans arrived again, demanding thousands of Jews to be rounded up for the "resettlement" program. When the news came, the Jewish fighters combined forces, attacked the German authorities, and pushed them out. They took control of the ghetto and created armed emplacements to ensure that any Germans entering would be gunned down. Meanwhile, inside the ghetto they prepared bomb shelters, medical areas, and barricades. The Germans tried to work with Jewish leaders, and they prepared their own assault. On April 19 the Nazis brought in police and SS forces to take control of the ghetto and to round up the death camp victims by force. A full-scale battle broke out within the ghetto, with German armored vehicles being hit by explosives and German troops gunned down. But over time the inevitable took its course. The Jews ran out of ammunition and supplies, and a German force of around 1,300 men was able to crush the rebellion. The principal method they used was simply to burn the ghetto to the ground, block by block. Those caught in houses and shops were burned to death, asphyxiated, or crushed by the collapsing rubble. By the final surrender on May 16, about 13,000 Jews had been killed and only about 300 German soldiers. Over 50,000 Jews would now pay the ultimate price, being rounded up and sent to the death camps. Those still in the burned-out shell of the ghetto hung on to life and hope by their fingernails, and some even rekindled their resistance groups for another day.

On June 30, 1943, the Poles sustained another tragedy when the commander of the Home Army, General Stefan Rowecki, was arrested by the Gestapo. He had been betrayed by Gestapo informants within the Home Army, most notably Ludwik Kalkstein. Kalkstein had been arrested by the Germans in 1942 and had been turned. Now he provided key information that led to Rowecki's arrest. Rowecki was taken out of Poland and imprisoned and interrogated for months in Berlin. During 1944, with the Nazis on the retreat in the Soviet Union, Rowecki was confronted with a remarkable proposal from Himmler's SS. Would he be willing to convince his Home Army to work with the Nazis against the advancing Soviets? Apparently he refused vehemently, and he was soon executed. The AK had lost a talented and commanding leader. He was replaced by General Tadeusz Komorowski, who would be the one responsible for the momentous decisions to be made the following year.

Only four days after the arrest of General Rowecki, the Poles suffered another disastrous loss when the legendary prime minister of the Polish government in London was killed. Władysław Sikorski was visiting Polish combat forces in the Middle East and meeting with that group's leader, Władysław Anders. A conflict developed between the two over the question of the Soviets. Sikorski believed that there was hope of renewing normal relations with Stalin's government, while Anders (who had been in

Soviet captivity and had seen the Stalin regime up close) was absolute in his refusal to support this. The issue was not resolved when Sikorski left and stopped at Gibraltar. When his plane took off from Gibraltar on July 4, the plane pitched over and dove into the sea, killing everyone on board but the pilot. The crash was deemed an accident due to shifting cargo, but there has been a question looming over the incident ever since, with some suspecting foul play, perhaps by the Soviets. He was replaced by Stanisław Mikołajczyk, a politician dedicated to a social republic. In his initial speech to the Polish people over the BBC, he made this clear and said clearly that there was "no place in Poland for any kind of totalitarian government in any shape or form." Joseph Stalin was no doubt listening.

HEROISM AND TRAGEDY: THE WARSAW UPRISING OF 1944

In one year, 1943, Poland had lost its beloved prime minister and its highly respected leader of the Home Army, severed relations with its largest and nearest ally, and seen the Warsaw Ghetto devastated in an inferno that took over 50,000 lives. Despite this string of disasters, the Poles could see some hope emerge during that vital year. Nineteen forty-three proved to be the year that the Nazi initiative was decisively exhausted in the Soviet theater, and that initiative now passed to the Russians. The German failure at Stalingrad by February 1943 and the failed offensive in the Battle of Kursk during the summer permanently turned the tide of the war in the east. During the final days of 1943 and into 1944, the Soviets began the long and painful process of pushing the Nazis westward and out of Soviet territory.

While this process played itself out, the Polish resistance was faced with an agonizing dilemma. It might be summed up with the following three questions they confronted: (1) Should the Polish people rise up to help finish off their Nazi occupiers? (2) If they did, would the cost in human life be justified by the Polish people taking control of their capital, ensuring an independent republic after the war? (3) Or, if the Polish people sustained serious casualties in an uprising, would this only make it easier for the Soviets to conquer and subjugate the Poles in place of the Nazis? The leaders of the Polish government-in-exile, the "Underground State," and the resistance all had to wrestle with the ultimate question of whether an uprising would lead to an independent future or a future of permanent enslavement.

The Home Army had been planning for such an uprising since its inception, and General Rowecki had defined the seven major objectives for the uprising in his "Operative Report 154" as early as September 1942. The goals were straightforward but slightly alarming, in that objective 7 called for not only restoring Poland's pre-1939 territory, but also taking other territory to make Poland larger and stronger in the future.

1. Crushing the German occupation by destroying administration, party organs, and German population, and by removing German troops by means of a "voluntary forced evacuation"

2. Securing weapons and other armaments through the voluntary or forced surrender of relevant stocks

3. Resistance against "Ukrainian claims" (southeast of the old state territories)

4. Restoration of law and order

5. Reconstruction of the regular army

6. Support for the new civilian administration

7. Occupation of areas within the old state territory that could not be occupied in the initial stages of the uprising, as well as new areas "whose occupation is imperative for a strong future Poland"[15]

Despite the aggressive language, circumstances in 1942 and 1943 did not remotely allow for any such rising to take place. The strength of the Home Army relative to the Nazi occupation apparatus made such plans purely theoretical. But in 1944 circumstances changed dramatically with the retreat of Germany's eastern armies.

One of the first decisive moves taken by the Polish resistance in early 1944 was the execution of a particularly despised Nazi occupation official, Franz Kutschera. Kutschera was an Austrian Nazi who found himself directing the operations of the Holocaust in Russia and, from September 1943, in Warsaw. As Jews and other Poles were rounded up, tortured, and sent to death camps, the Polish "Underground State" collected data on the man, and this was shared in an underground hearing by resistance officials. They found him guilty of his heinous crimes and secured approval from the government-in-exile for his execution. The sentence was passed and the execution order given to the Kedyw. A team was put together for the execution, led by the agent Bronisław Pietraszewicz (code-named "Lot"), including a special group that would hover nearby to provide cover fire after the assault. On the morning of February 1, 1944, the team moved into place at the SS headquarters, the Leszczyński Residence in downtown Warsaw. When Kutschera's limousine pulled up to the front entrance, two men fired on Kutschera, wounding him and then killing him. Nearby Nazi guards opened fire, and a gunfight commenced, with the other Kedyw team joining in. Four resistance men lost their lives in the firefight, but Kutschera was dead. The Nazis responded in their usual way, by choosing

100 Polish hostages held in local prisons and executing them on the spot the following day.

As the Soviets continued to push the Nazis backward and near Polish territory, the debate intensified among the leaders of the "Underground State." Eventually it was decided that a series of uprisings should take place in cities where resistance forces were strong and where Nazi forces would be weakened and chaotic. Uprisings took place then as part of wider strategy, known as "Operation Tempest" (*Burza* in Polish), which initially had been planned by Rowecki and his staff. As the Soviets advanced, the AK gave the signal for its armed members to rise up, which they did in places like Vilnius, Lublin, and Lviv. In each instance, casualties were high and weapons and ammunition supplies were quite low, impeding effective fighting. But victory was achieved by coordination with Soviet forces. The result of each of these actions was effective military operations, an initial but brief period of cooperation between AK leaders and the Soviets, but then the Soviet policy of forcing an "unconditional disarming of the AK."[16] With each area's liberation, there followed the disarming and dissolution of the AK forces. This was ominous for the leaders of the government-in-exile and the "Underground State"; they understood very well that Soviet occupation of Polish territory without armed Polish forces or Polish administrators present meant unopposed Soviet domination.

With the Soviets pushing toward the capital, Warsaw, it was clear that this action would be vitally significant and might hold the key to Poland's future. "Underground State" leaders worked with the new head of the AK, General Komorovski (known as Bór-Komorovski), to devise a plan that could defeat the Germans and give control of Warsaw to Polish authorities rather than the Soviets. They decided that a full-scale operation must be launched ahead of the arrival of Soviet forces, and that the uprising would have to fully defeat the Germans on its own. With this accomplished, the Polish authorities would seize control of all major institutions—transport, government ministries, the post, communications, armed defense, and so on. With a Polish government in place and functioning, it would take a Soviet attack and invasion to dislodge them. The thinking was that such aggression would be too blatant a violation for the other Allies to accept, and so Poland stood a strong chance of retaining its independence. With this scenario in mind, Bór-Komorovski made the decision to launch the uprising on the night of July 25, and the plan was implemented on August 1.

The AK had about 20,000 armed soldiers for the revolt and many thousands more with no arms. Of these, about 4,000 fighters were women, or about 10 percent of the combined personnel.[17] The attacks were launched by armed soldiers moving into office buildings, hotels, and post offices and seizing control while armed guards were stationed around the buildings. In the downtown area, they took the Prudential Insurance building, the

Labor Office building, the former Czech embassy, the electrical works, and some warehouses with food. Areas with German armed guards came under fire, and heavy combat followed. The Poles sustained frightful casualties for any successes gained. Despite this, during the first week, the insurgents were relatively successful and were able to take control of some large sections of the city, most importantly two sections in the very heart of the city known as the "Old City" and the "City Center." The river Vistula runs through Warsaw at nearly a 45-degree angle, from southeast to northwest. Most of Warsaw is on the west side of that river, including the Old City and the City Center. But German troops held on to strongholds throughout the city at places like their own command headquarters and the vital bridges across the Vistula. Although the first week's fighting had taken large blocks of the city, the Germans were not vanquished, and they held on to well-fortified defensive strongholds dotted throughout the city. From these strongholds, the Germans would very slowly and methodically expand outward in all directions. The man in overall command of the German forces was SS *Obergruppenführer* Erich von dem Bach-Zelewski. His troops numbered around 20,000, similar to the AK's number, but the Germans had superior arms and vast amounts of ammunition by comparison. They also had tanks and armored vehicles. In the weeks that followed, the Germans employed the strategy of using captured insurgents and especially innocent Polish civilians as human shields in their advances. They would round up 50 to 100 civilians, group them in front of tanks, and move forward into neighborhoods. Any AK members who fired upon the Germans would be killing their own people.[18] The Nazis also brought in two regiments for reinforcements. The first was known as the "Dirlewanger Brigade" after its notorious leader Oskar Dirlewanger. This regiment was known for its terrifying brutality and sadism and was made up of "German criminals, poachers, and SS men on probation."[19] The other regiment was a brigade of former Red Army soldiers who had gone over to the Nazis, known as the "SS Storm Brigade RONA," under Bronislav Kaminski. It was also known for its legendary brutality, and, as one historian puts it, it "had a terrible reputation, even among Germans."[20]

Over the course of August, the story was a fairly consistent one. The Germans made slow, deadly progress in recapturing areas of the city. The fighting was house to house and block to block. Von dem Bach-Zelewski had been given explicit orders from the German High Command and Himmler to destroy the entire city. As such, the Germans simply brought tanks and artillery to neighborhoods and steadily destroyed them house by house. A particularly important victory was won by the Germans on August 17 when they retook the Haberbusch brewery and food warehouses, which dramatically reduced the nourishment level for the Poles. Perhaps from this point, it was only a matter of time.

Members of Poland's Home Army in street fighting against the Nazis during August 1944. The Warsaw Rising ended in defeat and tragedy. (Jerzy Piorkowski [1957] Miasto Nieujarzmione, Warsaw: Iskry, p. 199)

Having reached late August without victory, the Poles were in deep trouble. Their plan had always been to win a fast and complete victory. No serious plans had been made for a long struggle regarding food, transport, replenishment of weapons and ammunition, or arrangements with the Allies. Now they were managing the situation on the fly. There were, however, two sources of hope. The first of these was the possibility of a large-scale Allied airlift to bring in supplies and weapons. Allied planes could also aid the Poles by bombing and strafing the Germans. Bombing and strafing the Germans by air, however, proved to be impossible, because of the configuration of the forces. German strongholds were dotted throughout the city, and any attempt to attack them would inevitably cause terrible civilian casualties. Since this strategy would not work, there remained the effort to drop large amounts of supplies and weaponry. There were certainly attempts to do this, some by the RAF and some by the Americans. But flying to Warsaw from the Italian base at Brindisi meant flying over hundreds of miles of enemy territory and was extremely dangerous. One RAF navigator recalls that it was not only Nazi aircraft that one had to worry about— Russian planes were an issue as well. He remembers, "We were engaged by Russian AA fire and Russian night fighters along much of the two and a half hour route. Disenchanted by this . . . (we) decided that if we survived the drop on Warsaw and were fated to be shot down on the way home, it would be by the enemy and not our Russian 'friends.'"[21] American planes also hoped to be able to operate from Russian-held territory east of Poland, but here again the Soviets did not allow American planes to land at their bases. Stalin, of course, had no interest in a successful Polish uprising and would do nothing that would help the Poles to take control of their own capital.

Indeed, the Soviets would play a decisive role in the tragedy that unfolded in Warsaw. By not allowing Allied planes to use Russia's airbases, the extent of aerial losses prompted the British to abandon the airlift all together. The Americans were only able to fly in large levels of supplies by mid-September. By that time the Nazis had reclaimed so much of the city that it was nearly impossible to find a safe landing area where supplies were sure to be in Polish hands. As one AK fighter remembers, by September 18, "three quarters of the supplies dropped . . . fell into German hands. Had the help come a few weeks earlier, the outcome of the Rising might have been very different. Now, it was too late."[22] But if Allied airdrops could not rescue the Poles, by September there was another option. The second great source of hope to the Poles was the arrival of the Soviet ground forces at the eastern rim of Warsaw. Having pushed the Nazis out of eastern Poland, the Soviet forces stopped just outside Warsaw, only a few miles away from the east bank of the Vistula. There they remained throughout the uprising and never intervened in the struggle. The Poles had launched their uprising to seize control of the city just ahead of the arrival of Soviet troops, and they had not planned on any material help from the Soviets. But having failed in this objective, and with the civilian population of Warsaw being destroyed day by day, the Polish government-in-exile now "pleaded desperately for Soviet support."[23] There has been debate about the Soviet response ever since. This is particularly due to the fact that documentary evidence does not seem to exist explaining who made what decisions and why.[24] The Soviet general Zhukov insisted that his troops needed to rest and regroup after the long push, and this was reluctantly approved by Stalin. But by September, certainly the Soviets could have intervened. They did not, and it would seem that Stalin's hostility to the Poles and his aims for Soviet hegemony after the war were the primary reasons. In his biography of Stalin, Robert Service writes,

> Stalin was already looking for ways to secure political dominance over Poland during and after the war . . . He was determined that whatever Polish state emerged from the debris of the war would stay under the hegemony of the USSR. This meant that the émigré government based in London was to be treated as illegitimate and that any armed organization formed by the Poles in Poland would be treated likewise.[25]

With the Nazis decimating the Polish capital's population, Stalin's aims for the postwar world were becoming much more easily obtainable. So the Poles were left to fend for themselves.

Perhaps the most enduring story from the uprising was the flight of the Poles from the Old City district. As early as mid-August, the area was being overrun by the Germans, and the Poles had no choice but to flee to the better-protected area of the City Center. But German tanks and troops blocked the way. To remain in place meant sure death, as the city itself was being wiped out steadily. The AK was able to organize a way out that was quite literally an underground movement. The plan was to use the sewer network, which would take them directly underneath columns of German troops in midtown. The sewers ran with filth and excrement, and the people had to run hunched over and at times to crawl. To make matters worse, the Germans grew wise to the tactic and would routinely toss grenades down the manholes or fire flamethrowers into the sewers. Many died in the flames, but the vast majority escaped to the safer areas of the city.

There are remarkable tales of heroism and astonishing courage from the uprising. Early in the process, in the middle of the city, what remained of the Jewish ghetto camp was liberated by the AK. One soldier remembers that, having freed the Jews inside, he saw an almost unbelievable sight: "In the middle of the camp square, at least a hundred prisoners had been drawn up military style in two long ranks . . . one of them came up to me and said, 'Sergeant Henryk Lederman, Sir, and the Jewish Battalion ready for Action.'" The soldier went on to wonder at their seemingly infinite store of courage, saying, "Not only had they not been broken by Nazi savagery, they had managed to organize themselves . . . and to ready themselves as soon as an opportunity occurred . . . [T]hose soldier Jews left behind them the reputation of exceptionally brave, ingenious, and faithful people."[26] Another heart-rending memory came from a soldier who had been injured and received medical care. He was astounded at the "high level of sterilization, or care over cleanliness in those insurrectionary conditions, where everything could be contaminated by the constant explosions." The trained nurses, he says, "carried out the bleakest work with a smile . . . Decisions had to be taken instantly. Skull trepanations, eye removals, and limb amputations were routine. Even so the death rate was relatively low." He remembered that the AK had decided to mark the hospital building's roof with a red cross so that enemy planes would not directly attack it. But, he says, having done this, "It precipitated an immediate bombardment by German Stukas."[27]

Through September the fighting went on, but steadily the Germans retook the town. All of the main sectors of the city were in German hands by the end of the month. Those who were left alive generally had no homes, only rubble and what sticks of furniture they could prop up in the gaps amid the heaps of debris. For the hundreds of thousands of civilians who had not been armed fighters, there were mixed emotions in the midst of the disaster. Some fought alongside the AK; many thousands lent aid, food, shelter, or whatever they could. Others wondered why on Earth these fools had brought destruction down upon them. One AK soldier, making his way through the rubble remembered the despair and contempt of an ordinary old man who had lost everything. He called to the unit and "pointing his hand at the rubble said bitterly: 'Look at what you have done!' We passed him without a word. What was there to say? . . . For us it was a question of dearly held 'ideals'; for him it was his house."[28]

By the end of September, the Polish rebels had run out of food, ammunition, and any real trace of hope. The German commander von dem Bach-Zelewski and Bór-Komorovski negotiated a truce on October 1, which was formally signed on the evening of October 2. The terms included plans for the removal of some 5,000 wounded to be evacuated to German facilities. Another result was that over 15,000 Poles were taken prisoner immediately and sent to death camps, labor camps, and forced factory work.[29] The uprising had been a disastrous failure. It had not defeated the Germans; instead it had resulted in horrendous casualties for the Poles. Estimates vary; between 150,000 and 200,000 Poles were killed in Warsaw between August 1 and October 2. The AK was entirely wiped out during and after the battle, and its network would crumble in the face of advancing Soviet troops in the days to come. The Poles had not been able to take control of their capital in order to secure their independence. Instead, the structure of the "Underground State" was all but wiped out, and Soviet control of Poland was virtually a fait accompli by the time of the Potsdam Conference in 1945. Poland would endure almost 50 more years of communist rule under the thumb of the Soviet Union. The historical questions that swirl around the Warsaw Uprising today, especially among Polish historians, mostly concern assigning blame. It might seem ridiculous to ask the question, "Was the Warsaw Uprising worth it?" In retrospect it might seem a poorly conceived, poorly planned suicide mission that made Poland's postwar independence all but impossible. Yet there are historians, like István Deák for example, who see in the extraordinary courage and selflessness of the Polish fighters the inspiration for Poland's eventual liberation from communism. Perhaps he says it best when he writes that despite the obvious truth that with no uprising, thousands would not have been killed, "Communist-run Poland and the Polish people would not have been able successfully to defy the Soviet Union as early as 1956, and then again in the 1970s and 1980s, without the self-respect gained and the worldwide admiration inspired by the Uprising and the Polish resistance."[30]

NOTES

1. Hans Frank, quoted in Włodzimierz Borodziej, *The Warsaw Uprising of 1944*, trans. Barbara Harshav (Madison: University of Wisconsin Press, 2006), p. 17.
2. Ibid., p. 19.

3. See Jan Rosinski, *The Warsaw Underground: A Memoir of Resistance 1939–1945* (Jefferson, NC: MacFarlane & Co., 2014).

4. István Deák, *Europe on Trial: The Story of Collaboration, Resistance, and Retribution during World War II* (Boulder, CO: Westview, 2015), p. 145.

5. Borodziej, *The Warsaw Uprising of 1944*, p. 20.

6. Ibid., p. 22.

7. Linderman, *Re-Discovering Irregular Warfare*, p. 153.

8. Borodziej, *The Warsaw Uprising of 1944*, p. 27.

9. For an in-depth discussion of the Katyn Forest massacre, see Victor Zaslavsky, *Class Cleansing: The Katyn Massacre*, trans. Kizer Walker (New York: Telos Press, 2008).

10. Stafford, *Britain and European Resistance*, p. 64.

11. Linderman, *Re-Discovering Irregular Warfare*, p. 153.

12. Borodziej, *The Warsaw Uprising of 1944*, p. 38.

13. Ibid., p. 149.

14. Ibid., p. 149.

15. Operative Report 154, quoted in Borodziej, *The Warsaw Uprising*, p. 42.

16. Ibid., p. 56.

17. Ibid., p. 74.

18. Ibid., p. 77.

19. Ibid., p. 78.

20. Ibid., p. 78.

21. See Norman Davies, *Rising '44: The Battle for Warsaw* (New York: Viking, 2003), p. 309. Davies's book is the closest thing to a definitive work on the subject in the English language; throughout his work, he includes firsthand testimony from those who lived through and fought in the uprising. I have relied a great deal upon his work for the firsthand recollections in this chapter.

22. Ibid., p. 378.

23. Service, *Stalin: A Biography*, p. 470.

24. See Borodziej, *The Warsaw Uprising of 1944*, p. 90. Here he writes, "Despite the relative openness of the Russian archives in the 1990s we still do not know what took place in Moscow between August 9–12 . . . There is a gaping hole." In *Stalin: A Biography* (p. 472), Service writes, "Almost nothing is known about who said what until the Warsaw Uprising was over."

25. Service, *Stalin: A Biography*, p. 471.

26. Davies, *Rising '44*, p. 262.

27. Ibid., p. 333.

28. Ibid., p. 368.

29. Borodziej, *The Warsaw Uprising of 1944*, p. 128.

30. Deák, *Europe on Trial*, p. 155.

7

Standing Against Hitler

The Resistance in Germany

In Nazi Germany resistance was very nearly impossible, whether during the 1930s or in the war years. First of all, the Nazi state built a monolithic state apparatus to smash any instances of internal opposition. Organizations like the Gestapo and the SD, all part of the larger SS organization, worked full-time to identify any real or potential challenge to the Nazi order. The state used extralegal means—truly extralegal because the SS received official status that placed it beyond the jurisdiction of the German legal system—to spy on its own citizens, identify its perceived enemies, and remove them from society. The network of concentration camps was begun immediately upon Hitler's rise to power. The leaders of trade unions and the opposition political parties, for instance, were arrested as early as the spring of 1933 and sent to the camps, some never to be heard from again.

But there was another dimension to this systematic oppression that is necessary to understand in order to fully grasp the reasons for the tiny level of organized opposition. The vast majority of the German population enthusiastically supported Hitler and his Nazi state, and despite its seeming excesses, like the oppression of the Jews, people generally believed that the good far outweighed the bad in the new regime. Crime amongst the citizenry virtually disappeared (though there was plenty of criminal behavior by those in charge!), the economy began to recover, and unemployment dropped, especially with the ramping up of rearmament. Workers and the family were glorified through the work of Joseph Goebbels's propaganda ministry, and Germans were constantly reminded that they were part of a racially superior people. The victors of the First World War (principally Britain and France) were no longer permitted to dictate Germany's policies. Germany had already stopped paying reparations, and in 1935 Hitler publicly announced the expansion of the German military and signed the Anglo–German Naval Agreement with Great Britain. In 1936 this reached a kind of pinnacle, with Hitler moving German military troops into the Rhineland region, in direct violation of the Treaty of Versailles. By demonstrating his complete contempt for the Treaty of Versailles, Hitler helped the German people to recover their sense of national pride, a sense that their nation was again in charge of its own future. For all of these reasons and more, the German people generally supported the Hitler regime and accepted its ideologically based policies, including racial discrimination and its brutality to supposed internal enemies. Historian Robert Gellately, for instance, has done important research on the inner workings of the Gestapo, based upon captured documents. His findings tell us that the Gestapo, in certain regions, was not driving the campaign to spy on internal enemies so much as constantly responding to the flood of denunciations it received from ordinary Germans. German citizens regularly reported their neighbors and even family members for their "antisocial" behavior—anything that suggested they did not support Nazi ideology or fit the Nazi definition of a German citizen.[1] The Nazis most assuredly created a smothering state apparatus to administer a regime of terror, but they were continually assisted by the cooperation of the majority of the German public.

In such an environment, large groups of coordinated resisters were virtually impossible. There were some important members of the clergy who refused to endorse Nazi cruelties, but these acts were necessarily tiny in scale and limited to questions of public endorsement or non-endorsement. The possibility of actual attacks on the Nazi state—burning offices, shooting members of the government, mass political opposition in the streets—was nonexistent. There were simply not enough people in German society who were disillusioned enough with the regime to constitute large organizations, and any such individual effort was suicidal. In the isolated cases where such an act was carried out, of course, it resulted in the state's savage reprisals against its own people. An example of this would be the assassination of the German diplomat Ernst vom Rath. A German Jew named Herschel Grynszpan was living in Paris and had received word from his parents back in Germany that they were being forced out of their home. His outrage was so great that he decided to kill a leading Nazi, and he chose the diplomat vom Rath at the German embassy in Paris. Vom Rath survived the initial assault but died on November 9 from his wounds. The Nazi hierarchy in Berlin reacted with fury, particularly Joseph Goebbels, the propaganda minister, who began to organize a mass reprisal against the Jews. It lasted for two days, as members of the Nazi SA destroyed Jewish businesses, arrested and murdered innocent people, and burned Jewish synagogues. More than 30,000 Jews were arrested and taken to camps, 1,200 synagogues were destroyed, and 7,000 Jewish businesses were ruined.[2] This was the infamous Kristallnacht, which earned that name because of the broken glass on the streets, which gleamed like crystal. Such could be the penalties for any serious act of resistance in Germany.

For all of these reasons, widespread resistance by ordinary people was practically nonexistent in Germany before and during the war. The only space where a secret resistance group *could* take shape was within the state apparatus itself. The story of the German resistance is mostly concerned with elites of the Nazi state, high-ranking army officers and political elites, who eventually determined that Hitler's regime must disappear. But the Nazi state was so completely dominated by a single man that it was clear that in order to bring an end to the war and to Nazism, its leader must be removed. The prevailing view among the small circle of resisters was that Adolf Hitler had to be killed in order to save Germany. As a result, this chapter will not be chiefly concerned with building secret armies, parachute drops, and wireless transmitters. The standard procedures of resistance didn't apply in Germany. Rather, this chapter will be primarily concerned with providing brief outlines of those involved in the resistance and their attempts to kill Adolf Hitler. The death of this one man would prove to be the most difficult challenge any of them would ever face. In the end, despite the outstanding courage of some of its members, the German resistance failed utterly.

A MATTER OF EIGHT MINUTES: THE ASTONISHING STORY OF GEORG ELSER AND HIS ATTEMPT TO KILL HITLER

Despite the state repression, despite the societal pressures, despite the seeming impossibility for one person to make a difference during the zenith of Nazism in Germany, one ordinary man did in fact undertake to kill the *Führer*. He came within minutes of changing history. Today his name is nearly forgotten, known mostly to historians and specialists, but had he succeeded, it is possible that Nazism could have collapsed in 1939. It is extremely difficult to project what might have happened if Hitler had been killed in November 1939 with the war only just beginning. But one thing seems certain: Had he succeeded, we would all know of the simple man named Johann Georg Elser.

Georg Elser was born on January 4, 1903, in the small town of Hermaringen in the state of Württemberg in Germany. His parents soon moved the family to the town of Königsbronn, and this is where Elser spent most of his childhood and school years. His father was a timber merchant who kept the family farm crowded with great stacks of wood, but he was also a heavy drinker, and he darkened Georg's childhood years with his drunkenness and violence. Georg was generally called on to work in his father's business and to care for his younger siblings, and he began to resent his situation. As his biographer Hellmut Haasis writes, "He wanted to get away from the misery of his parents' fighting, the constant control of his life and his wages, and the obligation as the eldest to always be at the family's beck and call."[3] He eventually took work in a number of other businesses in Königsbronn, including blacksmithing and carpentry, and excelled at the local technical school. He also traveled to the Swiss border regions, where he worked for a number of companies, including an aircraft parts company and in a few different clockmaking workshops. He continued his work as a craftsman through the 1930s and continually honed his skills. In his days as a woodworker, he had joined the fairly left-wing woodworkers' union, which seems to have colored his politics. He is said by Haasis to have revealed to a fellow leftist worker "that he was an ardent anti-Nazi."[4] In his testimony to SS interrogators in late 1939, he revealed that he had not been a member of the Communist Party but had been a supporter and generally voted for its candidates before 1933, when the party was suppressed. After Hitler took power, like many German workers, Elser watched with anger as the Nazis dismantled the German labor movement, making the Communist Party, unions, and strikes illegal. In that same interrogation, he explained that by 1938, he was determined to do something. As he said, "The dissatisfaction among the workers that I had observed since 1933 and the war that I had seen as inevitable since the fall of 1938 occupied my thoughts constantly . . . On my own I began to contemplate how one could improve the conditions of the working class and avoid war."[5] He seems to have been especially disturbed by the aggression against Czechoslovakia, and had resolved to take drastic action.

But how could one kill Hitler? The security around Hitler was airtight, and a particular problem was that one never knew where Hitler would be at a particular time. He and his schedulers took special precautions for him to maintain an erratic schedule. But there was one place and one day that one could count on the presence of Hitler every year without fail. This was the commemoration of the Beer Hall Putsch of 1923 in Munich at the very beer hall where it had begun, the Bürgerbräukeller. Every year on November 8, Hitler and the leaders of his inner circle returned to the beer hall and celebrated with a crowd of the Alte Kämpfer (Old Fighters), the legions of dedicated Nazis who had been with the party since its earliest days.[6] At these events Hitler would make a rousing speech on a small stage at the back of the long great hall. Elser seized on this location and decided that with his skills, he could kill the *Führer*. In November 1938 Elser went to Munich to observe the celebrations, and perhaps it was on this brief visit that he solidified his plan. After returning to his home region in April 1939, he got work in a quarry, where he learned about the intricacies of explosives. Experimenting on his own, he eventually perfected a method for an appropriate bomb.

On August 5, 1939, Elser traveled to Munich, where he intended to take up residency until the assassination. He took a large suitcase filled with the equipment for his explosive, but he was never confronted or checked. He eventually found a tiny room for rent, where he established himself, keeping his largest suitcases in the landlord's attic. On August 9 Elser started his work on the Bürgerbräukeller. Posing as an ordinary local worker, he became a regular customer, coming in most nights for a cheap meal and a drink or two. He even took the trouble to become friends with the proprietor's dog. After becoming a customary sight—part of the woodwork, so to speak—he began to steal away to the bathrooms and await closing time. After the establishment was closed and vacant, he would reemerge and go into the large beer hall. On the stage there was a central pillar support directly behind the speakers' area. Elser removed the paneling around the pillar and began carving out an opening in the concrete that would be large enough to accommodate a bomb. He would catch the refuse on a small piece of carpet and dump it in a box in the storage room. Then in the daytime he would transfer that debris into his own small briefcase and then dump it in a nearby river.[7] When he finished a night's work, he got the paneling back onto the pillar before opening time, and he would steal out of the place unnoticed or simply wait until mealtime and sit at the bar for a meal. Night after night he went through this routine until he was able to fit a bomb with a timer in the space and cover it with paneling so that it was completely invisible. By late October it was done, having taken him nearly two months of secretive work. His knees were deeply bruised and painful from so many nights kneeling on the hard floor. On the nights of November 1 and 2, he installed the explosives, and by the night of November 5 he was able to rig the entire mechanism. He used raw dynamite, packed tightly into the compartment he had created, but the bomb itself, which would ignite all the explosives, was quite complex. As historian Michael Thomsett explains,

> During the day, Elser worked in his room on the bomb's triggering device. The action involved two alarm clock works, so that in the event of failure, there was a backup system. By coordinating both clocks with a series of cog wheels and levers, Elser constructed a device he could pre-set up to six days. The complicated mechanism was flawless.[8]

During November 6 and 7, Elser made the arrangements to check out of his room, ship his things ahead of him, and leave Munich permanently. On the night of November 7, he made one last check of the bomb and found it satisfactory. All indications were that the bomb would go off at exactly the right time—during Hitler's long, haranguing speech about the glorious sacrifices of the early Nazi coup attempt in 1923. Elser left Munich on the morning of November 8 and began a long train journey to the town of Konstanz, just adjacent to the Swiss border.

On the evening of November 8, Hitler and his parade of adjutants converged on Munich for the ceremonies. But unlike years past, this particular ceremony was going to be affected by the war. Unbeknownst to anyone outside the Nazi inner circle and military command, Hitler was in the midst of planning the invasion of France and the Low Countries. He had almost canceled his appearance at the commemoration, but in the end he decided to make an appearance. But it would have to be quick; immediately after his speech, he would depart and head back to Berlin on his private train. To give him a head start on this schedule, his speech had been moved up. When Hitler and his key officials arrived at the Bürgerbräukeller, the hall was filled with celebrating old Nazis, who immediately fell silent, stood, and saluted as the *Führer* and his entourage moved through the central aisle and took their places on the stage. The celebration proceeded, and Hitler eventually took the podium for the keynote speech. It began at about 8:15 PM and lasted only 57 minutes. For Hitler this was quite short—he usually made a 90-minute speech—and it was obvious that he was trying to get back to Berlin as quickly as possible. His speech ended at 9:12, and immediately upon its conclusion, the group of high-ranking Nazis saluted, shook a few hands, and paraded out of the establishment, headed directly to the train station. At 9:20 the bomb went off with immense power. The ceiling caved in, and huge timbers fell, killing a number of people. One waitress, Maria Strobel (who later provided an eyewitness account), was blown from the stage the length of the hall to the crumbling front entrance. Incredibly she was not permanently injured. Hitler's table on stage was buried in six feet of rubble, and it seems virtually certain that he would have been killed or at least mortally wounded in the blast. But the *Führer* was safely arriving at the train station when he heard the news of the bombing. He had been eight minutes from death.

Elser, meanwhile, had arrived in Konstanz, and by 8:45 PM he was walking only meters away from the Swiss border. It is possible that he was waiting for someone, or maybe he was just hesitant to cross. But he was apprehended by local border security men and taken to their small guard post. There they forced him to empty his pockets. He had with him wire cutters, pliers, and most incriminating of all, a schematic drawing of the interior of the Bürgerbräukeller. At this time the bomb hadn't gone off, and though this was suspicious, it raised no particular alarm. But while he was still being interrogated, the news came across the radio of the bombing in Munich at the very same beer hall. He was soon sent back to Munich and taken into the custody of the Gestapo. He was intensely interrogated over months in both Munich and Berlin. While in Berlin, his chief interrogators insisted that he reconstruct the pillar and bombing mechanism setup, which he did, and photos of his reconstructions still exist in SS files. His family from Königsbronn was also brought in and interrogated in front of him for maximum effect. He was eventually sent to the Sachsenhausen concentration camp and kept in solitary confinement for years, always expecting death at any moment. He was later transferred to Dachau, and he lingered in captivity until the last moments of the war, when on April 9, 1945, not even a month before war's end, he was taken from his cell and shot. SS files claim he was killed by an Allied air raid.[9]

Who *was* Georg Elser, and how did he come to pull off such an extraordinary assassination attempt? These questions have fascinated historians to this day and produced a number of theories. One theory suggests that he may have been an agent working for Heinrich Himmler, who had arranged the bombing to demonstrate to the people that Hitler was protected by "providence" and to generate a wave of loving support among the people for their *Führer* at the very time he was leading them into a very questionable war.[10] It would also provide justification for another round of intensified Gestapo terror. The other major theory, insisted upon by Hitler himself, was that there must have been British agents behind the plot. This was the explanation most promulgated by the Nazi Party, and it served to discredit the British in the eyes of the German people. It could also be a blend of these two explanations; that is, a plot concocted by the SS to stage a fake assassination in order to generate extreme hatred among the German people for the British enemy. The questions persist: Could an ordinary carpenter with only moderate political enthusiasms really have planned and executed this operation on his own? Was he selected by British agents because of his skills and political affiliation (loose though it was) with the communists? Was he coached on how to pull off this extraordinary operation by British intelligence agents, communists, or perhaps the SS? Or did this young man really act alone? We shall probably never know the real answers, unless new evidence comes to light about the strange and lonely man who nearly changed history.

DRAMATIS PERSONAE: SOME KEY FIGURES AND GROUPS OF THE GERMAN UNDERGROUND

Elser's attempt took place in November 1939, by which time there had already been a plot for a coup attempt by the highly secretive underground functioning within the German High Command. From 1938 until July 1944, the underground network worked to arrange the assassination of

Hitler and the demise of the Nazi power structure, and to devise an alternative government to end hostilities. A large number of individuals were involved, even if some only functioned at a great distance, making a complete treatment of the underground unrealistic in a book of this size. The most thorough treatment of the German underground is Peter Hoffman's *The History of the German Resistance, 1933–1945*, which provides in-depth treatment of all the relevant individuals and groups. It runs to well over 800 pages. Obviously, then, in this book we must be far more selective. As such, what follows is a concise list of the most important figures and groups that actively resisted and eventually took on the harrowing mission to kill Hitler and end Nazism.

The White Rose

The White Rose was a group of students at the University of Munich who had become completely disillusioned with Nazism and who tried to run an underground press appealing to the German people to rise up against Nazi tyranny. There was a small core of students who were the heartbeat of the group, writing its pamphlets and working to find other sympathetic members. Among the most important of this group were Hans and Sophie Scholl, Alexander Schmorrell, Willi Graf, and Christoph Probst, as well as one professor, Dr. Kurt Huber, who taught psychology and music. A number of this core group were medical students and were sent as "medical student soldiers" to lend help on the Eastern Front. There these young men experienced the horrors of Nazi aggression and saw for themselves the Nazi project of mass murder and genocide. They returned home determined to take some kind of action against the regime. To this end, they formed an underground group to circulate written appeals, exposing the horrors of Nazism. Hans Scholl and Schmorrell wrote a series of four pamphlets that appealed directly to the German people. They used the moral and intellectual arguments of classic scholars but also reminded ordinary citizens about the lawlessness of Nazism, the unqualified and brutal men running the system, and the pressing need to stand up collectively to the regime's injustice. They ran off copies of their pamphlets on a hand-cranked duplicator and clandestinely distributed them around the university, stashing them in library books, phone books, and restrooms, and also mailing numerous copies anonymously. This went on through the last months of 1942 and into January 1943. In that month the German campaign at the Soviet city of Stalingrad had finally collapsed, and the major defeat there convinced many Germans, at least those who were willing to face it, that the war was now destined to end in a German defeat. The White Rose group pounced on this new development and issued two new pamphlets. The last of these pamphlets was written by Professor Huber, who had by now joined the group. His was a message that appealed to the patriotism of the German people, imploring them to reclaim their nation before the inevitable defeat dragged Germany into the abyss. The fifth and sixth pamphlets were copied in the thousands, and now the group began to ship copies to group members in other cities as it began to build the foundations of a nationwide movement. But it was in the process of distributing this last pamphlet at the University of Munich that a janitor detected their activities and reported them. On February 18 most of the core members were arrested by the Gestapo. What followed was a series of trials in the notorious "People's Court," with the fanatic Judge Roland Freisler presiding. Freisler was a despicable man who ignored any real adherence to trial law and spent a great deal of time shrieking malevolent condemnation at the defendants. Two principal trials saw the majority of the group's membership convicted of treason. Eleven others were subsequently jailed, and several trials would follow for other individuals whose subversion came to light later. The principal members found guilty were sentenced to death and quickly executed by guillotine. Today there are number of monuments to this group in Munich, but perhaps the most touching of all is that in Chamber 253 in the Justizpalast (Palace of Justice) in Munich. In that room, where the group was initially tried back in 1943, a lovely vase of flowers is constantly on display. In that vase is a bouquet of white roses, each one representing a member unjustly tried and killed in name of freedom.

General Ludwig Beck

Ludwig August Theodor Beck was born on June 29, 1880, in Biebrich in the Rhineland. He was educated in the time-honored Prussian military tradition and in 1914 went to war in the German army as a staff officer. Having lived through the war, Beck continued in the army through the years of the Weimar Republic, consistently rising in the ranks. By the time of Hitler's accession in 1933, Beck was promoted to head the Truppenamt, or "Troop Office," which was in reality the functioning General Staff. The Truppenamt was a cover organization to keep Germany in compliance with the Versailles treaty, but in 1935 Hitler famously reinstated conscription and announced the existence of the Luftwaffe. With the pretense gone, Beck now became the publicly acknowledged head of Germany's General Staff, an immensely powerful position. Beck earned that powerful position through his diligent work ethic and outstanding organizational abilities. He also had a striking and commanding personality, being an intensely thoughtful and intelligent man. Many called him more of a philosopher than a general. But Beck quickly became disenchanted with the Nazi system and Hitler in particular. He was horrified to hear about Hitler's plans for aggressive expansion in Eastern Europe and the possibility that this might drag Germany into a general European war that it couldn't win. As Thomsett writes,

> Beck was forced to admit by 1937 or 1938 that it was Hitler, and not just the Nazi Party, who was instigating terror in Germany. By then it was apparent that Hitler was seriously planning to make war on Germany's neighbors. Hitler issued a series of directives on November 5, 1937 that led to Beck's decision to actively organize a resistance to the Nazi regime.[11]

With his decision firmly made, and with his commanding presence, Beck soon emerged as the leading figure in the secret resistance network. If any plan to kill Hitler or to subvert the Nazi Party leadership could be brought off, it was clearly up to Beck to assure the military support and to convince other officers to assist in a coup. As the Czech crisis accelerated in August 1938, Beck's differences with Hitler became too much to bear, and Beck resigned as chief of staff. He would, however, remain as a crucial leader in the resistance circle, helping to plan future assassination attempts. He was among the planners of the July 20 plot to kill Hitler, and he was slated to assume the presidency of a new provisional government after Hitler's death.[12]

Carl Friedrich Goerdeler

If General Beck was the most influential member of the military involved in the anti-Hitler movement, then Carl Friedrich Goerdeler was the central civilian character. He was born in 1884 in Schneidemühl, Prussia, to a deeply conservative and Lutheran political family. His father served in Prussian political offices during his upbringing. Goerdeler was conservative, nationalist, and religious—all the characteristics of the right wing. But Hitler's Nazism was too radically nationalist even for Goerdeler; as Allen Dulles wrote just after the war, "It took a Hitler to make such a man a revolutionary."[13] By 1930 Goerdeler had been elected mayor of the industrial city of Leipzig, where he formed close associations with the city's most prominent business and political leaders. He was recommended as a possible leader of Germany during the political crisis of 1931–1932, but Hindenburg chose Franz von Papen instead. When Hitler came to power, Goerdeler refused to be part of the right-wing coalition cabinet, but he did serve in a bureaucratic position as "price commissar," working with Economics Minister Hjalmar Schacht. The two constantly feuded, and Goerdeler, quite rightly, accused Schacht of "aiding the Nazis' schemes for world domination."[14] His political career ended only shortly after he had been reappointed mayor of Leipzig by the Nazi government in 1936. There was a controversy over the great statue of the German composer Felix Mendelssohn that stood in downtown Leipzig. Mendelssohn, being Jewish, offended Nazi sensibilities, and local Nazis demanded that it be pulled down. Goerdeler refused, but while he was away from the city, Nazi storm-troopers removed the statue. In his outrage Goerdeler resigned his position. From that point forward, Goerdeler devoted all his energies to overthrowing the Nazis. In the years that followed, he would be the principal civilian figure in helping to plan the assassination plots, but also in devising the configurations for the post-Hitler governmental structure. Most often he was seen by those in the movement as the man to act as a new chancellor in the event of a successful coup.[15]

General Hans Oster

Hans Paul Oster was born in 1887 in Dresden, in Saxony, to Alsatian parents. He joined the German army in 1907 and fought on the Western Front during World War I until 1916. In that year he was promoted to the rank of captain on the General Staff. He was retained in the army's officer corps after the war and remained in the army through the years of the Weimar Republic. He was dismissed from the army, however, in 1932 for a rules violation and only got work again as part of the organization under Hermann Göring in the Prussian police force. Under the Nazi regime, he was able to use his military and police experience to join the Abwehr (military intelligence branch) in October 1933. He was reinstated in the army during 1935. But by 1938, after the horrors of Kristallnacht, he had firmly rejected Nazism and begun looking for ways to overthrow Hitler's terroristic regime. In his work in the Abwehr, he met several of the key individuals who would later work with him in anti-Nazi plots, such as Hans Gisevius and Arthur Nebe, and above all Admiral Wilhelm Canaris, who ran the Abwehr. His affiliation with the Abwehr was of tremendous importance for the movement, as he could provide false documents and travel passes, and arrange secret meetings, all with the authority of a secret organization, which other branches could not investigate. As Germany moved into the Second World War, Oster was firmly in the camp of those determined to kill Hitler and overthrow the regime.[16]

Admiral Wilhelm Canaris

Wilhelm Franz Canaris was born in 1887 in Aplerbeck in Westphalia to a wealthy middle-class industrial family. He joined the navy in 1905 and served in World War I on a ship that was engaging Britain's Royal Navy just off the South American coast. He and most of his fellow crewmen were captured and interned in Chile in 1915, but he was able to make a remarkable escape and make his way back to Germany. Back home, the military assigned him to intelligence duties, because of the remarkable enterprise he had displayed. He worked in numerous areas for the navy through the interwar years and traveled often to foreign nations. In 1935 he was made head of the Abwehr, the central military intelligence organization. But despite his strong nationalism, Canaris could not support the Nazi policy of attacking its neighbors and programs of racial persecution. By 1938 Canaris, deeply concerned over the Czech crisis, had become a quiet supporter of overthrowing the regime. But the wily Canaris kept such opinions strictly to himself and fooled the entire Nazi inner circle. His tactics were extremely subtle, for one, gradually staffing the Abwehr with those opposed to the regime. He would also occasionally intervene personally to help individuals avoid persecution. This sort of behavior eventually convinced his rivals, like Heinrich Himmler, that he was not a loyal Nazi, and the Abwehr was dismantled in February 1944, with Canaris sent to a much less prestigious post. With his loyalty in question, he was among those tried and executed after the failed plot of July 1944.[17]

General Friedrich Olbricht

Friedrich Olbricht was born on October 4, 1888, in Leisnig in Saxony. He was born to an academic family rather than a military family, but he eventually chose a life in the army. He fought in the infantry during World War I and continued in the army after the war. He was one of the very few military men who supported the democratic ideals of the Weimar Republic. Through the 1930s he worked his way to greater responsibilities, eventually becoming the chief of staff of the Fourth Army Corps in Dresden. Despite his success, it appears that Olbricht may have been anti-Nazi even during the early years of the Nazi regime, as he is known to have assisted some individuals in avoiding execution during the notorious "Night of the Long Knives" in the summer of 1934. When World War II broke out, Olbricht was among those leading troops into Poland, and he was decorated with the Knight's Cross for his bravery and enterprise. But Olbricht also then saw firsthand the murderous brutality of German occupation and "Germanization" in Poland. In February 1940 he was made a general and reassigned to a command of the Ersatzheer, or the "Replacement Army." This position would place him in an ideal position to help the resistance with a plot to seize the government from Hitler and his Nazis. He was physically present during the July plot to kill Hitler and was one of those working to coordinate its success. When the plot fell apart on the night of July 20, he was among those immediately arrested and executed.

Major General Henning von Tresckow

Henning von Tresckow was born January 19, 1901, in Magdeburg to an aristocratic Prussian family with a long record of military leadership. He joined the army when he was only 16 years old and fought at the Western Front during the First World War. In 1918 he won the Iron Cross for his bravery in the Second Battle of the Marne. After the war he left the military briefly, becoming a stockbroker, but he rejoined the Reichswehr in 1924. Working his way up, he joined the General Staff in the mid-1930s, where he became close to a number of Germany's top military minds, including some who would later turn against Hitler, like General Ludwig Beck. By 1939, Hitler's aggression and the coming of a general war convinced Tresckow that Nazism had to be eliminated and that Hitler must die. His convictions only strengthened in 1941 as he was assigned to serve under Field Marshal von Bock in Operation Barbarossa, as the head of Army Group Center, which struck deep into the heart of the Soviet Union. The atrocities and eventually the hopelessness of the Russian campaign deepened his anti-Hitler sentiments. Tresckow played a key role in the attempt to kill Hitler with a disguised bomb put aboard the *Führer's* plane as it left Russia, and later he would be a key organizer of the plot of July 1944, known as "Operation Valkyrie." After the failure of the Valkyrie plot, knowing well his fate, he drove to the front lines of combat, went into enemy territory, and blew himself up with a grenade.[18]

Colonel Claus von Stauffenberg

The most dynamic and courageous of the figures of the German resistance was also perhaps its youngest: Colonel Claus von Stauffenberg. He was born on November 15, 1907, in the region of Swabia in Bavaria. Born to a noble family with a very prestigious pedigree, he was born in their ancestral castle and given the title of count. This was eliminated after World War I, when Germany abolished noble titles and privileges. He joined the army in 1926 and became an officer (second lieutenant) by 1930. He was strongly nationalist but eventually found Nazism abhorrent, with its persecution of minorities, its terroristic tactics, and its anti-religious aspects. Stauffenberg remained a devoted Catholic. Like so many, he was alarmed at the Czech crisis but found himself assigned to the regiments that moved into the Sudetenland after the Munich Agreement of September 1938. When the war broke out, Stauffenberg seemed to be everywhere, serving in Poland, then France (for which he won the Iron Cross), then in the Russian Campaign, and later in North Africa. In North Africa he was badly wounded when his jeep was strafed by enemy aircraft; he lost his right hand, his left eye, and two fingers on his left hand. He was sent home to recover, and after hospital time, he recuperated at his family's estate. In these years, despite the overwhelming success of the German army until 1941, Stauffenberg had become convinced that Hitler was leading the nation into the abyss. Reemerging from his recovery, he was assigned as a colonel in the Ersatzheer, or "Replacement Army," stationed in Berlin. This group was a like a shadow army, training young soldiers to be ready to fill in for troops needed anywhere. The assignment placed Stauffenberg in a uniquely important position—he was in Berlin, the seat of government, and one of the officers in charge of the largest military force in the area. It was here that he was contacted by members of the resistance movement, including General Friedrich Olbricht. After the D-Day landings of June 1944, he became increasingly convinced that an assassination plot was the only way to save Germany from total destruction. He would go on to play the leading role in the plot of July 1944, which came as close as any to killing the *Führer*. He was also among those immediately executed when the plot unraveled on the night of July 20.[19]

CODE NAME "VALKYRIE": THE JULY 20 PLOT TO KILL HITLER

The plot of July 1944 was certainly not the first to have been planned or launched against the *Führer*. The first of the major plots had taken shape in the midst of the Czech crisis in late 1938, as members of the military, like General Beck, were becoming alarmed at Hitler's aggression in Eastern Europe. As military planners examined the data, they were convinced that Czechoslovakia could mount a stubborn defense, and that French and British intervention (most likely in the form of an invasion of Germany's western frontiers) might spell disaster. For those in the tenuous resistance group, it seemed like the moment had arrived to take action. Led by General Beck and General Oster (it became known as the "Oster Conspiracy"), plans were made, in the event of a German offensive, to have a German commando group move into the Chancellery and kill Hitler and as many Nazi officials as necessary. Other groups would storm the facilities of the SS to prevent their seizing power. With this in place, a provisional government would be installed after a brief military takeover to establish order. The whole plot rested, however, on the strong stand of the democracies against Hitler's aggression in Czechoslovakia. But instead of working with the conspirators, Neville Chamberlain's British government agreed to the last-minute negotiations that would produce the infamous Munich Agreement. When both France and Britain refused to honor their commitments, and Hitler was able to take the Sudetenland without firing a shot, the plot evaporated. How could one justify overthrowing the government immediately after one of the great diplomatic coups of history?

Any justification for eliminating Hitler only became more remote as he moved from success to success in the early years of the war. The period of European conquest made Hitler's position more and more secure at home, and by mid-1941 it seemed that Hitler was well on his way to realizing his ultimate vision. That vision was of a German-dominated Europe, purged of "inferior" peoples, and an unlimited supply of natural resources and slave labor for the German people. In June 1941, Hitler's forces rolled into the Soviet Union as Operation Barbarossa commenced. After months of initial success and a war of unparalleled brutality, the German effort stalled. During 1942, particularly with the devastating defeat at Stalingrad, the tide turned against the Germans, and the Soviet forces began to push them back in a long retreat that would take two years. In December 1941, of course, the United States had entered the war after the bombing at Pearl Harbor. The entry of the world's two mightiest industrial superpowers against the Axis completely changed the character of World War II. In Germany, the members of the resistance were only too aware of these developments and by 1942 were again making serious plans to assassinate Hitler before Germany was obliterated. If they could kill him, seize the government, dissolve the Nazi Party, and show the world that Germany had installed a reasonable government, perhaps they could save their country from annihilation.

In 1942 a new resistance group began to form away from Germany, within the staff of Army Group Center in the Soviet Union. The group revolved around Colonel Henning von Tresckow (later promoted to *Generalmajor*), who worked to find like-minded officers. No group was more aware of Germany's vulnerability than those facing the miseries of the Eastern Front. Tresckow made contact with General Oster, and they began to coordinate their activities, working together toward building a network large enough to make a coup a viable possibility. One of the most important men they were able to attract to the movement was General Friedrich Olbricht, who was chief of the Armed Service Reserve Office and one of those commanding the Ersatzheer (Replacement Army) in Berlin. It was Olbricht who had put together the initial plan for the Replacement Army seizing control in the event of extreme circumstances. If Allied bombing destroyed the municipal authority in Berlin, or if there was a mass uprising among the millions of foreign and slave laborers there, the Replacement Army had a clear plan for taking absolute control of the city. The plan was called "Operation Valkyrie." It would later form the basis of a plan to kill Hitler.

But still in 1942 Olbricht worked with Tresckow on a new plot. Hitler made flights to the Russian front occasionally for conferences, and this might be a perfect location to kill the *Führer*. They debated the merits of trying to poison Hitler, shooting him at the dining table, or possibly using a bomb. They decided on loading a bomb on Hitler's plane on one of his return trips to Berlin. Tresckow would be the man charged with arranging for the bomb to be aboard. He was able to get a converted plastic explosive that had been seized from the SOE. Using a timing device, he was able to set it for a time to blow up in the air, and the force of the explosion would certainly bring the plane down. They called the attempt "Operation Spark." Tresckow was able to pack the explosives in an elegant box made for two bottles of cognac. Tresckow asked a colleague, Lt. Col. Heinz Brandt, to take it with him on the journey and deliver it to a friend in Berlin, General Helmuth Stieff. Hitler and his party left Russia on March 13, 1943, and one of Tresckow's aides took the parcel to the airfield as they were boarding their plane to leave. The aide triggered the timer, and the bomb was scheduled to blow up in 30 minutes, just over the city of Minsk. In Berlin, when news came in about the plane crash and the death of the *Führer*, General Olbricht was to put the Replacement Army into action to suppress the SS and the Nazi Ministries, while seizing government control in the major cities of Berlin, Munich, and Vienna.

The men waited for news of the blast, but none came. The bomb's timer worked and clicked into place at the appointed time, but in the cargo section of the plane, the temperature was frigid, and thus the cap was too cold to ignite the explosion. The plane landed safely and without incident. Now Tresckow had a potential disaster on his hands. If anyone opened the box, the bomb would be discovered, and he would be dead. His aide flew immediately to Berlin and was able to get the package back from Col. Brandt before it was discovered; it was a tense and awkward scene, but Tresckow was saved. After this extreme disappointment, the group tried immediately for another attempt. Tresckow was aware that a museum exhibition was about to open in Berlin to put on display a mass of military equipment that the Germans had seized from the Soviet armies. The exhibition opened on March 21, and its first visitor would be Hitler himself, who would get a personal tour before it was opened to the public. One member of the resistance, a Colonel Gersdorff, was in a position to give that tour. Gersdorff volunteered to sacrifice his own life in order to kill Hitler. He would use the explosive, packed in his own coat, to kill Hitler and himself during the museum viewing. His plan was to embrace Hitler seconds before the blast in order to be sure that they both died. When the day came, Hitler did arrive as scheduled, but his security staff had notified him that he needed to go very quickly through the exhibit for security reasons. Gersdorff knew nothing of this and, having set his timer for 10 minutes, was very surprised when Hitler practically ran through the museum. Hitler was through the exhibit within two minutes, said his goodbyes, and left with his staff. Gersdorff was now about to be blown apart for no reason at all. He was able to sprint to a safe location and disconnect the bomb in the nick of time. But another seemingly sure attempt had failed.

In August 1943 Tresckow met the young Colonel Claus von Stauffen-berg and was deeply impressed. Stauffenberg's conclusions about the Nazi regime corresponded with Tresckow's own, and the young man was con-vinced to join the resistance. He had since joined the Replacement Army office, and one of his commanding officers was Olbricht. It must be said that Stauffenberg had a remarkable individual energy and boldness. He seemed far more determined and, while not reckless, brushed aside the nervousness and indecisiveness of many of the other plotters. He soon emerged as the leading force in devising a new plot to kill Hitler. The new plot that emerged relied heavily on the Valkyrie plan of the Replacement Army. Olbricht and Stauffenberg knew they were well placed to coordi-nate and command that force to suppress the SS and seize the government when the time came. Tresckow worked with them, but he worked himself to meticulously revise the Valkyrie plan to make it more adaptable to the events that were sure to come. Rather than focusing upon internal unrest, the plan was now adjusted to deal with the reality of Hitler's death and the vacuum of power. In addition to planning the actual process of the seizure of government, the military leaders worked with the civilian members of the resistance to plan a provisional government. The government that would take power and presumably negotiate with the Allies would include the venerable General Beck as president and Friedrich Goerdeler as chancellor, with men like Olbricht, Stauffenberg, and Tresckow in key positions of state security.

When all of the proce-dural pieces were assem-bled, two great questions remained. The first of these was who exactly would kill Hitler where and when. The second great question concerned the highest authority of the Replace-ment Army, *Generaloberst*

Colonel Claus Schenk Graf von Stauffenberg, the most energetic and courageous of the Ger-man resistance leaders, who placed the bomb that nearly killed Hitler on July 20, 1944. (AP Photo/goe)

Friedrich Fromm. Fromm was aware that a conspiracy was afoot and never reported any of his subordinates, but he also kept his distance from the plot. The orders to launch Operation Valkyrie and send the Replacement Army into action had to be signed by him. That meant when the time came, either he would have to take part and sign the orders or he would have to be eliminated. This could mean killing him or simply removing him from any possibility of sabotaging the coup—probably imprisonment until it was over.

In June 1944 the plotters got a boost when Stauffenberg was named Fromm's chief of staff at the Berlin headquarters of the Replacement Army.[20] This placed the young colonel even closer to Replacement Army operations, but it also meant he would be able to attend military conferences with Adolf Hitler present. As it turned out, this was a vital development. Another important development was the inclusion of General Carl-Heinrich von Stülpnagel, who by this time was the military commander of occupied France and governor of Paris. He had been involved in the resistance circles since 1942, and now he agreed to take action in Paris by shutting down the massive SS organization in France and seizing the government there. The one remaining problem was deciding who would actually carry out the assassination. Arrangements were discussed for various men to perform the task, including General Stieff. But it was clear that there was a lack of nerve, and eventually Stauffenberg stepped in and insisted that he was the man to do the job. This was slightly problematic, as he would have serious responsibilities controlling the Replacement Army and the coup in Berlin. Nevertheless it was decided that Colonel von Stauffenberg would take the next opportunity of a military conference to plant a bomb to kill Hitler, and then to figure out a way to get away from the scene and back to Berlin to continue the coup.

The plot now moved through some agonizing moments as two more attempts had to be aborted. On July 11 Stauffenberg traveled south to a conference at Berchtesgaden carrying a bomb and the timers. He brought with him an aide who would be prepared with an automobile to drive him away from the scene and back to Berlin. But at the conference it became clear that Heinrich Himmler would not attend, and so the attempt was called off. The plotters had wanted both Göring and Himmler to be present if at all possible, to eliminate possible replacements for the *Führer*. It could have happened that day, but it did not, and now the plotters agreed that this had been a mistake. They resolved that any future attempt should go forward whether Göring and Himmler were present or not. There was also an increasing sense that the Gestapo was closing in on the plot, and that their time was running out. Hitler called another conference on July 15, this time at his military headquarters in East Prussia, known as the Wolfsschanze or "Wolf's Lair." Here, Stauffenberg once again had his briefcase packed with explosives, an aide prepared to remove him from the scene, and co-conspirators in Berlin waited to send Operation Valkyrie into action. During the conference, Stauffenberg excused himself briefly to use the phone. He called Olbricht and confirmed that the plot was on. But when he returned, he found that Hitler had cut the meeting short and departed, and the conference was over. It took a panicked effort to eventually reach Berlin and call off the troop mobilization that was already in preparation. In Berlin the strange and abortive troop mobilization was called a "training exercise," and General Fromm was furious that orders had been placed without his directives. It seems that from this point, Fromm was categorically not to be trusted as part of the plan.

Another conference at the Wolf's Lair was called for July 20, 1944, and again Stauffenberg would take a flight to be present. After checking in with other attendees, and before attending the conference, Stauffenberg excused himself with his aide, Werner von Haeften, to change his shirt. He said he had blood on his collar from a shaving cut. In the cloakroom he and his aide worked to trigger the timing device. It was an extremely tense moment, as no less a figure than General Wilhelm Keitel was calling for them to hurry up and walk to the conference with him. If he stepped into the anteroom and saw the bomb, Stauffenberg and Haeften were dead men. But they eventually secured the bomb, ticking away, in the colonel's briefcase and made their way across the small compound to the wooden shed that functioned as the conference room. Inside, 24 men were distributed around an immense rectangular wooden conference table. Hitler sat at the middle of one of the long sides. Stauffenberg was able to get a seat fairly close to Hitler near the corner of the table to Hitler's right. His heart doubtlessly pounding, he stashed his briefcase under the table. The meeting started on time at 12:30 PM, and Stauffenberg sat through the first series of presentations. After seven minutes, he whispered to General Keitel that he had to make an urgent phone call before he delivered his own talk. He shifted his briefcase as close to Hitler as he could and then left the shed. Here something crucial may have happened. As Thomsett writes, "When Stauffenberg left, Colonel Brandt moved closer to the table so that he could see the maps. His foot nudged Stauffenberg's briefcase, so he moved it to the far side of the large table support. The heavy support shielded Hitler from the briefcase and its bomb."[21]

General Keitel sent an aide to find Stauffenberg, as it was nearly time for his presentation, but the aide received the message that Stauffenberg had left the building and had not used the phone. When this was reported to Keitel, he was bewildered. Then at 12:42 the explosion blew through the entire building. Men were torn apart, hurled backward against the walls, and some even knocked out through the glass windows. Hitler was blown to the left and onto the floor, where wood fragments tore into his legs. He sustained damage to his eardrums (as nearly everyone did) but otherwise suffered only superficial bruises and flesh wounds. In the hours after the explosion, he seemed to be reassured of his own immortality, saying to anyone who would listen, "I am invulnerable, I am immortal!"[22] He was even able to continue with his itinerary of daily tasks, which included a meeting with Mussolini.

Immediately after the blast, Stauffenberg and his aide Haeften made for their car and headed out of the Wolf's Lair compound. As he looked at the wooden building, Stauffenberg was convinced that no one could have lived through it. Certain that Hitler and most of his high level staff were dead, he and his aide sped to the sentry stations. Stauffenberg had to convince the sentries that he was on an urgent errand for the *Führer* himself to get past two different checkpoints, but he was eventually allowed to leave, and the two men headed for the airfield as quickly as they could. At the airfield they were able to take a plane for Berlin that left by 1:15 PM. On that flight, one can only imagine what was running through his mind—he had killed Adolf Hitler and his most senior generals, and now the task lay ahead of securing the government of the nation.

In Berlin, the conspirators had gotten a phone call from a subordinate at the conference, who relayed the unclear message, "Something fearful has happened. The Fuhrer is still alive."[23] In case the phone was tapped, this could be interpreted in a non-conspiratorial way. But the plotters were thrown into uncertainty. What had happened? Did the attempt succeed or fail? Where was Stauffenberg? Stauffenberg's plane landed in Berlin at 3:30 PM, and he quickly made his way to the War Ministry.

Back at the Wolf's Lair, the investigation began immediately. All communications were temporarily shut down, and all movement out of the compound was prohibited. Himmler's SS men immediately took charge. Through the questioning of the various staff members, one man, the telephone operator, Sergeant-Major Adam, suggested that Stauffenberg's behavior was strange and that he had left the room just before the blast. A wild search was conducted for Stauffenberg, but then it was discovered that he had left in the wake of the blast and headed for Berlin. He immediately became the leading suspect.

Stauffenberg, of course, was already in Berlin. Now meeting with his co-conspirators, he insisted to them that he had killed the *Führer*. They protested that they had received word that he was still alive, but Stauffenberg was adamant that there was no way he could have survived. The orders for Valkyrie were issued in General Fromm's name, without General Fromm's participation. The orders announced that Hitler was dead and that SS officers were trying to usurp power illegally. Fromm, meanwhile, was refusing to cooperate with what he was sure was a coup attempt. Fromm had also been in contact with General Keitel at the Wolf's Lair and heard from

Keitel that the *Führer* was very much alive. As the leaders of the conspiracy (Olbricht and Stauffenberg) met with Fromm and demanded his cooperation, he insisted that Hitler was alive and that he would have nothing to do with it. He then suggested that Stauffenberg shoot himself as the only honorable step, or the two men would both be under arrest. But Olbricht replied that it was *they* who were arresting *him*. Their aides came into the room and forcibly took Fromm and a staff member into a small office, where they were placed under arrest and locked in with no access to any communication.

At the Wolf's Lair, General Keitel had become suspicious after his phone call with Fromm, and he was confused about the operations going on with the Replacement Army. He began to suspect a larger plot and perhaps even a coup d'état under way. Officials now rushed from Prussia to Berlin, and calls were made to the key ministries in Berlin, including the SS and Joseph Goebbels. The hour-by-hour events of this chaotic night are tangled and complicated, but the general result was that SS troops, commanders of the Replacement Army, and key government ministers slowly became aware that the mobilization of the Replacement Army was a coup attempt and that the *Führer* was not dead. While the conspirators were managing their coup from the offices of the War Ministry, the forces of retaliation began to organize themselves, using Goebbels's home as their headquarters. Despite the efforts of Stauffenberg and Olbricht to keep the plan going by telephone, the military commanders of the Replacement Army gradually gave up their efforts, realizing that the plan was a sham. Eventually all the SS men who had been arrested were released, and the SS surrounded the War Ministry. They broke in, found General Fromm, and released him. Then a brief gun battle took place in the hallways of the War Ministry as the SS troops fought with the principal conspirators including Stauffenberg, his aide Haeften, Olbricht, and the retired General Beck, who had joined them earlier. The group was overwhelmed, and the SS men charged into the room, where General Fromm confronted them. They were all put under arrest, and Fromm demanded that they turn over their weapons. But old General Beck asked to keep his pistol, for the obvious purpose of shooting himself. Fromm agreed, and Beck attempted suicide. But in a gruesome scene, he misfired and blew off part of his scalp without the wound being fatal. He would try a second time, missing yet again and collapsing in a chair, bleeding profusely. Stauffenberg, Olbricht, and their small group of accomplices were taken to the interior courtyard of the War Ministry, put up against the wall, and shot one by one. Colonel Stauffenberg's last words are supposed to have been "Long live our sacred Germany."[24] With these men executed, General Fromm must have been proud of his part in crushing the coup. But despite his display of loyalty, he was called to account by Joseph Goebbels and executed himself that same night.

The coup in Berlin was all but over. However, there was another area where the coup had been in process, and this was Paris. In that city, when the coup had begun, General von Stülpnagel had acted upon his orders and arrested over 1,000 SS men around France, and secured the government. But then he found out, to his horror, that Hitler was still alive. He was eventually summoned to Berlin to face charges of conspiracy and treason. He decided that he could not face this, and so on his journey back to Germany, he stopped his car and attempted to kill himself. Like Beck, he failed, putting a bullet through his forehead and eye but surviving. He was taken to a hospital, where he recovered, and later he was forced to stand trial for his crimes.[25]

Hitler himself played a vital part in the collapse of the plot, by making phone calls to key commanders in Berlin personally. The sound of his voice reassured them that the plot was illegal and must be crushed. Later that night he delivered a radio broadcast to the German people to let them know he was still alive and unhurt. He told the German public,

> I regard this as confirmation of my mission by Providence to continue pursuing the goal of my life, as I have done up to now. Let me solemnly avow before the entire nation that since the day I moved into the Wilhelmstrasse I have had only one thought: to fulfill my duty to the best of my knowledge and belief. . . . [A] very small group was found in Germany, as in Italy, that believed it could carry through a stab in the back as in the year 1918. However, it was terribly mistaken this time. The claim of these usurpers that I am no longer alive is being contradicted at this moment, as I speak to you, my dear *Volksgenossen*.[26]

He went on to say that the culprits would be "mercilessly exterminated," and they were. In the days that followed, Himmler's SS took charge of the investigations and rooted out any figures even remotely associated with the resistance. The civilians who planned to form the new provisional government were identified and arrested, and any figures in the military still alive were rounded up and imprisoned, including Wilhelm Canaris. A special "People's Court" was presided over by the notorious Judge Freisler, who found them all guilty and sentenced them to death. The investigation rooted out some 200 resistance members, though surely most of these had nothing to do with the actual plot. Their fate was swift and terrible, as historian Peter Hoffman describes when he writes, "Most of them were executed within two hours of sentencing; appeals were a farce. The condemned men were strangled slowly with thin wire, and the first few dozen executions were filmed so Hitler could watch their agony."[27] Now with Hitler still alive and more than ever convinced of his special destiny, the war would stretch out for nearly another year, and Germany continued its march into oblivion.

NOTES

1. See Robert Gellately, *The Gestapo and German Society: Enforcing Racial Policy, 1933–1945* (Oxford: Oxford University Press, 1999).

2. See Martin Gilbert, *The Holocaust: The Jewish Tragedy* (London: Collins, 1986), p. 31.

3. Hellmut G. Haasis, *Bombing Hitler: The Story of the Man Who Almost Assassinated the Führer*, trans. William Odom (New York: Skyhorse, 2001), p. 120.

4. Ibid., p. 136.

5. Ibid., pp. 145–146.

6. Michael Thomsett, *The German Opposition to Hitler: The Resistance, The Underground, and Assassination Plots, 1938–1945* (Jefferson, NC: McFarland & Co., 1997), p. 98.

7. Haasis, *Bombing Hitler*, p. 174.

8. Thomsett, *German Opposition to Hitler*, p. 100.

9. Haasis, *Bombing Hitler*, pp. 202–203.

10. Ibid., pp. 178–192.

11. Thomsett, *German Opposition to Hitler*, p. 41. The meeting on November 5, 1937, to which Thomsett refers is known as the Hossbach meeting (notes were taken by Colonel Friedrich Hossbach). In that meeting Hitler revealed to the top military leaders his firm resolution that Germany must begin the process of conquest in Eastern Europe in order to sustain the German nation.

12. Boatner, *The Biographical Dictionary of World War II*, p. 33.

13. Allen Dulles, *The German Underground* (New York: Macmillan, 1947), p. 30.

14. Ibid., p. 30.

15. Boatner, *The Biographical Dictionary of World War II*, p. 188.

16. Ibid., p. 405.

17. See Richard Bassett, *Hitler's Spy Chief: The Wilhelm Canaris Mystery* (London: Wiedenfield & Nicolson, 2005).

18. Boatner, *The Biographical Dictionary of World War II*, p. 572.

19. Boatner, *The Biographical Dictionary of World War II*, pp. 534–536.

20. Thomsett, *German Opposition to Hitler*, p. 193.

21. Ibid., p. 203.

22. Ibid., p. 204.

23. Ibid., p. 206.

24. Ibid., p. 226.

25. Boatner, *The Biographical Dictionary of World War II*, p. 547.

26. Hitler's Radio Address, July 20, 1944, https://www.youtube.com/watch?v=LpCwuCzud-E, accessed November 11, 2016.

27. Peter Hoffman, *German Resistance to Hitler* (Cambridge, MA: Harvard University Press, 1988), p. 125.

8

Red Resistance

The Partisan Movement in the Soviet Union

Each European nation occupied by the Axis powers generated a resistance movement unique to its own set of particular national circumstances. One nation, however, stood out as even more distinctive than others, and this was the Soviet Union. Militarily, the Soviet Union had been Germany's closest ally in the war from its beginning. But on June 22, 1941, Nazi Germany invaded the USSR with the commencement of Operation Barbarossa. It remains the most extensive land invasion ever launched. What was so remarkable about this was the fact that up to that moment, the Nazis and the Soviets had been alliance partners—allies in a war that brought them both extensive new conquests. The Soviet Union was also the largest nation in the world by area, and the massive amount of Soviet territory occupied by the Germans added up to nearly the same area as the rest of the Eastern and Central Europe. While the Soviet military was in no condition to match the Nazi war machine at the beginning of the conflict, its population was enormous at nearly 197 million people relative to a German population of around 70 million. Indeed, the German campaign into the Soviet Union would be like no other, and the scale of the fighting there dwarfed the destruction elsewhere in the war. Although estimates continue to vary, access to Soviet records indicates that the Soviets lost nearly 26 million human beings in their "Great Patriotic War" against Nazi Germany and its allies.

The resistance movement that developed in the occupied territories of the Soviet Union was unique as well, and it closely resembled the title of this book—*Hidden Armies*. Certainly fighting squads existed elsewhere in occupied Europe and were especially prevalent in France, Yugoslavia, and Greece, but in the Soviet Union, a true civilian army was formed. And in yet another unique feature, it was recruited, trained, supplied, and directed by its own sovereign government, which was still in existence and still fighting the war. Unlike anywhere else in Europe, save Italy after 1943, the Axis powers controlled only parts of a nation they occupied for extensive periods of time.

The Soviet partisan movement, as it was known, has not yet been extensively researched to this point. Again, documentary sources have only become available to international scholars after 1991, and so the study, outside Soviet control, has only been going on for about 25 years. Even with archival access (though this is now increasingly limited), the amount of documentary sources is quite limited and there are precious few journals and memoirs to use as countering corroboration. The shortage of formal scholarship, then, has led to the movement being less widely understood by professional scholars and general readers alike. Another reason for this is that the partisans did not produce any particularly famous or consequential individual operations that have lived in memory. There is no single Soviet operation that has been celebrated like the Norwegian missions to sabotage the German heavy-water supplies, or the Greek mission to blow up the Gorgopotamos bridge, or the Czechs' assassination of Heydrich. As one scholar has written, there is no partisan operation with the "horrific glamour of a Kursk or a Stalingrad."[1] Another important reason that the partisan movement has not been well understood has to do with the ideology of Soviet leadership through the 20th century. Joseph Stalin was the man who took control of the Soviet Union almost immediately after its creation and led that nation into full-scale communism between 1924 and his death in 1953. He would stop at nothing to reinforce his communist ideology, which in turn reinforced his own almost godlike power. The partisan movement was treated in Soviet sources after the war in a way that complemented Stalin's claims about mass popular support for communism and for his personal regime. The story went along the following lines: The Nazi German armies, representing the reactionary fascists, had come to destroy the people's revolution and the people's system. While there were initial conquests made, the great Soviet people rose up spontaneously against the fascist aggressors in their outrage and played an extremely important role in harassing the invaders, destroying their communications and transport, and killing the enemy. Their love for the communist system, for their leader, Stalin, and for their beloved Russian nation drove them to endure any hardship to save the Soviet fatherland. This was the myth perpetuated by Soviet historiography, as dictated by Communist Party leadership. As such, the contributions and heroism of the partisans have been seriously exaggerated in Soviet historiography. The developing research now being produced, however, is already painting a modified picture, and that picture often deviates from the Communist party line.

OPERATION BARBAROSSA AND GERMAN
RULE IN THE EAST

The Nazis launched Operation Barbarossa at around 3:15 on the morning of June 22, 1941. The length of the front was thousands of miles, reaching from the Baltic Sea near the Lithuanian border in the north all the way to the Black Sea coast in the south. The Germans organized the overall attack under three principal military units: Army Group North under General Wilhelm von Leeb, Army Group Center under General Fedor von Bock, and Army Group South under General Gerd von Rundstedt. Within each of these groups were several entire armies. The level of initial penetration into the Soviet Union was astonishing, and Soviet defenses seemed nearly helpless. The principal reasons for Soviet unpreparedness lie almost entirely with Stalin himself. For one thing, Stalin's paranoid brutality had resulted in an extensive gutting of the officer corps of the Red Army during the purges of the 1930s. Thus there was a serious shortage of experience and talent in the top echelons of the Soviet High Command. But what forces the Soviets did have were held back by Stalin, because he refused to accept the possibility of a German invasion. After signing the Nazi–Soviet Non-Aggression Pact in August 1939, Stalin had scrupulously followed its stipulations and worked with the Nazis. In the process, his Soviet Union had absorbed eastern Poland, the Baltic nations, and part of Finland without any challenge from Hitler. In early 1941, however, reports came in from Soviet intelligence suggesting that Hitler was preparing to invade the Soviet Union. Stalin could not and would not believe it. He was certain that Hitler would never do so unless his war in the west was completed, and the war against Britain was still raging. As Stalin's biographer Robert Service writes,

> How had he let himself be tricked? For weeks the Wehrmacht had been massing on the western banks of the River Bug as dozens of divisions were transferred from elsewhere in Europe. The Luftwaffe had sent squadrons of reconnaissance aircraft over Soviet cities. All this had been reported to Stalin by his military intelligence agency . . . Richard Sorge, the Soviet agent in the German Embassy in Tokyo had raised the alarm. Winston Churchill had sent telegrams warning Stalin . . . Yet Stalin had made up his mind. Rejecting the warnings, he put faith in his own judgement.[2]

Stalin had prevented serious defensive measures from being taken, and now he and the Russian people would pay the price. The Germans, with their combination of aerial bombing, tanks, and mechanized transport, moved well into the Soviet Union in a remarkably short period of time. From late June to early September 1941, the Germans occupied Soviet territory running from the Baltic Sea to the Black Sea along a front nearly 1,500 miles long. All along that front, the Germans had penetrated to a depth of around 500 miles. Major Russian cities like Kiev and Leningrad either had been taken or were under siege. By late September the final phases of the plan were ready, as Operation Typhoon was prepared. This was the final push to Moscow to claim the capital. Hitler's ultimate objective was to take Moscow and push the Soviets beyond the Ural Mountains before stopping the invasion. Once the Soviets had lost all of their western territory, population, natural resources, and industry, mounting any future defense would be impossible. The Germans meanwhile would consolidate their gains, build airfields, and commence bombing the Soviets into submission for however long that would take. For the Soviets, then, the defense of Moscow was absolutely essential—losing the city might well mean the end of the Soviet system.

But Stalin, his people, and his military rose to the challenge. Near Moscow, the Russian people followed Stalin's directives assiduously, burning their fields, destroying water supplies, and even killing livestock. The German supply lines were now stretched to the extreme, and living off the available resources would be nearly impossible given the scorched earth around them. Stalin and the Soviet general staff or Stavka had also been frantically training and equipping soldiers and now could throw nearly 800,000 men at the Germans. Still the German advance continued, and on October 13, the 3rd Panzer Group famously reached a position only 87 miles from the capital. But now a significant contribution was made by Russia's perennial ally, the weather. Snows came, and then rains, which turned every road into a treacherous sea of mud and trapped the German tanks, trucks, and horses in a quagmire. The advance slowed to a crawl, and on October 31 the German High Command called a halt to reorganize. During this pause of over two weeks, the Soviets were able to transfer eleven new armies into the area from the Far East, which transformed the battlefield situation. In the weeks after November 15, the Germans renewed their offensive but were stopped and driven back by superior Soviet forces, which included 1,000 new tanks and aircraft deployed into the region. Struggling for every yard of territory by the beginning of December, the Germans were then hit by severe winter weather with freezing blizzards. The Germans had not equipped their armies for a winter war, never having forecast the conflict lasting into the winter months. Now German soldiers froze along with the engine blocks of their tanks, planes, and equipment. On December 5 the Soviets launched a coordinated counteroffensive against the weakened Germans, and this forced the Nazis into retreat. By the end of December, it was clear that Operation Typhoon was a failure and that Moscow would be held for the foreseeable future. The Germans retreated nearly 200 miles in the center of their front. Now the war settled in for nearly three more years of tortuous fighting.

Despite petering out by December, in the months from June to December 1941, Barbarossa had given the Germans an enormous area of Russia for occupation. As the conquest progressed, its commanders divided occupied territory into three zones. First, the "Front Line Area" extended from the battle lines to a distance of about 25 kilometers behind. This area was obviously devoted to combat operations. The second zone was the "Army Rear Area," extending from around 25 kilometers to 50 kilometers behind, and was mostly used for services like airfields, reserve troops, maintenance, and supply. The third zone was the "Army Group Rear Area," which extended from 50 to 100 kilometers deep and was designated to be converted to formally occupied territory.[3] In the first two zones, the commanding officers of the army were in absolute control, but in the third zone and all territory behind it, the SS took charge. In these areas the SS was given its special duties—the identification and execution of all Communist Party leaders, the confiscation of all Soviet papers and archives, inventorying resources and assets for German confiscation, and identification of undesirable ethnic groups, particularly Jews. Under the SS, the infamous Einsatzgruppen were put to work as early as 1941. The Einsatzgruppen were specially formed police squads that were tasked with identifying Jews and moving them into ghettos where appropriate, but mostly rounding them up for mass executions. The Einsatzgruppen got on with their murderous work, sometimes enjoying cordial cooperation from military leaders, while at other times having to curb their activities if they interfered with military operations.[4]

This brings us now to perhaps the most astounding feature of the massive catastrophe that was the eastern war. The fanatical ideological objectives of Hitler's Nazis determined the nature of the war in the east. Hitler had written as early as 1925 (in his autobiographical manifesto, *Mein Kampf*) that it was the German destiny to attack and colonize Eastern Europe and the Soviet Union. This would extinguish the fountainhead of world communism, accomplishing one central Nazi objective. But there was something even more fundamental. His vision of the future was frankly *centered* upon the German conquest of the Soviet Union to provide the land, space, and natural and human resources for the expansion of the Germanic people. With a massive contiguous empire consisting of all of Eastern Europe and Russia, the Germans would create the most powerful nation on Earth. They would need nothing from any other nation, and they could dictate to any other nation whatever they chose.[5] To reach this objective, Russia's land had to be conquered in war; that much was obvious. But what of the enormous population of the Soviet Union? Nazi ideology saw the vast majority of the Russian people as biologically subhuman—an eastern branch of the genetically inferior "Slavic" race. Therefore, the vast majority of the Russian people would have to be exterminated like vermin, and a small population kept alive to act as slave labor for their Germanic masters. This was Hitler's vision for the future of the Soviet Union, and it colored his directives as to how commanders were to fight the conflict there. He gave specific instructions that brutality was to be used, that mass executions were necessary, and that women and children were not to be spared. This hateful ideological approach has proven, under historical scrutiny, to have been not only morally despicable and a crime against humanity, but also disastrous in practical terms. To be direct, it was a catastrophic mistake that seems very likely to have cost Hitler the war in the east.

When the German tanks rolled across the borders and rivers into Russia in June 1941, many thousands of Soviet citizens did not see them as a source of terror. For these citizens, the Germans represented a miraculous opportunity to be rid of the Soviet system and Stalin forever. There were citizens in every region of Russia who were persecuted by the Soviet system. Those who came from middle-class backgrounds were constantly in fear of their heritage being used against them to justify their banishment to the gulags. Successful farmers who had built up productive estates had been under threat throughout the 1920s and 1930s as Stalin pursued his strategy of agricultural collectivization. This project dispossessed peasant landholders and conglomerated their lands into enormous state-owned and state-run farming collectives. Those who worked on them were merely wage laborers and worked under Soviet rule. The peasant farmers who had built successful operations had become known as "kulaks" and had been publicly declared enemies of the state. Just how many millions of them died in gulags or summary executions may never be known. Other victims were non-Russians who despised their forced "Russianization," former political prisoners, and those who simply hated Stalinist rule. But in June 1941 such citizens saw a glimmer of light as German forces approached their towns and villages. As the scholar Matthew Cooper writes, "Over large areas of the Soviet Union, the German invaders had initially been greeted by the population as heroes, as liberators rather than as conquerors."[6] In the very early stages of conquest, when the Germans had no manpower available for local administration, they were even able to use local dissidents to act as district supervisors.[7] This willingness to cooperate with the Nazi invaders was echoed by a similar level of unwillingness to fight for the Soviet cause. General Anders, commanding the Free Polish Army, said of that time that the conflict "disclosed the widespread disinclination of the Soviet soldier to fight in the defense of the 'fatherland and proletariat,' . . . Many soldiers, seeing the war as an opportunity for a change of order in Russia, wished for a German victory and therefore surrendered in great masses."[8] This is a long way from the Soviet-era myth of total national unity against the aggressors. Despite his later twisting of the narrative, Stalin at the time recognized this reality, and it was this widespread disloyalty that convinced him to position the conflict as the "Great Patriotic War." The people might well have refused to fight for the artificial Union of Soviet Socialist Republics, they might have refused to fight for communism, but they were much more likely to fight for "sacred Mother Russia."[9]

More than any public relations positioning by Stalin, the actions of the German invaders turned the general opinion of the people of Russia. The Soviet soldiers that General Anders reported as surrendering in such huge numbers, eventually stopped doing so. By 1942 it had become clear that surrender might spell instant execution, or a journey to a Nazi prison camp, where the conditions were unspeakable and produced horrific death rates. Such extreme conditions were deliberately created by the Nazis for the east. It was certainly not the reality for the war in the west, where prison camp conditions were at least passable; there the Germans believed they were fighting mostly racial equals. But the prison camps in Russia were notorious, and of the 5,000,000 Soviet prisoners taken by Germany during the war, some 3,000,000 died in captivity.[10]

When the German forces moved far enough forward and the SS had completed its "cleansing" of the area, the permanent administrators moved in. These were the men from the newly created Reich Ministry for the Occupied Eastern Territories. These officials took control of the areas and laid down extremely rigid restrictions and regulations. Such laws and directives got into every aspect of people's lives, including "such intricate details of everyday life as the prices of geese, with or without heads."[11] These local administrators collected food from the population and often withheld it in favor of meeting German requirements, along with any other vital supplies. Part of their responsibility was to exploit every available resource for German use. Anyone who protested, who was caught resisting, or who even acted suspicious was generally shot without any kind of investigation. Anyone caught involved in resistance activity was generally hanged in a public square, and the Nazis regularly hung signs around their dangling corpses that declared they had been partisans and had been killed for it. This was meant to be a powerful deterrent to any kind of resistance activity. But under such a wide range of abusive policies, one can see how the Soviets grew to hate their occupiers with burning intensity and how that hatred could be translated into resistance.

Of these repulsive German policies, one might ask the question, did the Germans *need* to behave in this manner? Was this the best and only way to manage an enemy in occupied territory in order to secure victory? From

German sources the scholar Matthew Cooper has identified areas of German occupation that provide an instructive example. In one area, between the Bobruysk-Roslavl highway and the Berezina River, the German front line commanders used a different approach. They ruled with a relatively enlightened and cooperative approach, using local leaders' expertise and renewing free-market exchange in their communities. The result, says Cooper, was a "rebounding economy," while "disaffection and resistance were unknown; cooperation was widespread."[12] But in August the German troops moved on, and the SS and then the administrators moved in with their death squads, labor levies, and draconian restrictions. "[The] persecution of the Jews and conscription of labor transformed the area, within six months, into a hotbed of partisan activity."[13] It was this ideologically based German sadism that turned potentially cooperative communities into furious enemies and made possible the creation of a robust and extremely dangerous Soviet resistance.

THE EARLY PARTISAN MOVEMENT

The partisan movement in the initial phases of the war was very tiny indeed and almost completely uncoordinated. When the German invasion began and immediately made territorial gains, there were no formal preparations in place for such a development. During the late 1930s, Stalin had been certain that if war came with Germany, it would be fought in Eastern Europe and not on Russian soil. His military advisers urged him to prepare for an invasion, create resistance bases, and prepare underground weapons stores. But Stalin, says Nik Cornish, "increasingly suspicious of the military establishment from the early 1930s, decided that the offensive was now preferable to the defensive and that the next war would be fought exclusively on enemy soil."[14] The result, writes Cornish, was that "plans for bases and the like were shelved indefinitely; conventional warfare was the order of the day."[15]

With no solid preparations having been made, Stalin was stunned and bewildered in the first days of Operation Barbarossa, but he recovered himself soon after. He spoke to the nation on the radio to explain the situation and to give the Soviet people a directive for a scorched earth policy and an appeal for popular resistance. In his broadcast he said,

> In areas occupied by the enemy, guerilla units, mounted and on foot, must be formed, diversionist groups must be organized to combat enemy troops, to foment guerilla warfare everywhere, to blow up bridges, and roads, damage telephone and telegraph lines, set fire to forests, stores, transports. In the occupied regions conditions must be made unbearable for the enemy and all his accomplices. They must be hounded and annihilated at every step and all their measures frustrated . . . All forces of the people for the demolition of the enemy![16]

This was a clear and fairly detailed message, and it inspired those who were fired with the love of communism and loyal to their leader. But scholarship has indicated that in these first months after Stalin's broadcast, only a tiny number of people were forming into resistance groups in these territories. The majority of people were either hoping to cooperate with the invaders or had adopted "a 'wait and see' attitude."[17] There were generally two kinds of people who were busy organizing and leading resistance groups during 1941. These were mostly local Communist Party leaders, who had now been given a specific directive by their leader, and the others were Red Army soldiers who had found themselves left behind and trapped behind enemy lines. Their central mission was to fight their way back to the front and to their original units, but this was no easy task, and nearly impossible without assistance.[18] Those military or partisan leaders generally only found willing compatriots in those fired by patriotism and particularly among those who were trying to avoid being rounded up and deported to work in German factories. Just as in France with the formation of the Maquis, it was the mass conscription of young men for forced labor that left them no choice but to take to the wilderness. Stalin made choices even starker for such people when he issued Order 270 on August 16, 1941. In the text of the order, it stipulated that "commanders and political workers surrendering to the enemy were to be deemed deserters and if necessary shot."[19] Those who might have hoped to surrender to avoid fighting for the Soviet system found that they would most likely be shot by their Russian friends or their German foes—it became far safer to continue fighting partisan warfare than to surrender.

In September 1941 the Soviet government formed a special group to boost the efforts to form partisan bands in occupied territories. The group had the rather cumbersome name of the "Separate Special Purpose Motorized Rifle Brigade," with its Russian acronym OMSBON. This group helped mold formal organizations and regional partisan groups in Karelia, Crimea, Ukraine, Leningrad, and Moscow, though OMSBON provided no centralized or coordinated command structure for them. OMSBON also formed the earliest beginnings of formal recruiting, training, and supply organizations. But to be sure, the movement was still small and not particularly significant. During 1941, as scholar Alexander Hill writes, "the damage done to the German war machine was . . . very limited."[20]

THE MATURATION OF THE PARTISAN MOVEMENT, 1942–1944

The partisan movement struggled on through the last months of 1941, during the desperate struggle to protect Moscow, and through the winter months of 1942. But it was in the spring of 1942 that the movement was given a tremendous boost by the Soviet government and reorganized. From this point forward, the partisan bands became much deadlier to the German invaders and kept them constantly on the alert for raids. On May 30, 1942, the Soviet High Command created the "Central Headquarters of the Partisan Movement," or TsShPD. The regional groups (or oblasts) that had already been formed were now made into more formalized organizations, with a district headquarters and appointed leaders. Inside the "Central Headquarters" in Moscow the TsShPD was divided into four specific directorates: Operations, Information/Reconnaissance, Political, and Supply.[21] With the organization completed, the objective was to dramatically increase the level of centralized support and command for the men in the field. In Russia the resistance was supplied and directed not by foreign allies, like the SOE, or by governments in exile, but instead by its own still-functioning government.

In the field, the groups controlled by their district headquarters were organized as follows: the largest organizations that reported directly to the district headquarters were battalions, and each battalion was made up of four companies. A company, in turn, was composed of four platoons. A platoon would be made up of two or more sections, which were the immediate organizational groups that fighters belonged to and in which they took direct commands. A section would contain around 70–100 men, though this was not consistent and varied widely. Each organizational unit had its own officers in increasing order of rank and consistent with the conventions of the Red Army. However, each level of the organization had a designated "political officer," and this man would ensure the unit's commitment to the Soviet cause and its dedication to the Communist Party. He had the authority to "ensure the unit's reliability and curb any 'deviationist' tendencies."[22] Within this organization there were self-contained units of those with specialized skills, like machine gunners, mechanics, and especially communications operators. These groups might move around from section to section as needed. Partisan sections took on patriotic names for their groups, including the "Red Banner," "Lenin," "Stalin," "People's Avengers," and "Death to Fascists" groups.[23]

Fit and politically reliable young men were recruited in the unoccupied territories and given extremely rigorous training in camps outside Moscow, where they received training in how to infiltrate enemy positions, the use of their own and enemy weapons, the use of explosives, how to cut communications links, how to sabotage railroad lines, how to take prisoners, and methods of interrogation. A great deal of time was devoted to training them to live in the wilderness, including skills like using maps and compasses and identifying water supplies, and endurance training.[24] When a young recruit was deemed ready for action, he would be transported into his assigned region, usually by airplane, and either parachuted or landed in the area. He would join his group, but he was not immediately given fighting responsibilities. New recruits entering a partisan section were given a probationary period of four weeks during which they were not given a weapon and had to tend to more menial tasks like digging trenches, building shelters, or tending livestock. From here a new recruit would graduate to doing guard duty, though still without a weapon. An armed supervisor monitored new recruits and only after a period of a few months made the determination that a recruit was absolutely loyal and could be trusted to fulfill his duties, even under duress. If that recruit deserted, it was reported and "his family were immediately killed."[25] Apparently the system worked, as partisan groups tended to be quite reliable and desertions low. One Nazi report on the partisans written in 1943 said of this practice, "This procedure is effective. It makes infiltration by our agents difficult, gives sufficient time for screening out undesirables."[26]

In terms of where the partisans operated, the battle plans were always conditioned by geography. Russia's vast areas of steppe and open grasslands were absolutely unsuited to partisan activity. Without a place to hide, and without a terrain to inhibit German mechanized equipment, partisans were highly vulnerable. Thus partisan camps could only be established in areas where there were extremely thick forests and in marshlands. In such areas the Germans could not detect them from the air, nor could trucks and tanks move into the area quickly. This geographic reality had serious implications for the overall character of the partisan movement, as the majority of Russian territory was untenable for resistance. It is estimated that the resistance movement could only operate in about one third of the German-occupied territories.[27] But in such forested or swampy environments, partisans established camps, sometimes for one section, sometimes larger camps for multiple sections. Campsites were chosen especially for their proximity to fresh water supplies and their protection by dense foliage. Typically, a central area was created with a shack built or rooms dug into a hillside for a command headquarters. The hospital was also usually at the center of the camp, as well as workshops for repairs and equipment. Around this center were built barracks for troops, again sometimes wooden shacks, dugouts, or tents. Latrines were dug away from the center of activity. Around this camp a network of trenches was dug, sometimes with barbed wire and sandbagged machine gun nests. Beyond that ring was an area where sentries would patrol constantly; beyond the range of the sentries, the partisans laid mines, with safe avenues in and out that only they knew.

Food was always an issue, as hunting, fishing, and gathering could never hope to feed the kind of numbers of these groups. Thus the partisans relied upon regular supply deliveries from the TsShPD, which were brought in by air; sometimes these were delivered after an aircraft landed, but mostly they were dropped in metal canisters. To give us an idea of the scale of these kinds of operations, Alexander Hill has calculated statistics for the food dropped to the Leningrad partisans during 1942. He says that the TsShPD dropped 25,000 kilograms of biscuits and 7,000 tins of meat or fish, and the total weight of food dropped in this area during 1942 was 151,777 tons.[28] Partisans also received voluntary help from local villages at times, but they were notorious for demanding and seizing resources from villages. Even with this, food remained in short supply, and partisans often went without. Winter clothing and especially boots were also constantly in demand, and their shortage presented regular challenges to partisan operations. Food, clothing, and weapons were all brought by aircraft, and the plane most often used for these operations was the LI-2, a license-built version of the American DC-3, comically nicknamed the "heavenly slug." The LI-2 had the ability to land and take off on the kind of short, improvised runways that were common in deep forest clearings.[29]

The weapons used by the partisans varied widely for several reasons. First, the highest-quality weapons the Soviets could manufacture were being given to the Red Army for direct combat operations, and the partisans often had to take whatever remained. But partisans gleaned weapons wherever they could, accepting them (or stealing them) from local villages, and also using captured weapons from the Germans. Nik Cornish estimates that only about 25 percent of the weapons used by partisans were captured German weapons. Ammunition was also a nagging problem for captured German weapons. Soviet weapons included rifles used in the First World War, including the Mauser 1898, the Mannlicher 1895, and the Mosin–Nagant 1891.[30] The most common light machine gun, so vital to partisans, was the Degtyaryov or DP Model 1928, which had a flat, cylindrical magazine mounted on top of the weapon. It looked a bit like a small trash can lid, and the troops soon came to call it the "record player." It was a bit heavy and cumbersome to transport, but it had the redeeming quality that it could withstand dirt and muck and continue to perform. In addition to weapons, the TsShPD also delivered radio equipment in larger quantities after 1942. This was vitally important to keep sections in the field in constant contact with their command centers. It also allowed local sections to receive official news broadcasts from Moscow and redistribute the news when possible. Partisan groups often would copy down the content of the Moscow news to print in makeshift newsletters for distribution to local villages. Such news was cherished by Russians under German rule. As Cornish writes, "The fillip news from the 'Great Land' provided to morale was incalculable as was the support it gave to reinforcing the Soviet regime's authority."[31]

Partisan groups that were somewhat near to towns and villages monitored their relations with their German oppressors whenever possible. If the Germans found partisans in a particular village, or designated it for reprisals for some other reason, the partisans made every effort to help evacuate the village into the forestlands. Having gotten to relative safety, they could move to other regions or be flown out of the area by TsShPD aircraft. Capturing German soldiers was a rarity. It was routine for partisans to capture individual German soldiers in sneak raids, or to take one or two in a firefight. This was done in order to interrogate them. But the partisans simply did not have the resources or facilities to feed and maintain prisoners. This meant that they generally killed all enemies, even if they surrendered.[32]

NOTABLE OPERATIONS

The partisan groups were sometimes used to facilitate undercover operations and assassinations. Such an operation was launched in late August 1942. The Soviet High Command had determined to assassinate the German *Reichskommissar* for the Ukraine, a German officer named Erich Koch. Koch was a notoriously fanatical Nazi whose brutality to ordinary Ukrainians, and especially Ukrainian Jews, was unspeakable. He is infamous for statements like, "I will draw the very last out of this country. I did not come here to spread bliss. We are a master race which must remember that the lowliest German worker is racially and biologically a thousand times more valuable than the population here."[33] The Soviets assigned a special operative named Nikolai I. Kuznetsov to assassinate Koch. Kuznetsov spoke perfect German and was even tested by being placed in a POW camp with German captives to see if his accent could be detected. He parachuted into the land of the Ukrainian partisans on August 26, 1942. With partisan help he scouted the city of Rivne, which Koch and his inner circle had made their capital. According to historian Leonid Grenkevich, Kuznetsov was so adept at playing the role of a German that he was able to go inside the German *Reichskommissariat* office and pose as a German officer. While playing this role, he is said to have heard about the impending German offensive at Kursk, and to have passed that information on to the Soviet military.[34] He carried on this way through much of the summer. After weeks of monitoring Koch's activities, Kuznetsov made two attempts at the assassination, but both were called off because of Koch's extensive personal security team, which made a close approach impossible. The Soviets then changed the mission and instructed Kuznetsov to kill Koch's deputy, Paul Dargel. Again local informers and Kuznetsov worked together to chart out the new target's activities and a plan to shoot him. They found that Dargel was always accompanied by an adjutant who carried a red leather briefcase, and that he was accompanied by security police that made sure the area was secure before Dargel proceeded to his vehicle. On

September 20, 1943, Kuznetsov, wearing a German officer's uniform and driving a disguised German car, pulled up to the *Reichskommissariat* building at exactly 2:30 PM, when Dargel would exit. He had evaded the security scouts, and now, seeing two men leaving the building, one carrying a red briefcase, he leapt from his car and shot both men dead. He scampered back into his car, and his driver, another operative, sped away to safety. Back at the Ukraine partisan camp, he got the news that the man he had killed was not Dargel but a German economist named Hans Gehl. In late October Kuznetsov made a second attempt, this time leaping from his car and throwing a grenade. The blast shredded Dargel's legs and put him in the hospital, where later both legs were amputated.[35]

Such stories of individual operations are quite rare in the literature of the Soviet resistance and rarer still in English-language sources. The most prominent Soviet resistance operations were described as large-scale campaigns. The largest of these campaigns was the organized blitz on the railroad system as the Germans moved into their offensive at the Battle of Kursk during July and August 1943. As the German offensive progressed, Stavka ordered the partisans to "conduct a large-scale operation to disrupt the German railroad communications network."[36] Soviet analysts estimated that the German offensive would require approximately 100,000 tons of cargo per day in food, petrol, weapons, ammunition, shells, transport wagons, horses, and so on. All of this cargo would have to move to the front by train. The partisan mission then was clear: The rail system was to be attacked so heavily that German equipment would be stranded in the rear areas, never making it to the front. The operation was named Rel'sovaia Voina or "Operation Rail War," and it was carried out during the period from July 21 to September 15. On the first day of the operation, July 21, some 430 demolitions took place involving 11 partisan brigades throughout the Bryansk forests. Grenkevich says, "According to German prisoner of war testimony and partisan intelligence reports, it took the Germans up to three days to re-establish traffic along those lines."[37] The assault continued all across the Russian front for nearly two months. Obtaining reliable statistics for the results of this massive campaign is problematic because different analysts have used various methods to measure—some counting locations, some counting specific detonations. But Grenkevich provides the following statistics: By September 15 the partisans had disabled some 214,704 sectors of railway lines, and if the portions of destroyed track are taken together, this adds up to some 1,000 linear kilometers of track.[38] The net result was that much of the German logistics effort behind their all-important Kursk offensive was slowed to a crawl, and much of what did get through ended up going to different locations than intended. This included not just equipment, but even combat troops. In the final analysis, says Grenkevich,

Partisan performance in Operation *'Rel'sovaia voina'* represented a major contribution to the Red Army's achievement of victory at Kursk and in subsequent operations . . . This massive sabotage put these major communication arteries out of action continually, and in the time required to repair the damage seriously impeded German supply of needed material and personnel . . . In essence it prevented the Germans from carrying out planned force regroupings in timely enough fashion to meet and defeat the growing Red Army offensive.[39]

In direct combat, the partisans could be of little help against the Germans at the front. But the contributions they made during the Kursk offensive make clear the value of the partisan movement to the overall military effort. In the battle that proved to be the end point for the German advance into Russia, the partisans played a vital role in that victory.

After the disaster at the Battle of Kursk, the Germans would never again be on the offensive in the USSR and were merely reacting to Soviet initiatives. Thus began a long retreat, lasting a year and a half, that would finally see Soviet troops enter Berlin in late April 1945. As the occupied territories were liberated, the partisan units were gradually disbanded and the men and women in them reassigned to the Red Army. Some partisan groups, though, were kept intact to hunt down and eliminate prominent collaborators.

* * * * *

In evaluating the Soviet partisan movement, there are a number of questions that scholars will continue to examine and discuss well into the future. The first of these questions revolves around the Soviet myth of the resistance: Was the partisan movement truly reflective of popular support of the communist/Stalinist system, and did such patriotism truly contribute to the war effort? Most international scholars seem to agree currently that Stalinist propaganda about the partisans is extremely misleading, and that the large numbers of Russians who welcomed the Germans suggests that their eventual move into resistance was motivated by something other than loyalty to the Soviet system. The degree to which the movement caused real problems for the Germans is still under investigation, but it would certainly seem that, at a minimum, in the places where it did operate, the partisan movement was a genuine problem for the Germans. First of all, it made necessary the use of large numbers of German troops in the rear areas. Here, Grenkevich has estimated that the Germans used forces of 200,000 to 250,000 men for rear area security in 1943 and 1944.[40] This, he says, "was a tremendous drain on German manpower resources," for a German force that was already well below its estimated requirements to complete its mission. The contribution made by the actual killing of German troops is difficult to estimate, but certainly the damage done to railways and communications infrastructures was significant, at least after 1942.

Another major question is whether or not the partisan war was even necessary at all. As we have seen, the initial German surge into the Soviet Union was met by many of the Russian people with enthusiasm and hope for liberation. In some areas German front line commanders were able to cooperate with locals and gain loyalty, increasing economic activity and producing no partisan resistance. It was only after the Germans implemented their murderous ethnic cleansing and repressive rule that ordinary Russians were *forced* into partisan activity. They made the choice to fight to avoid the immediate danger of death, to avoid the deadly German prison camps, to avoid labor conscription, or simply to rid the land of such savage oppressors. As historian Matthew Cooper says, "The guerilla war was so unnecessary. Its very existence proved the futility and brutality of German occupation policy, which squandered the valuable potential that lay in the East."[41] The fanatical racial hatred of the Nazis and the brutality it produced may have been Germany's greatest strategic mistake. Instead of widespread cooperation and quite possibly access to an enormous reservoir of manpower, the Germans created a new enemy force—the resistance army, which eventually grew to be a serious adversary. Perhaps Cooper sums it up best when he writes that, in the end, "the partisan movement was blessed with the advantage of being the lesser of two evils."[42] Indeed Stalin's directive that all people should rise up in resistance was one that paid no attention to the potential risks. Other governments and resistance movements in Europe focused on underground, clandestine organizations to reduce the loss of life that would result from German reprisals. This was seemingly of no concern to Stalin, who instructed his partisans to confront the enemy and to fight in direct combat, whatever the cost. Both the Nazi ideology and that of the Stalinist communists saw populations of ordinary people as utterly expendable. Stalin would prove this again as he not only created a partisan movement in the Soviet Union but also directed the network of communist organizations around Europe to create their own partisan groups. Their mission was not to secretly store weapons for a future date, or to conduct secret sabotage—their mission was to confront and fight the enemy in open combat whenever possible, regardless of the sacrifices and the potential loss of life.

NOTES

1. Nik Cornish, *Soviet Partisan, 1941–1944* (New York: Osprey, 2014), p. 4.

2. Service, *Stalin: A Biography*, pp. 411–412.

3. See Alexander Hill, *The War Behind the Eastern Front: The Soviet Partisan Movement in North-West Russia, 1941–1944* (London: Frank Cass, 2005), p. 41.

4. Ibid., p. 43.

5. See Manuel Sarkisyanz, *From Imperialism to Fascism: Why Hitler's "India" Was to Be Russia* (New Delhi: Deep & Deep, 2003).

6. Matthew Cooper, *The Nazi War Against Soviet Partisans, 1941–1944* (New York: Stein and Day, 1979), p. 19.

7. Hill, *The War Behind the Eastern Front*, p. 49.

8. General Anders, quoted in Matthew Cooper, *Nazi War Against Soviet Partisans*, p. 20.

9. Ibid., p. 20.

10. Ibid., p. 22.

11. Ibid., p. 23.

12. Ibid., p. 24.

13. Ibid., p. 24.

14. Cornish, *Soviet Partisan*, p. 6.

15. Ibid., p. 6.

16. Radio broadcast of Joseph Stalin, July 3, 1941, quoted in Cornish, *Soviet Partisan*, p. 7.

17. Cornish, *Soviet Partisan*, p. 7.

18. See Hill, *War Behind the Eastern Front*, p. 70.

19. Stavka Order 270, August 16, 1941, quoted in ibid., p. 76.

20. Ibid., p. 83.

21. Ibid., p. 124.

22. Cornish, *Soviet Partisan*, pp. 18–19.

23. Cooper, *Nazi War Against Soviet Partisans*, p. 73.

24. Cornish, *Soviet Partisan*, p. 16.

25. Cooper, *Nazi War Against Soviet Partisans*, p. 74.

26. Ibid., p. 74.

27. Ibid., p. 35.

28. Hill, *The War Behind the Eastern Front*, p. 125.

29. Cornish, *Soviet Partisan*, p. 28.

30. Ibid., p. 24.

31. Ibid., p. 28.

32. Ibid., p. 49.

33. See Shirer, *The Rise and Fall of the Third Reich*, p. 1225.

34. Leonid Grenkevich, *The Soviet Partisan Movement, 1941–1944* (London: Frank Cass, 1999), p. 298.

35. See Cornish, *Soviet Partisan*, pp. 46–47.

36. Grenkevich, *The Soviet Partisan Movement*, p. 241.

37. Ibid., p. 247.

38. Ibid., p. 248.

39. Ibid., p. 255.

40. Ibid., p. 225.

41. Cooper, *Nazi War Against Soviet Partisans*, p. 162.

42. Ibid., p. 72.

9

Resistance in the Mediterranean

The Resistance Movements in Italy and the Balkans

There is no question that Adolf Hitler's Nazi Germany played the leading role in initiating the Second World War and in conquering and subjugating the nations of Europe from 1939 to 1945. But Italy was also a prominent attacker and oppressor of the peoples of Europe. Under Benito Mussolini, fascist Italy had been the first of the dictatorships to launch an aggressive conquest when, in October 1935, Italian forces invaded the Empire of Abyssinia. This illegal invasion of a fellow League of Nations member state caused a diplomatic crisis and eventually resulted in economic sanctions against Italy. But Mussolini used such sanctions to mobilize a spirit of defiance among the Italians as he celebrated his nation's new status as a grand imperial power. The condemnation of the invasion and sanctions also pushed Mussolini into closer relations with Nazi Germany. In 1936 Mussolini joined Hitler in sending considerable military aid to Francisco Franco's Nationalists, who fought against Spain's Second Republic (and later its Soviet allies) during the Spanish Civil War. Generalissimo Franco would use that German and Italian help to win the war and establish his own military dictatorship that lasted until 1975. Mussolini's Italy, however, was not finished with its efforts to expand Italian territory and power. In April 1939 Mussolini moved Italian troops into the nation of Albania, forcing that country's king to flee into exile. By the commencement of the Second World War in September 1939, Italy's empire included territories in East Africa including Eritrea and Abyssinia, the vast territories of Libya, territories on the Yugoslav coast, a collection of small Mediterranean islands (the Dodecanese), and Albania. The fascist Italian Empire was taking shape, and it must be said that Italy had been the most violent of the aggressors before the start of the war. Germany had certainly used intimidation and force to accumulate the lands of Austria and Czechoslovakia, but there had been no major military conflict. Italy, on the other hand, had fought a long war in Abyssinia and used poison gas on the military and civilian populations to win their conquest.

Now, in the Second World War, fascist Italy would again prove to be a brutal and abusive aggressor, but its entry into the war was delayed. Italy had joined Nazi Germany in a treaty alliance in 1939, known later as the "Pact of Steel," as part of Hitler's maneuvering against Britain and France. But when war came in early September 1939, Italy did not honor its treaty obligations and stayed out of the conflict. It was a dishonorable but wise choice, as Italy was in poor condition militarily to take part in a war of that scale. As such, Germany fought alone in its conquest of Poland, Denmark, Norway, Holland, Belgium, and Luxembourg. But in the later phases of Germany's conquest of France, Mussolini made the cynical and opportunist move of joining Germany as an ally. He was anxious to gain territorial prizes in a conflict he thought was already won. As a result, Italian armies moved into the south of France and became the occupiers of a small border region that extended from the Swiss border to the Mediterranean coast at Nice. Hitler meanwhile continued his fight against Britain and his tightening of the noose in continental Europe. With Germany in control of the vast majority of Europe and Italy in possession of only Albania and a tiny scrap of France, Mussolini was determined to demonstrate to the world that Italy too could be a first-class conqueror. On October 28, 1940, he launched an invasion into Greece from his territories in Albania. The invasion, however, was repulsed by the Greek armed forces, who pushed the Italians back to the Albanian border. When the British joined the fight to help the Greeks, Hitler decided that he must intervene. If the British won a victory in Greece, they could use the Greek mainland as a staging area to launch attacks on Germany's territories in Eastern Europe, and this, he felt, could not be allowed.

Just as Hitler was planning Germany's intervention into the Greek situation, complications arose in nearby Yugoslavia. The Yugoslavs had agreed to act as German allies in the war, signing on to the Tripartite Pact. But this controversial decision had caused a military coup in Yugoslavia, and the new government, led by General Dušan Simović, reversed the decision to ally with Germany. He announced that Yugoslavia would remain neutral. This infuriated Hitler and convinced him to invade Yugoslavia as well. On April 6, 1941, an enormous German invasion force crashed simultaneously into Yugoslavia and Greece. In less than a month's time, both nations were defeated and their governments dissolved. In Yugoslavia the Italians were given some areas to administer along the Adriatic coast, in Montenegro, and in the areas adjacent to Albania. The Germans occupied most of Serbia. Croatia, notably, was given virtual independence as an Axis ally, with its own fascist regime under the dictator Ante Pavelić. In Greece the situation was similar, with the Italians occupying the vast majority of the Greek mainland and its islands. The Germans, however, occupied the northern zone surrounding the important industrial port city of Thessalonica and the majority of the island of Crete. The Bulgarians occupied and adminis- trated other parts of northern Greece and some small areas in Yugoslavia. But in Greece, the Germans were also in primary control in the capital city of Athens, where both German and Italian officials were present. This pro- gression of invasions and the subsequent configuration of occupation cre- ated strange scenarios for the resistance movements in the Balkans. Some fought the Italians, others the Bulgarians; some fought the Germans, while still others might have to fight indigenous authorities. This tangled config- uration became still more complicated with the collapse of Italy's fascist regime during 1943.

ITALY, THE RESISTANCE, AND THE QUESTION OF CIVIL WAR(S)

In the summer of 1943, the Allies launched the invasion of Sicily and began the long advance onto the "toe" of the Italian peninsula and north toward Rome. As the Allies advanced, the Italian government did some- thing startling. On July 25, the Grand Council of Fascism, technically the only committee with power over the duce, convened and voted to remove Mussolini from power. They voted to restore full powers to the king, Vic- tor Emmanuel III, who immediately ordered Mussolini's arrest. Mussolini was put in a mountaintop prison, the Hotel Campo Imperatore, in the Apennines, to ensure that none of his supporters could rescue and restore him. With Mussolini safely jailed, the Italians created a provisional gov- ernment under their top general, Pietro Badoglio. Badoglio's government began prolonged negotiations with the Allies, which resulted in an armi- stice on September 8. From this point the Italians worked with the Allies, and on October 13, Italy formally declared war on Nazi Germany. Ger- many responded to the armistice by sending a commando raid to break Mussolini out of jail and bring him to safety in Germany. After this, Hitler was convinced that he could not allow the Allied conquest of Italy, and so he sent a massive invasion force that occupied the Italian peninsula to a point a few hundred miles south of Rome. The Italian army was disarmed,

ITALIAN SOCIAL REPUBLIC, 1943

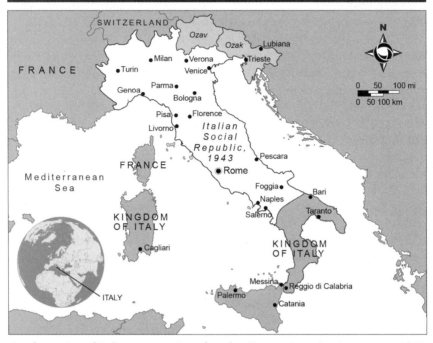

Configuration of Italian occupation after the German invasion in autumn, 1943. (ABC-CLIO)

and the majority of its troops were interned in German POW camps. Hitler reinstalled Mussolini as the nominal head of Italy and renamed the German-occupied zone in the north the "Italian Social Republic." It would also be referred to as the "Salò Republic," because Mussolini's administration was set up in the small town of Salò in the north. Now the Allied forces in the southern half of the peninsula would fight alongside Italian troops against the Germans as they began the long, bloody process of pushing the Axis forces north and eventually out of Italy. That process involved some of the bloodiest fighting of the war and lasted until the war's very last days.

Like Nazi Germany, resistance in Italy, as we have seen in the introduction to this book, was almost nonexistent in the years leading to the Second World War. Most of the leadership of the opposition political parties or labor organizations had been arrested and deported to "confinement," or had been forced to leave the country. The few dissidents who remained were limited to a secretive existence, and only the tiniest of gestures could be accomplished, such as the release of a militant pamphlet. Organizing a large group and mobilizing the resources for armed resistance simply was not a realistic possibility. But the nightmare of the war began to change the collective mood of the people by 1942. Italy established a consistent pattern during the war for its military expeditions: attacks on weaker territories, abject failure on the battlefield, the necessity for German intervention, and then abusive occupation practices while leaning on German strength. The Italian people had little to celebrate in terms of national pride, and by 1942, with the Allied victories in North Africa, they had a new menace to face—vigorous Allied bombing that would last throughout the war. The mounting losses and now the regular terror of Allied bombing made large numbers of Italians question the fascist regime and even contemplate resistance.[1]

When Mussolini was deposed on July 25, 1943, there were sporadic attacks by groups of individuals all over the country upon Fascist Party offices and newspaper shops, including 36 offices in Rome alone.[2] Such attacks were soon suppressed by the remaining authorities, but meanwhile the leaders of Italy's opposition parties began meeting in secret to prepare for the new situation. The vast majority of these party leaders were hiding out in France, and so their meetings took place in Lyons, where they laid preliminary plans for the construction of a functioning resistance organization. In the days to come, both Badoglio and King Victor Emmanuel negotiated with the Allies, trying to get favorable terms for a formal armistice. Eventually, terms were agreed and announced on September 8, which placed the nation of Italy immediately in a hostile relationship with Nazi Germany. The very next day, September 9, the heads of the parties formed the umbrella organization that would oversee Italy's resistance. It was called the Comitato di Liberazione Nazionale (CLN): in English, the National Liberation Committee. This organization would be the ultimate authority of the overall resistance apparatus, based in the south in liberated territory. In the north of the country, in the lands of the occupied Italian Social Republic, a separate council was created later in 1944. This was the CLNAI or the National Liberation Committee for Northern Italy. The most important of Italy's former political parties were all represented within these organizations, including the Communist Party (PCI), the Socialist Party (PSI), the Action Party (Social Democrats, PdA), the Christian Democrats (DC), the Labor Democrats (PDL), and the Italian Liberal Party (PLI). There was also, of course, representation from the existing royal government under Badoglio. This group of seven factions could be divided into three different tendencies, depending on each group's visions of Italy's future. As historian István Deák writes, "The monarchists supported restoring the prewar regime minus the Fascists, moderates wanted democracy, and the Communists and left wing Socialists hoped for a social revolution."[3] This multitude of political factions and convictions meant that generally resistance groups formed within their own party affiliations. There was unity at the top of the CLN, but each faction formed its own proprietary set of combat groups. The communist fighters were known as the Garibaldi Brigades, after the legendary 19th-century Italian revolutionary Giuseppe Garibaldi, who had fought to unify Italy. The socialists called their fighters the Matteotti Brigades, after the Italian socialist Giacomo Matteotti, who was murdered by the fascists for speaking up against Mussolini's brutality in 1924. The Action Party's groups were known as the Justice and Liberty Brigades, after an earlier iteration of the Action Party.

Just as this organization was in its preliminary stages of formation, events thrust the resistance into action in the southern city of Naples. Immediately after the Italian armistice with the Allies, the Germans moved large numbers of troops into Italy and occupied the peninsula all the way south to Naples. The Allies, meanwhile, were landing troops in the south and fighting their way north. In Naples itself, on September 23, the Germans ordered thousands of Italian families out of their homes near the coast, in fear of an Allied landing there. The Nazis also announced a massive call-up for Italian men to join the Nazi forced labor program. Posters were put up all over the city calling for men to show up at the appointed registration points. The Germans expected a crowd of perhaps 30,000 young men but found that only 150 men showed up. This sent the local authorities into a rage, and they responded with a second announcement that anyone not showing up for mandatory labor service would be executed.[4] This forced the men of Naples into an almost impossible choice—go to work for the Nazis or become an outlaw. As historian Thomas Behan writes, "These continuous turns of the screw pushed people's backs to the wall, and the only potential outlet was popular resistance."[5] Those made homeless and those who now had to fight to preserve their families grouped together in safe houses in the city and began to gather whatever weapons they could find. As they planned and gathered weapons, news was arriving of the Allied advance, suggesting that the Allied armies might be in the city within days. The trick was not to attack too early and get slaughtered, but instead to attack the Germans just before the Allied arrival, to help make them ineffective. On September 26 the Germans forced events by raiding all the shops they could find for food, and rounding up thousands of men (even hospital patients!) for forced labor. The outraged people of Naples exploded and attacked the Germans in the streets. All over the city, German columns were rushed by ordinary people shooting guns, throwing rocks, or tossing Molotov cocktails. Coordinating this mass rising was extremely difficult, and the resisters had to rely on couriers and even children on bicycles to transmit information. It was a necessity, as the Germans had cut all phone lines days before.[6] For four days the attacks went on, and eventually the German commander in Naples, Colonel Walter Schöll, withdrew to the suburbs and began to shell the city from a safe distance. This was a serious situation and could have seen the city destroyed, but on October 1, the Allied columns arrived at the city's southern gates. In the face of such an enormous invading force, the Germans retreated north. It now appears that 663 Italians were killed in the uprising, but the city was saved.[7]

It was a heroic effort from mostly ordinary citizens and with only marginal guidance or direction from the resistance organizations. There was no significant help given to the city from Allied air flights or nearby armies. Making the uprising even more remarkable is the fact that the citizens of Naples were not only fighting the German troops. The hardline Italian fascists fought alongside the Germans. It was impossible at times to know just who the enemy was. There were times, says Behan, when "those fighting the Germans had often suffered sniper attacks from the rear from Fascist snipers."[8] This was the reality in Naples but also throughout occupied Italy during the long fight to liberate the country. It made for a tangled and confusing situation, one that can be difficult for students of the war to fully understand. A new work of scholarship has recently appeared in the English language that provides important insight into the Italian resistance effort. In 1991, Claudio Pavone produced perhaps the most thorough treatment of the subject when he published his book *A Civil War: A History of the Italian Resistance*. It has now been fully translated, and in 2013 it was published in English. According to Pavone, the Italian situation was never as simple as native Italians fighting against Nazi Germany—the conflict involved Italian resisters fighting against the Germans, Italian formal military troops fighting against the Germans, Italian resisters fighting against the committed fascists of the Salò Republic, and of course it also involved power and strategy struggles between the various factions of the resistance. Pavone explains that the Italian conflict from July 25, 1943, to May 1945 took the shape of three simultaneous civil wars. He uses these three separate civil wars to provide the structure for his analysis and calls them the Patriotic War (Italians of all hues and the Allies versus the occupying Germans), the Civil War (non-fascist Italians versus the fascist faithful), and the Class War (those desiring a Marxist future versus reactionaries).[9] Viewing the conflict in this new light has been vital for scholars trying to make sense of the period, and as Stanislao Pugliese writes in his introduction to the book, it has been "a true paradigm-shifter in Italian historiography . . . the single most influential piece of scholarship in the last generation."[10]

While the combat between the various groups could be confusing, another layer of this complexity surfaced in one of the most infamous attacks of the resistance. In March 1944, one of the communist brigades in Rome planned to attack a German column that marched down the same street every day. They were military policemen, and on their daily marches through the city, they passed down the narrow Via Rasella. The Roman communists watched their exercises and decided to plant a bomb to go off during the march. The resisters were able to disguise themselves as street cleaners and get the bomb into position in a group of trash cans. The blast was ferocious and killed 33 of the Germans and wounded hundreds, the shrapnel tearing bodies and blinding many permanently. All of the Italian partisans were able to escape to safety.[11] What they may not have known was that these German troops, in Nazi military police uniforms, were in fact Italians. They had been recruited from the mostly German-speaking region of South Tyrol, which had come into Italian possession after the First World War. This would not likely have made any difference to those resisters who had to attack German forces, but it again highlights the many levels of complexity in this conflict—even Nazi-uniformed troops could be Italian. Like so many successful resistance attacks, the Via Rasella bombing had a tragic epilogue when the Nazis carried out a brutal reprisal. The SS chief in Rome at the time was Colonel Herbert Kappler, and he was ordered to execute 10 Italians for every German killed. In the end 335 Romans were gathered from the jails or on the streets and taken to an area known as the Ardeatine Caves in a rural suburb of Rome, where they were gunned down. The severity of the retribution horrified many Romans, some of whom condemned the bombing, and according to István Deák, for the Germans it "had not been unsuccessful; Roman resistance was weakened for the duration."[12]

For the rest of 1944 and into the early months of 1945, the various resistance factions attacked German columns, destroyed railroads and other transport networks, and disrupted communications wherever they could. Mostly these resistance groups lived in the mountain regions and relied upon the local peasant communities for help. They could not have survived without the food and clothing they received from the efforts of local people. The communist Garibaldi Brigades were the largest and lived primarily in the mountain regions, coming down to make attacks and then fleeing again into the hillside. Their brigades were led by a military commander who had absolute authority during military operations, and a political commissar (in the fashion of the Soviets) who was generally in command of the brigade while in its quarters. The political commissars ensured loyalty and focused on educating the young fighters on Marxist theory and the communist vision for the future. Communists and non-communist groups enjoyed a high level of success by keeping their groups constantly on the move and not generally using permanent bases. They were also now supplied by both the SOE and the OSS and got a steady supply of weapons, ammunition, food, and communications equipment. They also got agents. The SOE, for example sent in 125 British agents and 92 Italians they recruited and trained, to help direct and expand the combat brigades.[13]

SOE records also indicate that some 3,000 tons of supplies were dropped to the various CLN brigades.[14] These mountain brigades enjoyed a high rate of success in their operations despite chronic shortages of guns and ammunition. As Behan writes, partisan ammunition levels were so low that they "did not allow more than an hour's firing in any engagement."[15] Despite this, he says, using one division (the Lunense Division in northwest Tuscany) as a representative example, "the scale of success is undeniable." He reports that from August to December 1944, this one brigade made 50 sabotage raids against rail lines, destroyed 90 German vehicles, and killed about 1,000 enemy soldiers. This was against their own losses of about 150 men.[16] The Italian resistance joined the fight later than any other major resistance group, but its efforts lent tremendous support to the Allied ground troops who gradually pushed the Nazis and Salò fascists northward to the German border. In the final days of the Allied offensive in the spring of 1945, resistance action emerged into full combat against the fleeing Germans and fascists. Resistance fighters were able to take some 40,000 German and fascist prisoners and "liberated over a hundred towns before the Allied armies reached them."[17]

There remains one final controversy regarding the Italian partisans, and this is over the role they played in the death of the dictator Benito Mussolini. In the final days of the war, Mussolini and his administrative staff had gone on the run from Salò. He had established himself in Milan temporarily, but with the Allies marching toward the city, he abandoned Milan and attempted to escape into Switzerland. In the very north of the country, he was tracked down by Italian partisans. On April 15, 1945, the CLNAI had issued the equivalent of a death warrant on Mussolini. The order read, "The members of the fascist government and those fascist leaders who are guilty of having suppressed constitutional guarantees, destroyed the people's freedoms, created the fascist regime, compromised and betrayed the country, bringing it to the current catastrophe are to be punished with the penalty of death." Two days later, near the village of Dongo on Lake Como, a partisan group came upon a German column traveling in a group of trucks. The partisans searched a truck and, to their surprise, found an exhausted and addled Mussolini dressed in street clothes slumped in the back. Accompanying him were other fascists and his mistress, Clara Petacci. The partisans arrested the Italians, including Mussolini and his mistress, and took them into Dongo. Worried that fanatic fascists might try to stage a rescue, they secretly moved Mussolini and Petacci to an even smaller farming village nearby called Giulino di Mezzegra. There the orders came through from the resistance leaders to execute both Mussolini and his mistress. The two were put up against a small wall and shot on April 28. Their bodies were taken to Milan, and now the city's population, celebrating liberation, hung the bodies of Mussolini and Petacci upside down in a town square. There, people derided and vilified their corpses, spitting on them and tearing their clothes. It was a grotesque and igno-minious end for a man who, at the height of his power, had seemed invin-cible. In the weeks afterward, the communist newspaper *L'Unità* ran a series of articles under the headline "How I Executed Mussolini." In the articles, an agent from one of the Garibaldi Brigades code-named "Colonel Valerio" describes how he personally shot Mussolini. These descriptions were endorsed by Luigi Longo, the top commander of all the Garibaldi Brigades and a prominent communist politician after the war.

Since that time there have been competing claims regarding the execu-tion of Mussolini. Other agents have claimed to have been the ones to have shot him. But perhaps the most compelling conspiracy theory involves the British SOE. This theory has been pieced together primarily by the Ameri-can journalist and OSS spy Peter Tompkins.[18] The theory says that Musso-lini was traveling with a cache of secret documents, which included extensive correspondence between him and Winston Churchill. The cor-respondence would have revealed the extent to which Churchill was willing to work with Mussolini in exchange for help defeating Germany. This would have been a potentially explosive and scandalous revelation. The theory goes that Churchill sent in a secret agent from the SOE, whom the Italian partisans simply called "John." It was his responsibility to get the docu-ments and ensure Mussolini's death. A communist partisan from the time named Bruno Lonati spoke in an Italian television documentary in 2004, saying quite plainly that he had worked with "John." "John" had apparently insisted that an Italian must be the one to kill Mussolini, for historical and political reasons. Lonati says that he agreed to do that, but that he did not want to kill Ms. Petacci. "John" said that he would do it. In the documentary Lonati pointed out the exact spot where the shootings took place and claimed that both were shot in the chest rather than the head. He says with firmness in the film, "Colonel Valerio could not do what we had already done!" With the two dead and the documents safely in his hands, "John" departed.[19] There are serious problems with the claim, the most damaging of which is that no evidence of the secret correspondence has ever surfaced. Regardless of who precisely pulled the trigger, or if an SOE agent was pres-ent, there is no doubt that communist Italian partisans were able to track down and kill Mussolini. In the very land where fascism was born, it was the masses of ordinary people who had risen up to end it.

THE RESISTANCE MOVEMENT IN GREECE

The configuration of Italian occupation and resistance was certainly complex, but the Greek situation was every bit as complicated and can be quite confusing for non-specialists. With the defeat of the Greeks and the

British during April and May 1941, the Axis powers established an intricate occupation administration. The Germans directly occupied northern regions of the Greek mainland surrounding the important industrial seaport of Thessalonica. The Germans, who had used the armies of their Bulgarian allies during the invasion, now gave the Bulgarians a large portion of the northern territories in western Thrace. The Italians occupied and administered the bulk of the Greek mainland from Macedonia to the coast of the Peloponnese. The island of Crete was mostly occupied by the Germans, but the Italians occupied the east end of the island. Finally, the capital city of Athens was occupied and administered by the Germans, though an Italian occupation administration was also present in the city. Having chased the existing Greek government from the country, the Germans and Italians helped establish a pro-fascist collaborationist regime based in Athens. Under the Greek general Georgios Tsolakoglou, the collaborationist government cooperated with Axis security policies and attempted to promote the full cooperation of the Greek people. Tsolakoglou failed utterly in this attempt and was dismissed and replaced in late 1942.[20] The various iterations of the Greek puppet government that followed would establish a new organization known as the "security brigades," a sort of paramilitary police force whose principal function was to root out members of the Greek resistance. So, for a Greek person contemplating joining the resistance, one might be fighting the Italians, the Germans, the Bulgarians, or the Greek police.

Further layers of complexity were added by internal political rivalries and the collapse of fascist Italy in 1943. The Greek king, George II, had gone into exile in British Egypt and established a government-in-exile. Churchill and the Allies generally supported the king and his plans to return to Greece after the eventual defeat of the Axis. But inside Greece there were precious few who supported the monarchy; one officer who escaped the country and became minister of defense in the government-in-exile, Panagiotis Kanellopoulos, estimated that only about 2 percent of the Greek public supported the king.[21] The rest generally sided with the communist-run resistance organizations or the republican resistance groups. On top of all of this confusion, in the summer of 1943 Mussolini was deposed, and by September of that year, the Italians were siding with the Allies. Thus Italian troops in Greece suddenly changed from enemies to captives and then to potential allies. It was a chaotic and almost bewildering political configuration. But for those ordinary Greeks simply trying to stay alive during the occupation, the situation was much more fundamental.

Conditions in Greece during the occupation were extremely difficult, with supplies of the most basic commodities shriveling into nonexistence. The farming communities of Greece were devastated, and food production was minimal. What was produced was, naturally, appropriated by the Axis powers, and the Greeks were left with only the barest of necessities. Clothing, shoes, eyeglasses, automobiles, gasoline, and especially food were all in desperately short supply. The period of occupation from 1941 to 1944 lives in Greek tradition as the years of the "Great Famine." An SOE report of the time describing the conditions in Greece provides statistics that speak to the extent of the difficulty:

> After 3 years of Axis occupation, the Greek people's chief problem is, more than ever—how to live. The great majority spend their time and energy looking for some means to solve this particularly unsolvable problem . . . Let the following figures speak for themselves.

	Per oke [2.8 lbs.]
Bread	7,000 dr.
Ordinary goat-cheese	12,000
Sugar (when available)	30,000
Meat	12,000
Olive Oil	12,000
Milk (w/ large pct. of water)	2,000
Eggs	1,000 dr. apiece

> A worker's daily wage is between 2,000 and 3,000 drachmas . . . How he manages to feed himself and his family is not in the power of Source.[22]

One of the most powerful accounts we have of the years of the Greek occupation is the diary kept in Athens by Ioanna Tsatsos, the educated wife of the prominent university professor and dissident Konstantinos Tsatsos. She worked to coordinate an informal network of assistance to the poor and especially worked with the families of those in the resistance. Her entries tell us of the widespread poverty, the infuriating injustice of the raids, arrests, and executions, and the shattering anguish of the family members who saw their relatives tortured or executed. On the subject of hunger she wrote almost constantly, as deprivation was never far away. In November 1941 she wrote of her growing desperation in dealing with the problem of child hunger that was all around her.

> It is night. Cold, snow, hunger.
> What will this hunger do to us? How shall we feed the starving children?
> I had a most wonderful dream. A long, long table, covered with the most beautiful food and sweets. At the head sat the Christ Child and around Him the countless Greek children. . . . I woke up . . . and fully awake I sank slowly into the familiar nightmare . . . Around me gather all the little faces of Plaka, but as they really are, skeletons, all eyes. Eyes full of bewilderment, eyes that do not understand. . . . What shall we do about the mothers? I see them every day, and I am in despair . . . Oh God let the children live! Let not one of them die![23]

Tsatsos went on to work directly under Archbishop Damaskinos of Athens and rendered him vital aid in managing numerous efforts to raise money for the poor and to solicit charitable contributions of clothing, metal, food, and other necessities for resistance fighters and civilians alike. Her diary remains a crucial source describing the conditions of the Greek occupation.

Such conditions of oppression and deprivation forced thousands of Greeks into resistance activity. During 1941 and into 1942, such organizations were loose and somewhat random. The first resistance priority emerged immediately after the Axis defeat of the combined Greek and British forces. The Germans actively sought out any remnants of the British force. Greek civilians were called upon to find safekeeping for British servicemen on the run. A family might stash someone in their attic or create a safe house from a rental property they owned. Then, through a network of these safe facilities, the servicemen moved by night until they reached the coast. Once there, fishing vessels could be paid to get the men to safety in Egypt.[24]

By 1942 the organizations for the principal resistance organizations were taking definitive shape. The Communist Party of Greece (KKE) took the leading role in working to combine the most prominent left-wing organizations (including communists, socialists, and the People's Democratic Party) into a single body. In September 1941, its leaders had created an explicitly anti-Axis political group known as the National Liberation Front (EAM). The EAM was adamant about its aims to rid Greece of all foreign occupying powers, and at the same time to prepare the way for the Greek people to choose their own government after the country's liberation. At first, the true political nature of the EAM was not widely understood, but over time it became obvious that the group was dominated by the Greek Communist Party and had every intention of forcing a communist system into place by whatever means necessary. A little over one year after its founding, the EAM created an explicitly military division to carry out sabotage and combat against the enemy. This group was named the Greek People's Liberation Army (ELAS). This group became Greece's largest resistance army in the fight against the Axis until liberation.

The second of the principal resistance groups was founded by a Greek ex-officer named Napoleon Zervas. Zervas had been a passionate republican and had participated in several political actions during the 1920s and 1930s that culminated in the creation of the republican government under Eleftherios Venizelos from 1928 to 1932. But from 1936, under the Metaxas dictatorship, prominent republicans lost their influence, and Zervas was reduced to an irrelevant retirement.[25] In 1941 there were calls for him to step forward and establish a resistance army that could rid the country of the occupiers and pave the way for a new republican government after liberation. The British negotiated with him and eventually turned over a large sum of money (24,000 gold sovereigns) to help him create the group. Even then he hesitated to take action. C. M. Woodhouse, who eventually ran the British military mission to Greece, tells us, in what he calls a "distasteful story," that what finally convinced Zervas to move was the British threat to "expose him to the Germans."[26] It worked, and in the autumn of 1941, Zervas worked with other Venizelist officers to form an armed resistance band. They called themselves the National Republican Greek League (EDES). The EDES began working from the wild mountain terrain, sabotaging German vehicles, cutting communication lines, and occasionally attacking German and Italian troops. Like the ELAS, the EDES could only survive and function with the help of local mountain villages and with occasional excursions to the cities for supplies. Unlike the ELAS, we are told, Zervas's organization always paid for supplies. The ELAS, meanwhile, tended to terrorize the local populations. As a British Foreign Office report stated in comparing the two armies, "The efficiency and wide extension (of ELAS) were in the early days built up by force, all goods and services being conscripted as needed . . . this unpopular conscription was backed up when need be by looting, burning, torture, rape and murder. These are no longer practiced, but they have left a certain legacy of bitterness and suspicion among the survivors."[27] One prominent reason for this, not mentioned in the report, was that the ELAS received no financial support in its earliest days from either the British or the Soviets.

A third organization operated in the hills of Greece, and particularly around the city of Athens. This group was known as National and Social Liberation (EKKA). The band was formed by two prominent personalities: the Greek ex-officer Dimitrios Psarros, who was the principal military commander, and the fiercely republican politician Georgios Kartalis. The armed soldiers of the group were known as the 5/42 Evzone Regiment, named after Psarros's old army unit. EKKA was much smaller than the other two groups, made up of only about 1,000 men at its peak, while the EDES by comparison controlled about 5,000 armed men. The communist ELAS organization was by far the largest and most powerful of the resistance groups, boasting somewhere between 15,000 and 20,000 men.[28] EKKA was formed in the fall of 1942, with its military arm fully formed by early 1943. Its political aims were described as pursuing a "radical social democratic platform very similar to that of EDES."[29] With such similar aims, one British Foreign Office official asked Kartalis why the two organizations did not merge and form a larger, more powerful group. The answer came back that they "had not sufficient confidence in Zervas personally" and considered Psarros to be the most able of the military commanders.[30] Still, both organizations represented the popular desire for the dissolution of the monarchy and a multiparty parliamentary system to be constructed in Greece after liberation. A Soviet-style single-party dictatorship, as sought by the EAM, was abhorrent to them, and thus the three resistance organizations were constantly on the edge of conflict.

The organizations were brought together briefly in the early days of the movement, chiefly due to the work of the head of the SOE's military mission in Greece, Colonel E. C. W. "Eddie" Myers.[31] Myers was able to secure signatures on a cooperative agreement between the ELAS and the EDES on October 11, 1942, and from there began to plan a major operation involving both groups.[32] The mission was code-named "Operation Harling," and it was a brilliant success. SOE agent C. M. Woodhouse (known to the Greeks as "Major Chris") would later call Harling "the most important single success of the Resistance, and the only one in which ELAS cooperated with other guerillas under a single command."[33] The plan centered upon the transport network running through Greece, and especially the enormous railroad bridges that connected Thessalonica to Athens. At this time, October–November 1942, the war in North Africa was at a crucial stage. The British were engaged in a fierce conflict with the German Afrika Korps under General Erwin Rommel. Operation Harling was intended to interrupt the German supply line from Europe to North Africa, which relied upon moving supplies through Greece and then from Greek ports across the Mediterranean to Africa. Three chief viaducts crossed tremendous mountain valleys on this transport route—the Gorgopotamos, Asopos, and Papadia bridges. All three were massive steel structures and quite difficult to damage. A team of 12 SOE agents was dropped into Greece on September 30, 1942. The leader of the British force, Myers, did secret reconnaissance and eventually chose the Gorgopotamos bridge as the best chance for success, based on its geography, engineering, and security. There was an Italian contingent of about 80 guards in the area. Myers's second-in-command, Woodhouse, went into the mountains to negotiate with Zervas and the commander of the ELAS at the time, Aris Velouchiotis. He eventually convinced each group not only to participate in the mission, but also to cooperate with each other in the operation.

The team assembled for the operation numbered 150 men: 12 from the SOE, 86 from the ELAS, and 52 from the EDES. On November 25 they approached the bridge under the cover of darkness at around 11:00 PM. A fighting force of 100 men began the operation by engaging the Italian security force in an attack. It turned into a rather prolonged firefight, and so Myers gave the order for the demolition team to move into action while the shooting was still raging. Despite this, the engineers were able to affix the plastic explosives and the charges. The first blasts damaged the main steel support beams, and then a second round of explosions tore through the bridge itself. By about 4:00 AM the job was complete; the bridge was rendered useless, and the men withdrew into the surrounding mountain forests. The supply route was interrupted for several weeks, but in the end this was not greatly consequential. During the months the mission was in process, the British Eighth Army had won significant victories over Rommel, and with British troops securing the Libyan coastal areas, says István Deák, "the supplies would not have reached Rommel in any case."[34] Still the German supply line had been badly damaged, and in early 1943 a team of British agents magnified the problem by disabling the Asopos bridge as well. Operation Harling marked one of the earliest and most spectacular of the accomplishments of the SOE, which at that time was still fighting to justify its own existence. By demonstrating that it could help coordinate local resistance and pull off major operations, its leverage was greatly increased.

Another major accomplishment of the Greek resistance, in cooperation with the SOE mission, was the acceleration of resistance attacks during the first half of 1943. This overall operation, made up of numerous small operations, was code-named "Operation Animals." Its purpose was to tie up both German and Italian troops in Greece and to create the illusion that, after the victories in North Africa, the Allies were intending to invade Greece. In fact the Allies had agreed to invade Italy, using Sicily as the initial strike point, and that invasion took place during July 1943. It paved the way for the larger invasions of mainland Italy in September. But in the spring of 1943, as the North African campaign was concluding, Allied intelligence suggested that Hitler and Mussolini both were concerned about an Allied landing in Greece. "Hitler was virtually convinced," writes historian Mark Mazower, "that Greece was the Allies' intended target, for the Führer believed that Churchill wanted to wipe out memories of the Dardanelles fiasco with a successful Balkan campaign."[35] Axis leaders were also convinced that the Allies had their eyes on the many raw materials available in southeastern Europe—both gaining them for themselves and depriving the Germans of them—including chrome, bauxite, and especially Romanian oil.[36] The repeated attacks on German troop carriers, the constant cutting of telephone lines, and attacks on the railroads all reassured Hitler that Greece was preparing for a major invasion. As a result Hitler sent numerous divisions into Greece, including the 11th Luftwaffe Field Division, the 117th Jaeger Division, the 1st Panzer Division, and the 1st Mountain Division. All of this, says Mazower, "represented a considerable strategic investment for an army which was scattered across the vast expanse of Fortress Europe."[37] All of these German troops were waiting in Greece when the Allies moved into Italy. Furthermore, the existing German and Italian troops in Greece that could have been transferred to Italy remained in place. In the months that followed, as Mussolini's regime in Italy collapsed, the Italian soldiers in Greece were left with no orders or direction. In an instant they found themselves enemies of the Germans, their former allies. Italians were taken prisoner by the Germans by the thousands, but Greek resistance groups also moved to capture and disarm Italian soldiers wherever they could and in the process greatly expanded their supply of weapons.

But it was after this, as the war moved into late 1943, that the positive contributions of the Greek resistance began to fade away, and increasingly the factions fought against themselves. The ELAS and the EDES were already fighting each other before the end of 1943. In the spring of 1944, ELAS guerillas made a deadly attack on the forces of EKKA and killed that group's leader, the very popular Colonel Psarros. His body is said to have been beheaded by the communists and left to rot, and his assassination appalled resistance members and civilians alike. Ioanna Tsatsos wrote of her community's shock in her diary:

> The doorbell rang! Kartalis came into the house without speaking to any-one! He threw himself on the bed! . . . Yesterday the ELAS guerillas killed Psarros and more than 150 of the officers and men of the 5/42 Regiment . . . Anguish chokes us . . . Every day we hear descriptions of the catastrophe which befell Psarros and his men, and they are nightmares. Extreme suffer-ings, degradations. But why so much hate? Why all this evil?[38]

Greece was falling into a civil war. The leaders of the EAM and the ELAS were absolutely driven to gain a full monopoly of the resistance forces by the time the Germans were driven out of their country. This had been prevented earlier by the British efforts to fund and grow a republican resistance group. But in preventing a full communist monopoly of popular resistance, writes C. M. Woodhouse, the British ended up "creating the conditions of civil war."[39] In February 1944 the Allied mission was able to convince both the ELAS and the EDES to sign the so-called Plaka Agreement, which pledged both sides to cooperation in exchange for increased arms supplies. But that cooperation was very short-lived, as both sides could see that the Germans were in full retreat and that after their departure, the greatest enemy would be one another.[40] And so, the Greek Civil War would rage on through the eventual withdrawal of the German and Bulgarian forces in October 1944 and continue through the end of the Second World War. Despite the establishment of a republican government and British oversight immediately after the war, the tragedy of the conflict and all its atrocities would not end until 1949.

Despite all the horrors to come after the end of the war, nothing could take away from the joy that Greeks felt upon their liberation in October 1944. Ioanna Tsatsos writes of the ecstasy of her family and friends upon the German retreat, as she saw the German flag taken down and the Greek flag once more raised on the Athenian Acropolis:

> And we see the German flag slowly, slowly descend, see it disappear as if the Sacred Rock had swallowed it. And there begins to rise in its place the beloved color of our sky. . . . Greece is once more our own, our very own. We have won her with our blood, our toil, with daily privation, but above all we have won her in the dark grief of all our years of slavery. Greece is once more our own. This is justice.[41]

That night, she tells us, Archbishop Damaskinos recited a prayer that he had composed for those who had fought the Axis, for those who had suffered, and for those who had died:

> Ye Shades of the heroic dead,
> Ye hosts of the living,
> Ye myriads of victims,
> Ye rows of graves,
> Ye swarms of mourners,
> With tears rejoicing,
> Bless ye the Lord![42]

THE RESISTANCE IN YUGOSLAVIA

The nation of Yugoslavia was born out of the long periods of ethnic conflict leading up to the First World War and the subsequent dissolution of the Austro-Hungarian Empire at that war's conclusion. The Pan-Slavist movement that had seen so many acts of violence, including the assassination of Archduke Franz Ferdinand in June 1914, now reaped its reward. As part of the peace settlements, the Slavic peoples were given their own great nation, initially known as the Kingdom of the Serbs, Croats, and Slovenes, but commonly referred to as "Yugoslavia." In 1929 its name was officially changed to the Kingdom of Yugoslavia. But the new kingdom was racked by internal conflict from its birth. Its governments were dominated by a Serbian political and religious elite, which alienated the Croatian and Slovene populations. There were also religious divisions, with the Croatian population being predominantly Catholic and the Serbs mostly Orthodox Christians. There were also Muslim minorities within the mix, making the situation even more complicated. All of these ethnic and religious rivalries would be present as the nation dealt with life and resistance under Axis occupation.

In the years leading up to the war, Yugoslavia was thrown into political turmoil. Its monarch, King Alexander, was assassinated in 1934 when the crown prince, Peter, was only 11 years old. To deal with this, the former king's cousin, known as Prince Paul, took on the duties of the monarch as regent, ostensibly serving until young Peter came of age. Prince Paul's regency was still controlling the country when Mussolini and Hitler began their series of aggressive conquests, straining the balance of power in Europe. As Europe lurched into war, Prince Paul had declared Yugoslavian neutrality, but now Germany put increasing pressure upon the Yugoslav government to sign on as a formal ally. Eventually Prince Paul's government gave in and signed the Tripartite Pact on March 17, 1941, but this was an extremely controversial move. Yugoslavia erupted in street protests and popular outrage across the country. The move also convinced a group of military officers to carry out a coup d'état, seizing the government in the name of Crown Prince Peter, now 17 years old. Prince Paul and his ministers were swept away, and the new government, headed by the young King Peter, announced its intention to withdraw its signature from the Tripartite Pact and return to its policy of neutrality. This was all happening while the Italians were attempting to conquer Greece. The Greeks stood up to the Italian invasion and pushed the Italians back to their bases in Albania, and by this time British troops had arrived to help. It appeared that the Italians would soon be routed. Adolf Hitler had decided that such a thorough and visible embarrassment to the Axis powers could not be allowed, and he was already planning his intervention in the Greek situation. With the Yugoslavian coup and policy reversal added to this mix of problems, Hitler decided to handle both problems with one decisive strike. On April 6, 1941, he sent a massive German invasion into Yugoslavia and Greece simultaneously. The result was the rapid defeat of both nations, with Yugoslavia capitulating within 12 days. Young King Peter and his government escaped to Athens, then to Jerusalem, and finally on to Britain, where the Yugoslavians would set up a government-in exile at Claridge's Hotel in central London.

By May 1941, then, Yugoslavia was entirely under Axis control. The nation was carved up into separate occupation districts. The Italians administered areas on the Adriatic coast, in Montenegro, and in the regions bordering Albania. The Germans directly controlled the Serbian regions in the central part of the country, including domination of the capital city of Belgrade. This area was allowed to create its own collaborationist government, known as the "Government of National Salvation," under General Milan Nedić. But this government was mostly symbolic, having no meaningful input with the Germans and no control of police or security. The region of Croatia, however, was given the status of a sovereign and independent state under its own fascist dictatorship. The party of Ante Pavelić, by then known as the Ustaša Croatian revolutionary movement, had long been pressing for the creation of an independent Croatian state with the implementation of hardline fascist policies. The Ustaša police forces would become notorious for their genocidal policies, persecuting, deporting, and executing thousands of Serbs, Jews, Romani, Bosnians, and Muslims. As the Yugoslavian people moved into the terrifying period of occupation, these were the principal forces ranged against them—the Italian occupation authorities including the OVRA secret police, the German occupation troops including the Gestapo, and the Croatian Ustaše.[43]

As in most of the other occupied territories, resistance took shape early in the occupation as so many thousands were forced into an impossible position. Ethnic and religious minorities faced persecution almost immediately, and soon after, German and Italian plundering of resources sank many into destitution. Particularly the Germans also began programs of forced labor, which forced thousands of young men into the hills. Also, like several other examples around Europe, the first resistance groups formed around the remnants of the shattered defeated armies. Several of these floating bands eventually gelled into the two principal resistance groups that would endure through the end of the war. The first of these two groups took form under the leadership of an escaped military officer, Colonel Draža Mihailović. Having eluded capture, Mihailović took to the hills and labored to find other officers and units that might come together to form an intelligence network to provide information to the Allies. After a time, the group grew so large that it was necessary to move to the safer region of the Ravna Gora forest in the mountains of central Serbia. There, Mihailović would establish a genuine armed resistance movement, who called themselves the "Chetniks." The Chetnik movement represented Mihailović's own political convictions—fiercely supportive of the Yugoslav monarchy and loyal to King Peter in exile, anti-Axis and pro-independence, and deeply anti-Marxist. The ultimate objective of Mihailović and his group was the formation of a completely independent Serbian state for the Serbian people, led by its traditional royal family.[44]

The Chetniks conducted small-scale sabotage against the Axis, but these operations were quite limited. Mihailović was quite aware of the publicly announced German policy of killing 100 Serbian hostages for every German killed by resisters. As such, armed attacks were almost unheard of from his group. Instead, Mihailović determined early on in the conflict that the greatest challenge to his ultimate goals lay in the rival resistance organization—the communist partisans. That partisan movement, under the leadership of Josip Broz Tito, had grown to considerable size and was actively waging war on the Axis forces. As a result innocent Yugoslavians were being killed in German reprisals, and the partisans were becoming more powerful every day. If they continued to grow in power and influence, when the liberation finally came, they would be in position to assert their political will, making Yugoslavia a communist nation. This was even more terrifying to the Chetniks than the Nazi occupation. Mihailović then began to focus his sabotage and military action on the communists rather than the Axis. As with Italy and Greece, the Yugoslavian resistance situation evolved into a simultaneous civil war.

The SOE and the OSS both sent their own agents into Yugoslavia to get concrete information about the two major movements. One of the most influential of these agents was the American OSS officer Linn Farish, who sent reports deprecating the level of active resistance among the Chetniks and praising the fierce fighting of the partisans. His reports were among the many that eventually convinced both the United States and British governments to move their support away from Mihailović and toward Tito. But while Farish was visiting the Chetnik base, he did help in the construction of airstrips. These would become very important in one of the most important Allied operations involving the Chetnik base. This was Operation Halyard, a plan to airlift hundreds of downed airmen out of Yugoslavia during August 1944. After the Allies took control of southern Italy in the summer and fall of 1943, that region became a key location for airbases that would send missions into Axis-controlled Europe. Planes would take off, mostly from the airbase in Brindisi, on the "heel" of Italy's boot, and fly missions to bomb Germany, Poland, and particularly the German-controlled oil fields in Romania. Most of these bombing missions took the planes over Yugoslavia. As a result, many Allied airmen were shot down in the region and eventually found refuge with the Chetniks or the partisans. By August 1944 the Chetniks had nearly 250 Allied airmen within their base, and they worked with the Allies to fly dozens of missions to evacuate them, using the Chetniks' mountain airstrip. Many of those airmen remained thankful for the rest of their lives, and they lobbied the U.S. government for recognition of Mihailović and his group for that assistance in Operation Halyard. One scholar, Marcia Kurapovna, asserts that the Chetniks were responsible for saving around 500 Allied airmen over the course of the war.[45] For such contributions, the Eisenhower administration decided to give Mihailović a posthumous award—the highest American award that can be given to a non-U.S. citizen—the Legion of Merit, for his efforts in this operation. But this remains highly controversial. In fact the Mihailović resistance movement seems to have done only a small amount of active resisting against the Axis. Most of its combat operations were focused against the partisans, and in that fight he was at times willing to fight alongside the Axis forces. We shall return to this question momentarily.

The second of the great resistance movements in Yugoslavia, as mentioned above, was the communist partisan movement led by Josip Broz Tito. Josip Broz (Tito was an adopted nickname) was born in Croatia in 1892. As a young adult, he fought in the First World War in the Austro-Hungarian army, and after the war he became a metalworker and a member of the Communist Party of Yugoslavia (CPY). The CPY was then outlawed in Yugoslavia, and as a result, Tito lost work and was even arrested for his political advocacy. He later left Yugoslavia and spent most of the late 1930s in the Soviet Union, working within the Comintern. The Communist International, or Comintern, was the Soviet-run agency that labored to create and manage the various communist parties and agendas to help spread the communist revolution throughout the world. While still in Russia, Tito was named secretary general of the CPY by the Soviets, and arrangements were made for him to return to Yugoslavia to continue building the party. When the Axis invasion of the country dissolved the Yugoslavian government and all political parties, Tito took to the forests with his party faithful and immediately began constructing an army to begin the active battle against the Axis. But Tito could not engage in any fighting against the Axis for the moment. Tied to Soviet policy, Tito had to respect the Nazi–Soviet treaty alliance and so could not initially attack the Nazis. But the Yugoslav partisans did not have to worry about this predicament for long. On June 22, 1941, only two months after the defeat of Yugoslavia, the Nazis rolled into the Soviet Union, commencing Operation Barbarossa. Immediately Yugoslavians began to flock to the partisan movement, and Tito began preparing for battle in earnest. The first armed guerrilla attacks against the Axis were launched as early as July 7.

The Axis policies (along with those of the of Nedić government and the Croatian Ustaše) of plunder, work conscription, and outright brutality drove thousands of Yugoslavs into the partisan ranks. One estimate says that Tito's partisan force had reached 20,000 able fighters by 1942, "including quite a thousand young women, who fought alongside the men."[46] Tito and his partisans gravitated to areas where there was little to no Axis military presence, in the great forested mountains in the center and west of the country. The partisans tended to have widespread support, because their identity was defined by ideology rather than with religion or ethnicity. There was outwardly no discrimination between Serbs, Croats, and Slovenes, and the religious conflict between Orthodox and Catholic was dismissed. With this support the partisans were able to take huge areas of territory and declare their own authority. The first area where this was implemented was in the center of the country. It was an enormous area that overlapped three occupation districts—parts of German-occupied Serbia, parts of Italian-occupied Montenegro, and the southern regions of the Independent State of Croatia. The bulk of Tito's headquarters staff set up shop in the town of Užice, where there was rail transport, several nearby villages for resources, and in Užice itself, an armaments factory, which the partisans used to replenish their guns and ammunition. The partisans declared the entire territory the "free republic of Užice," infuriating Axis occupying authorities. It was governed, as other partisan territory later would be, by a "people's committee," similar to the soviets formed during the Russian Revolution of 1917. The partisans took full control of the area in September 1941 and here formally established their organization as the National Liberation Partisan Detachments of Yugoslavia. That name would be changed four more times by 1945, but the name most commonly used by Yugoslavs was the National Liberation Army (NOV). During that same month, Tito and the NOV leaders met with Mihailović for the first time to discuss possible cooperation. Their talks were inconclusive, and so a second conference was convened at the town of Brajići on October 27. Here they reached a tentative agreement to work together and share resources, including some of the arms produced at the Užice arms plant. It was at this point that the Germans moved into the area to attack and eliminate the resisting "republic." Given the enormous size of the territory, the Germans used two entire infantry divisions and parts of several others, along with Serbian troops. The fighting took place on hillsides, in dense forests, and in villages, with the Germans using overwhelming force and the partisans trying to kill them through guerrilla attacks. On November 1, the Chetniks violated whatever shaky agreement they had with the partisans and launched their own attack on Tito's forces. They were pushed out of the area. With that, Mihailović began talks with the Germans to see how they could work together to rid the area of the communists. Eventually Tito's soldiers were forced to retreat and flee the area. They initially retreated to the southwest into Italian territory in the region of Sandžak, but within a year they had moved north along the coastal regions to set up a new, massive "liberated territory" within Croatia.

This new territory was also given a name that suggested that it was completely independent of Pavelić's Croatian government or Axis authority. They called it the "republic of Bihać," after the principal town where Tito and his staff created their new headquarters. It was in this newly established territory that the next major battle of the war in Yugoslavia would take place. From January 20 through March 1942, the Axis powers attacked the partisans and attempted to encircle and destroy them. The partisans decided to escape with their forces south across the river Neretva. To effect this escape, they would have to cross the river themselves and then destroy four major bridges to prevent the Axis forces from following. But there was a major concern in pulling off this escape. William Deakin, an SOE agent in Yugoslavia at the time, fought alongside the partisans and tells the story in his important book on the subject, *The Embattled Mountain*, published in 1971. When the battle took place, more and more badly wounded partisan soldiers were being distributed throughout the network of villages near Bihać. When the Axis forces hit the partisans, Tito had to make seriously difficult decisions about what to do with the wounded. One option was to leave them where they were, but this would almost surely mean execution, or at the least, capture and internment. So the partisans launched a major operation to move the wounded as their entire force moved south. Would the decision to transport the wounded across the river slow down the army and lead to its destruction? Deakin writes that in this harrowing march,

> Three thousand wounded had been brought from the forests and mountains of Bosnia out of reach of the pursuit of the German and Italian divisions, with their Chetnik auxiliaries, and the specialized assassins of the Ustaša brigades, to the territories in Hercegovina and on the borders of Montenegro . . . Most survived, but the cost was grim . . . But a revolution had been achieved.[47]

It has been often suggested that Tito followed the Soviet directive to fight the enemy directly with a callous disregard for the consequences to his own people. The historian Marcia Kurapovna, for example, says that his "reckless disdain for German reprisals against the civilian population formed part of his path to power."[48] Like all communists, he followed Stalin's clear directive to fight the Axis regardless of the consequences, which was consistent with the more general communist disregard for human life in the pursuit of the victory of the ideology. His decisions regarding the wounded at the Battle of Neretva must, however, temper this assessment to some degree. The partisans were forced from some of their territory, but now they moved into new areas. They left very few behind, which is why the battle is sometimes remembered as the "Battle of the Wounded." Today in the city of Jablanica on the Neretva river, the Museum of the Battle for the Wounded at Neretva commemorates the conflict.

It was to this newly established territory that both the SOE and the OSS would send emissaries in the summer of 1943, to assess the situation in Yugoslavia and begin a program of accelerated assistance. The SOE and the OSS had also sent missions to the Chetniks, but with the reports returning about both groups, Allied policy began to change. Winston Churchill was, by 1943, increasingly intrigued by the stories of large-scale combat carried out by the partisans. The SOE was supporting both the Chetniks and the partisans, though the Chetniks were receiving the lion's share of the support. But overall, British and American support at this point was minimal. In June 1943, Churchill sent his own personal envoy, the ex-diplomat Fitzroy Maclean, to work with Tito and assess the Yugoslavian situation and the partisan movement in particular. Later a full SOE military mission would be assigned to Tito, led by William Deakin. Both Maclean and Deakin would fight alongside Tito's partisans, and both have written fine histories of the resistance movement in Yugoslavia.[49] Also in 1943 Linn Farish, mentioned above, was sent by the OSS and evaluated the situation. The reports from both SOE and OSS agents suggested that the Chetnik groups did not generally fight the Axis powers, as they were exceedingly concerned about reprisals. They did, however, tend to attack the partisans, who were the only group taking the fight to the Nazis. In fact, the partisan will to fight was quite strong, and they were concerned less with sabotage and intelligence (although they certainly pursued these as well) than they were with outright guerrilla combat. These reports clarified the situation for the Allied strategists, and during late 1943 a shift in policy was effected. An SOE report from the autumn of 1943 illustrates how the British support in Yugoslavia was being shifted. The update on operations reported with satisfaction that "the most important development was the successful running in by sea of 1,450 tons of weapons, ammunition, food and medical supplies to the Partisan force in Yugoslavia."[50] For the Chetniks, though, things had changed; as the report stated, "Supplies to Mihailović were at present confined to food and medical stores."[51] By late 1943 Allied support to Yugoslavia was being dramatically ramped up, but armaments and supplies to the Chetniks had been cut. This policy, already being implemented, became even more official as a result of the conference of Allied leaders held from November 28 to December 1 at Tehran. Among the leading decisions taken at the Tehran Conference was that the full support of the Allies should be given to the Yugoslav partisans and that support to the Chetniks should be suspended. Churchill and Stalin, here, had to convince Roosevelt and the American diplomats to abandon their clear preference for Mihailović and their aversion to the communists. But the Americans reluctantly agreed.[52]

As this was happening in the last months of 1943, another major development had taken place. In Italy the fascist regime had collapsed, and the Italian soldiers in Yugoslavia were overwhelmed by partisan forces. The result was that the partisans were able to capture significant amounts of Italian weapons and ammunition.[53] By 1944, then, the partisan movement was armed better than ever, and Allied supply shipments continued to increase their stocks—though, as M. R. D. Foot comments, the Italian capitulation "released (Tito) from much dependence on SOE for supplies of arms."[54] The partisan movement was also growing at an exponential rate in terms of personnel. Though the partisans had never won a decisive victory over the Axis forces, they had continued to move into vast areas of territory and survive. From these areas, the partisans launched continual guerrilla actions, regularly killing Axis soldiers. All over the country, Yugoslavs of all ethnicities saw that the partisans were successful and offered a viable way for individuals to fight their oppressors. Estimates of partisan strength by 1944 suggest that Tito had nearly a quarter of a million men and women under his command.[55] By the autumn of 1944, the Germans were in retreat all over Europe, and the Soviet armies were making their way into Eastern Europe. The Soviets had invaded and conquered Bulgaria, setting up a communist government there and creating a "Bulgarian People's Army."

Joseph Stalin was able to meet with Tito and plan a final offensive in Yugo-slavia. Together the Soviet army, Tito's partisans, and sections of the Bul-garian People's Army engaged in a bloody final battle for Yugoslavia. The culmination came with the final liberation of Belgrade, which was overrun by partisan forces on October 20, 1944.

Tito and his communist partisans had wedged themselves into a domi-nant position by the end of the war. There is no question that the partisan movement became the preeminent resistance force in the country and that the Chetniks shrank into insignificance. Tito entered into a number of negotiations involving the British, the government-in-exile, and the Sovi-ets. This is a deeply complicated story and cannot be embarked upon here, but in the end Tito and his CPY took control as the ruling power in Yugo-slavia. Famously, during the years of the Cold War, Tito broke with Stalin and kept Yugoslavia independent from Soviet influence, although the com-munist system remained in place. Tito himself remained a dictator until his death in May 1980.

But what of Mihailović? The break between Mihailović and Tito and the subsequent conflict between them, which can certainly be seen as a civil war, remains perhaps the most heated controversy surrounding the Yugo-slav resistance movement. Tito and his supporters saw Mihailović as a traitor, as a man who had willingly collaborated with the Axis powers in order to advance his own personal power. After the war was over, Mihailović took to the hills, but he was eventually found and arrested. He stood trial for treason and war crimes, was found guilty, and was executed in July 1946. But today some scholars, particularly in Serbia, are arguing that the Mihailović story has only been told by the communists, his sworn enemies. The distinguished American historian Sabrina Ramet explains that the Chetniks' plan for the future was vitally linked to the question of collaboration and their ultimate fate. Mihailović and his Chetniks planned to create a Greater Serbia after the war, claiming vast territories then occu-pied by other ethnic and religious groups. If their plan had been put into effect, they would have expelled some 2.6 million Yugoslavs from Serbia. Their intermittent collaboration with and attacks upon the Axis were sim-ply based on whatever, at the time, best served their ultimate purpose.[56] Mihailović himself simply tried to use the Axis powers in his effort to eventually create a free and independent Serbia with a restored monarchy and a purified Serbian population. Non-Serbians and non-monarchists would have seen his vision as itself quite fascist. The historian Marcia Kurapovna, however, has also written a new analysis of the relationship between the Allies and Mihailović, pointing out what she sees as the irra-tionality of the Allied policy to reject a willing ally and embrace a commu-nist dictator. She is clearly telling her story from the Serbian point of view, but, as she writes, her analysis tries to explain how a Royal government (Great Britain) betrayed a Royalist government (the Kingdom of Yugoslavia) to exclusively support a Communist government (that of Tito) against the wishes of an ally and a Democratic government (the United States) in order to keep another Communist government (of Stalin) from gaining control, while that Communist government (of Stalin) betrayed its own Communist partners (the Yugoslav Partisans) to support the Royalist government (the Kingdom of Yugoslavia).[57]

It is a twisted story indeed, and historians and political scientists will continue to debate these issues for years to come. But one issue is clear. Between them, the Chetniks and the partisans saved nearly 1,200 downed airmen, and their resistance activity meant the Germans were forced to use an enormous occupation force of over a quarter of a million men (some 15 divisions) as well as 100,000 native troops.[58] Many of these men could have been fighting in France or on the Eastern Front, but with the level of resistance combat in Yugoslavia, such redeployment was never an option for the German High Command.

NOTES

1. See Thomas Behan, *The Italian Resistance: Fascists, Guerillas, and the Allies* (New York: Pluto, 2009), p. 21.

2. Ibid., p. 27.

3. Deák, *Europe on Trial*, p. 167.

4. Behan, *The Italian Resistance*, p. 35.

5. Ibid., p. 35.

6. Ibid., p. 37.

7. Ibid., p. 38.

8. Ibid., p. 37.

9. Claudio Pavone, *A Civil War: A History of the Italian Resistance*, trans. Peter Levy with David Broder (London: Verso, 2013).

10. Stanislao Pugliese, in ibid., pp. ix–xi.

11. Deák, *Europe on Trial*, p. 167.

12. Ibid., p. 168.

13. Linderman, *Re-Discovering Irregular Warfare*, p. 156.

14. See Foot, *European Resistance to Nazism*, p. 227.

15. Behan, *The Italian Resistance*, p. 75.

16. Ibid., p. 75.

17. Foot, *European Resistance to Nazism*, p. 227.

18. Peter Tompkins was an undercover agent for the OSS in Rome during 1944. He went on to write a number of books about the mysterious properties of the pyramids in Egypt and in Central America.

19. See the documentary film *Mussolini: The Churchill Conspiracies*, directed by Marie Luisa Forenza (Shanachie Entertainment Corp., 2007).

20. Tsolakoglou was arrested and tried after the war and sentenced to death for his role in the Axis occupation. His sentence was commuted to life imprisonment,

and so he died of natural causes in jail in 1948. He was dismissed by the Axis powers in December 1942 and replaced by Konstantinos Logothetopoulos. Logothetopoulos was himself replaced during April 1943 by Ioannis Rallis, who was instrumental in creating the "security battalions," the Greek police who actively sought out the Greek resistance.

21. C. M. Woodhouse, *The Struggle for Greece, 1941–1949* (London: Granada, 1976), p. 22.

22. "Conditions in Occupied Greece: A British Intelligence Report," August 25, 1943, British National Archives, SOE Papers, HS5/242, p. 1. Reprinted in Richard Clogg, ed., *Greece 1940–1949: Occupation, Resistance, Civil War: A Documentary History* (New York: Palgrave, 2002), p. 113.

23. Ioanna Tsatsos, *The Sword's Fierce Edge: A Journal of the Occupation of Greece, 1941–1944* (1965; trans. Jean Demos, Nashville: Vanderbilt University Press, 1965), pp. 12–14.

24. Ibid., pp. 3–4.

25. Boatner, *The Biographical Dictionary of World War II*, p. 635.

26. Woodhouse, *The Struggle for Greece*, p. 29.

27. Major D. J. Wallace, "British Policy and Resistance Movements in Greece," July 14–August 9, 1943, British National Archives, Foreign Office Papers, 371/37213, R8419. Reprinted in Richard Clogg, ed., *Greece 1940–1949*, p. 121.

28. Ibid., pp. 120–126.

29. Ibid., p. 127.

30. Ibid., pp. 126–127.

31. Myers was the single most important British agent in organizing and building the Greek resistance. He was later recalled for having worked too closely with the communists, and he was replaced by his second-in-command, Chris M. Woodhouse. See his memoir, E. C. W. Myers, *Greek Entanglement* (London: Sutton, 1955).

32. Woodhouse, *The Struggle for Greece*, p. 26.

33. Ibid., p. 26.

34. Deák, *Europe on Trial*, p. 161.

35. Mark Mozower, *Inside Hitler's Greece: The Experience of Occupation, 1941–1944* (New Haven: Yale University Press, 1993), p. 144.

36. Ibid., p. 144.

37. Ibid., pp. 144–145.

38. Tsatsos, *The Sword's Fierce Edge*, pp. 97–98.

39. Woodhouse, *The Struggle for Greece*, p. 26.

40. Stafford, *Britain and European Resistance*, p. 124.

41. Tsatsos, *The Sword's Fierce Edge*, p. 124.

42. Ibid., pp. 125–126.

43. See Marcia Christoff Kurapovna, *Shadows on the Mountain: The Allies, the Resistance, and the Rivalries That Doomed World War II Yugoslavia* (Hoboken, NJ: John Wiley, 2010), pp. 48–78.

44. Sabrina P. Ramet, *The Three Yugoslavias: State-Building and Legitimation, 1918–2005* (Bloomington: University of Indiana Press, 2006), pp. 145–150.

45. Kurapovna, *Shadows on the Mountain*, p. 270.

46. Foot, *European Resistance to Nazism,* p. 195.

47. F. W. D. Deakin, *The Embattled Mountain* (New York: Oxford University Press, 1971), pp. 42–43.

48. Kurapovna, *Shadows on the Mountain,* p. 62.

49. See ibid. See also Sir Fitzroy Maclean, *Disputed Barricade: The Life and Times of Josip Broz-Tito, Marshal of Jugoslavia* (London: Jonathan Cape, 1957).

50. "SOE Report on Operations," November 1943, British National Archives, CAB/119/43, p. 1.

51. Ibid., p. 1.

52. O'Donnell, *Operatives, Spies, and Saboteurs,* p. 83.

53. Foot, *European Resistance to Nazism,* p. 196.

54. Ibid., p. 196.

55. Ibid., p. 196.

56. See Ramet, *The Three Yugoslavias,* pp. 145–150.

57. Kurapovna, *Shadows on the Mountain,* p. xii.

58. O'Donnell, *Operatives, Spies, and Saboteurs,* p. 101.

10

"The Sun of Our Grandeur"

The French Resistance and the Liberation,
from D-Day to the Paris Uprising

The elaborate network of organizations and individuals that collectively
made up the French resistance had overcome much by the late spring of
1944. *Résistants* had withstood repression, arrest, torture, and deportation,
but they had also managed to work through their own prolonged internal
struggles over structures, strategies, and command. Throughout the four
years of war, those who made the courageous choice to be a part of the
resistance had lived lives of extreme hardship and stress. Most had been
cut off from their families and all the comforts they had previously known.
For many, particularly those maquisards encamped in the forests, joining
the resistance had meant living like a hunted animal. Through it all, however, there had emerged a principal source of control—de Gaulle's Free
France—and a central command organization with the Conseil National
de la Résistance (CNR), under the legendary André Dewavrin, or "Colonel
Passy." Smaller groups working independently from the CNR still existed,
as well as groups working directly with Britain's SOE. But there had
emerged something like a unified and coordinated effort. While they conducted raids on electric plants, blew up rail tracks, and stealthily reported
reams of intelligence to the Allied High Command, collectively they were
all looking forward to an ultimate objective. It was well understood by this
time that the Allies were planning a massive invasion of the continent and

that that invasion would likely strike somewhere on the north coast of France. When it came, the French were convinced, the moment of their liberation would be at hand. The weapons they had been storing, the ammunition they hijacked from German convoys, the specially trained personnel they had cultivated would all now be thrust into a mass uprising that would see their beloved nation through to liberation.

The fighting, of course, would have to take place not just on the coasts of northern France, but all over the country. The Germans would naturally mobilize in whatever landing zone the Allies chose, but they would need to move tremendous numbers of troops, equipment, and infrastructure to the coastal zone from all over France and the Low Countries. This would require a massive operation on the French railways, highway system, and airfields. To coordinate it all would require intensive use of the telephone and telegraph networks. In view of this, the Allied High Command began to discuss plans with the resistance for its interference in all of these areas. Those in the resistance would find that they were to play an extremely important role in the invasion, a role every bit as dangerous and deadly as any veteran *résistant* expected.

THE RESISTANCE AND OPERATION OVERLORD

The plans for a great invasion of the continent had been in formulation for many months after Allied leaders agreed that a new front had to be opened to relieve the monumental destruction in the Soviet Union. Stalin's insistence on a new front led to the eventual conception of a mass invasion on the northern coast of France and the subsequent master strategy of a convergence upon Germany itself—the Americans and the British pushing east and the Soviets pushing west. The ultimate goal was for these two great forces to enter Germany and meet at the capital city of Berlin. But for this to happen, there would need to be an all-out assault on Hitler's famous "Atlantic Wall," the network of coastal fortifications that protected his western continental empire.

The great expedition was code-named "Operation Overlord," and it remains to this day the largest military expedition ever launched. Obviously, the planning of its logistics, manpower, equipment, strategy, and so on were all matters of extreme importance and involved months of argument and debate. The question of where exactly to land was among these essential issues. Eventually those in charge, primarily supreme Allied commander General Dwight D. Eisenhower, decided upon the series of flat beaches on the northern coasts of the peninsula of Normandy. This was counterintuitive, as the coastline at the northernmost tip of France, near the city of Calais, was geographically the closest point to Great

Britain. Landing there would only require a 90-mile crossing of the English Channel. Because of this, Adolf Hitler remained convinced that this area was the primary landing point for any large-scale invasion to come. The British and the Americans helped Hitler and his staff to maintain this conviction. On the coast of Great Britain just across from Calais, the Allies staged an enormous army. There were miles of barracks, of trucks, tanks, and airplanes lined up as if in preparation for a great offensive. Any aerial reconnaissance by the Germans would reassure the German High Command that Calais was the strike point. This enormous invasion force, however, was almost entirely a phantom. The Allies had used a fake army made up of dummy buildings and equipment to create the illusion of a massive force headed for the north coast of France. It remains, says David Schoenbrun, "one of the most successful hoaxes ever played in the art of intelligence warfare."[1] When the Overlord forces hit the beaches in Normandy, the fighting was fierce and should not be trivialized, particularly at places like "Omaha Beach," where the casualties were horrifying. But in general the landings were made much more viable because the Norman coast was relatively lightly defended by the Germans—the bulk of their defenses were focused around Calais. Even for weeks after the landings, the Germans hesitated to move their forces away from the far northern coast.[2]

The French resistance played a vitally important role in facilitating the landings at the five beaches of Normandy. Those beaches, moving west to east, were codenamed "Utah," "Omaha," "Gold," "Juno," and "Sword." The Utah and Omaha beaches were taken by primarily American troops, Gold and Sword by primarily British troops, and Juno by primarily Canadian troops. For planners, a thorough knowledge of the coastline was absolutely necessary, and a current map including German defenses was not available. The earlier rehearsal for Overlord, the amphibious landing at Dieppe in August 1942, had used aerial scouting and, infamously, *holiday snapshots* to try to assess the landing areas. The Dieppe landing (Operation Jubilee) was an operational disaster, but it taught many lessons. Now, in early 1944, members of Marie-Madeleine Fourcade's Alliance network ("Noah's Ark" to the Germans) combed the coast for intelligence. One figure in particular, a draftsman and high school teacher, Maurice Dounin, risked his life to chart every inch of that coastline. Schoenbrun writes about this forgotten hero, saying that he

> walked and bicycled up and down the coast, sketching every German fortification and taking copious notes for weeks and months.... [I]t proved to be a more than fifty foot map of the beaches and road nets ... Every German gun, every beach obstacle, all military units and their strengths, the most complete, detailed military picture of what had already been selected as the landing sites, were on that map. It was a colossal achievement in espionage.[3]

When the map was completed, an Alliance agent flew it out of France on a Lysander and delivered it to Marie-Madeleine Fourcade. "It was," says Schoenbrun, "one of the proudest moments in the life of Marie-Madeleine Fourcade when she brought the map to the British Secret Service."[4]

With the Allies in possession of a clear and accurate picture of the landing zones, the *résistants* began to plan the actions they would need to carry out for a landing to be effective. They established a series of operations, whose code names are listed below:

Primary Operations

1. Plan Green (*Vert*)   Attacks on the Railway System
2. Plan Blue (*Bleu*)   Attacks on the Electrical Grid and Power Stations
3. Plan Violet (*Purple*) Attacks on the Telephone and Telegraph Systems
4. Plan Tortoise (*Tortue*) Attacks on the French Highway System to Halt Traffic

Secondary Operations

5. Plan Red (*Rouge*)   Attacks on German Ammunition Supplies
6. Plan Yellow (*Jaune*)   Attacks on German Command Posts
7. Plan Black (*Noir*)   Attacks on German Fuel Depots[5]

For each operation, the appropriate staff was assigned and equipment assessed and distributed. The objective was clear—to completely paralyze the Nazi defense effort outside Normandy, in order to minimize the men and equipment facing Allied troops in their initial efforts to secure a foothold.

As the time for launching the invasion approached, the Allied High Command informed Charles de Gaulle that the invasion was imminent but did not share with him the precise details. This led to further rancor between him and the Americans and especially Churchill. De Gaulle consistently requested more information, personal participation, and a prominent role for the Free French troops. All these things were considered secondary and of minimal importance in the face of such a daunting operation. Among the issues of disagreement was the question of a radio address to the people of France at the moment of the invasion. Eisenhower would give this address and insist that the Allied military forces were in command and their orders must be followed. De Gaulle resented not delivering the primary message, and above all he wanted to insist that the people of France would follow only the Free French leadership. When Eisenhower offered him the opportunity to take part in a set of broadcasts from the various leaders of the governments-in-exile, de Gaulle refused and insisted upon his own separate address later. He eventually got his way, though once again causing resentment on all sides. On the evening of June 6, with fighting still raging on the beaches and in coastal towns, he spoke:

> The Supreme battle has begun. It is the battle in France and it is the battle of France. France is going to fight this battle furiously. She is going to conduct it in due order. The clear, the sacred, duty of the sons of France, wherever they are and whoever they are, is to fight the enemy with all the means at their disposal. The orders given by the French government and by the French leaders it has named for that purpose [must be] obeyed exactly. The actions we carry out in the enemy's rear [must be] coordinated as closely as possible with those carried out at the same time by the Allied and French armies. . . . The Battle of France has begun. In the nation, the Empire and the armies, there is no longer anything but one single hope, the same for all. Behind the terribly heavy cloud of our blood and our tears here is the sun of our grandeur shining out once again.[6]

The people of France responded all over the nation.

Before the landings took place, on June 4 officers of the French government in London received their first notifications that the invasion was on. That evening just after 11:30, the BBC delivered its usual broadcast "Personal Messages," which was generally loaded with coded messages to the various resistance groups around Europe. Amongst the strange code phrases, one rang out in the ears of French officials: "It is hot in Suez." This had been the agreed-upon phrase to launch a general mobilization of the resistance all over the country. Later that night the BBC announcer pronounced a second coded message: "The arrow will not pierce." This was the specific signal to put operations Green and Violet into immediate action.[7] The chiefs of the resistance in London began sending their signals to the men and women in the field, and the resistance charged into action.

According to a top-secret report compiled after Operation Overlord, the French resistance performed magnificently in the hours leading to and immediately after the landings on the Norman beaches. The report says, "The D-day plans were executed with efficiency and dispatch. Prearranged railway targets were attacked all over the country and the general chaos was enhanced by spontaneous acts."[8] In addition to freezing German troops in place and cutting communications, the resistance sabotage did something else that contributed to more effective assaults by Allied aircraft. The report goes on to say, "The local congestion built up valuable targets for the Air Force: For instance, at Lille 51 trains were held up at once."[9] Such buildups on the railways and roads produced clear targets for Allied bombing and strafing. In all, says the report, 486 rail lines were cut by sabotage and 180 different German trains were derailed in the period during and immediately after the Overlord landings. And the pace of attack only grew. In the months that followed, says the report, "the nine main arteries in the North were still being cut from two to five times daily; and by August, 668 locomotives had been destroyed and 2,900 attacks on railways had been reported . . . The confusion on the railways drove the enemy to the employment of road transport."[10] But here again the French were waiting; they constantly blocked the highways by cutting hundreds of trees and stacking them across the roads. When a German convoy was stopped and had to disembark to clear the road, an armed resistance group could open fire on it in open ambush. What was the overall effect? According to the report,

> The effect of all this activity, combined with the action of the Allied Air Forces, was tremendous. The German troops moving to the bridgehead area found their communications everywhere in a state of chaos, and it was esti-mated that the normal delay on the forward movement of their advance was between 48 and 72 hours, while in exceptional areas it was much longer. When they finally reached the battle area, they were frequently in a state of considerable disorganization, short of vehicles, equipment, and men.[11]

Years later, the overall commander of Operation Overlord, General Eisen-hower, shared his perceptions with Schoenbrun, who had been an Ameri-can operative in France. Eisenhower said, "I knew as much and probably more about German rail transport than Rommel or von Runstedt. The French Resistance was magnificent. The railway men not only kept us informed of all the movements but, over and over again, they impeded the transport of German trains, holding them up as much as thirty-six hours, enough to help turn the tide of battle in our favor, particularly when we were still inside the beachheads of Normandy."[12] General Omar Bradley, who was in overall command of the forces on the ground in Nor-mandy, recalled, "I don't know how many divisions the Resistance shot up or bottled up. But I can tell you this: the French Resistance was worth a hell of a lot of divisions to us. We needed them, and they were there when needed."[13]

There is little debate about the effectiveness of the overall resistance contribution to the Allied military effort in establishing its beachheads and then advancing eastward into France. During June, July, and August, the Germans were constantly hampered by resistance sabotage that kept thou-sands of Germans from timely arrival for battle. But sabotage and interfer-ence was not the only kind of action taking place. Nearly all shades of the resistance did what they could to mobilize armed soldiers against the Nazis in combat. Here the reports are far less inspiring and the statistics generally grim. Allied and Free French leaders had never intended for the resistance to come out into the open in direct combat with large Nazi armies. This strategy had always been far too costly and would prove so again.

The leaders of Free France had made yet another organizational change in the days leading up to Operation Overlord, creating an umbrella organization to unify all of the armed resistance fighters. The organization was named the Forces Françaises de l'Intérieur (FFI) and put under the command of General Marie-Pierre Kœnig. Kœnig's command was formally recognized by Eisenhower on June 23, 1944. But in the days immediately after the Overlord landings, Kœnig and his staff were busily attempting to unify all of the many armed factions of the various movements. These included the main branches of the CNR but also some independent communists and Maquis groups. All armed groups were now collectively referred to as members of the FFI, but in reality many of them were still operating independently as local circumstances dictated.

Now, as the Allies made their way west from the beaches of Normandy, armed civilian resisters challenged the Germans in combat. It was almost always a bloodbath. As a result, the Free French, worried about these "ill-armed and ill-prepared *résistants*," tried at once to "stop the wave of action."[14] General Kœnig issued a general notification as a telegram that read as follows:

> Put Maximum brake on guerilla action stop Currently impossible to supply arms and ammunition in sufficient quantities stop Wherever possible break off attacks to allow reorganization stop Avoid large groupings Form Small isolated groups.[15]

In some places the action was curbed, but in others it went on. In the village Oradour-sur-Glane, such fighting resulted in a tragic massacre. The local German commander of the "Das Reich" battalion (2nd Panzer Division) learned that a Waffen SS officer had been taken prisoner by the resistance in the fighting. A standoff ensued. The Germans immediately took 30 hostages, and on June 10 they sealed off the town. They rounded up all the inhabitants, putting most of the women and children in the town's church and the men in a group of barns. The Nazis gunned down the men with machine guns; many were shot in the legs so they couldn't move. Then the Germans set the barns on fire, where as many as 190 men burned to death. The Nazis then moved on the church. They threw in firebombs, which forced the women and children to run out of the exits, only to be gunned down. When the massacre was over, some 642 people lay dead. Only a single woman, Marguerite Rouffanche, survived to tell the awful story. She played dead after she had been hit by gunfire. Hours later, after the Germans left, locals from a nearby village came to inspect and check for survivors. Mme. Rouffanche was the only survivor they found, and she was taken to safety and medical care.[16] Incidents like the one at Oradour-sur-Glane were the inevitable cost if French civilians, with only small arms, were going to rise up instead of a fully prepared army.

At this same time, the Maquis in southeastern France made a stand of its own that has passed into legend. The region known as Vercors had been a magnet for the Maquis from its inception. Its geography consisted of a vast plateau with large expanses of wild forests, which was a perfect location for their secret army. With the coming of the D-Day landings, the leaders of the Vercors Maquis began preparations for a large-scale uprising. Their principal contacts were the Free French leaders in Algiers in French North Africa. After receiving messages from Algiers about the beginning of the liberation, the highest-ranking commander of the Maquis, Colonel Marcel Descour, began to secure the entire area. Roads were sealed off with barriers, trenches dug, and troops dispersed to turn their vast area into a sealed camp. They were preparing to declare the area under their control as a "liberated" part of France. In these days of early June, hundreds of locals began to flock to the plateau to join this resistance group. The historian Matthew Cobb says that in just weeks, the Maquis there grew from a force of only about 400 to over 4,000.[17] They brought with them the resources they could. In the days that followed D-Day, the Maquis leaders declared Vercors a liberated zone and an independent republic. They produced uniforms for the fighting men, began printing their own "national" newspaper, and even established their own court system. In a provocative move, they raised the French tricolor flag every morning on a hilltop, well in view of the German troops massed around them. While the maquisards gloried in their defiance and scrambled to secure and organize what resources they had, the Germans watched and planned. The Allies, made aware of the Vercors "liberation," dropped supplies, most being delivered, symbolically, on Bastille Day, July 14. But the Germans had aircraft to chase away the Allied planes, and to bomb and strafe any of the maquisards who tried to collect the supplies. As a result, only about half of these supplies and weapons ever made it into resistance hands.[18]

On July 21 the luck of the Maquis ran out. The Germans launched an all-out attack on the Vercors plateau including about 10,000 troops, tanks, and heavy artillery. SS troops were flown via gliders right into the heart of Maquis territory and began destroying the French resistance from behind the lines. Over the course of about one week, the Germans wore down the French defenses, and the French suffered from their customary handicap—they had neither the heavy weaponry nor the ammunition supplies to survive a fight in open combat. Just as it had always been, when the maquisards faced full Nazi battalions in the open, they lost whatever advantages they possessed; stealth, mobility, and surprise were all lost in conventional combat. Predictably, the maquisards were savagely defeated, with the survivors fleeing into the hills, and much of the civilian community was massacred in retribution by the infuriated Nazi commanders. In all, 326 resistance members and 130 civilians were killed, and the independent state of Vercors evaporated.[19]

But heavy fighting in the southern part of France did not end with the Vercors defeat. In fact, it was only beginning. On August 15, another massive Allied landing force hit the beaches on France's southern Mediterranean coast. This second mass landing was code-named "Operation Dragoon" and had been initially planned to take place alongside the Overlord landings. The shortage of resources prompted Allied planners to abandon it, but with Overlord's success and the early initial push into the French interior, it was clear that supplying the advancing armies from the overwhelmed Normandy ports would be a challenge. A new supply line would be extremely helpful, as would a second front that would divert German troops away from the north. The Mediterranean landings also provided an opportunity for Free French troops to play a more important and visible role in the recovery of their own country.

The actual landings were lightly defended, but the advances into major cities generated serious combat. Two areas of particularly fierce combat were the seaports of Toulon and Marseille, both strongly defended by German troops. In the fighting for these two cities, however, the secretive armed French resistance (now nominally under the FFI) suddenly rose up in the middle of the cities. Instantly, German troops found their enemies not just at the gates of the city, but all around them. The French FFI fighters fought valiantly and played significant roles in defeating the Nazi occupation troops in both cities, each seeing liberation by August 28. Such intense combat was not the norm, and in many French cities the resistance was not called upon. Either the Allied armies overwhelmed the German forces very quickly, or the Germans simply left on their own as part of larger retreats. Cobb tells us that during the period of liberation of 212 major French towns, 84 percent were liberated without any intense fighting required from the local resistance forces.[20] On September 2, the Germans evacuated the large city of Lyon, which had been almost a headquarters for the French resistance. In the south, the major cities of Toulon, Marseille, and Lyon were liberated with relative ease, but Paris, the nation's political and spiritual capital, would not come so easily.

THE UPRISING AND THE LIBERATION OF PARIS

Paris was of the utmost importance to the French people and particularly to the leader of Free France, Charles de Gaulle. Perhaps in no other large country in the world are the nation's identity and its affairs so bound up with a single city. When Paris fell in 1940, it was a clear indicator that France had fallen and that there was no reason to continue the fight. Now, de Gaulle believed, the liberation of Paris would signal and symbolize the liberation of all France. Unfortunately for him, the Allied High Command did not share his view. The long and tortuous path from the Norman beaches, across northern France, and across the German border would bypass Paris, which lay miles to the south. It might seem that Paris would be a key supplier of resources to the Allied armies, but in fact Paris represented a logistics and supply nightmare. If Paris were liberated, its vast population of ordinary people would become dependent upon Allied supplies of food, clothing, policing, medical care, and so on. It would mean the Allies diverting tons of desperately needed food and supplies away from their armies to feed a great urban population. Simply put, Paris may have been of *symbolic* value, but it was of no *strategic* value—in fact it was a great strategic liability. As General Omar Bradley remarked, "Behind its handsome façades there lived four million hungry Frenchmen"; he said that "food for the people of Paris meant less gasoline for the front."[21] Allied commanders hoped that de Gaulle and his staff would come to understand this.

But of course there never was any chance that General de Gaulle would agree to bypassing Paris, leaving its liberation to a later date. He and the Free French leadership continued to pressure the Allied commanders for the liberation of Paris as an urgent priority. Both the supreme headquarters and the Free French agreed, however, on one important point: that there should be no popular uprising in Paris. Eisenhower issued strict orders to this effect to de Gaulle and the FFI.[22] De Gaulle was in full agreement, for he harbored deep fears about the size of the communist political organization within the resistance in Paris. Should a rising occur outside the control of his own government, the communists might well elbow themselves into control. Likewise, should an Allied military force liberate Paris without de Gaulle himself or Free French troops present, any number of groups might be in a position to displace de Gaulle's authority. For these reasons de Gaulle's government did not favor a popular uprising in Paris. But events overtook both de Gaulle and the Allied commanders.

Inside Paris, the German authorities remained in control and the routines of Nazi repression continued. As late as August 15, the SS deported some 3,000 jailed *résistants* to the concentration camps.[23] But the D-Day landings and the reality of the Allied advance had changed the atmosphere among the people. On Bastille Day, for instance, there had been an enormous popular demonstration with nearly 100,000 Parisians celebrating in the streets. There were also a number of workers' strikes, in which the workers linked their professional objectives to liberation. The man tasked with maintaining German authority against such agitation was Major General Dietrich von Choltitz. Von Choltitz had made his reputation in the brutal fighting on the Soviet front and had come to be known as a man who would follow orders to the letter. He was later involved in the fighting in Italy, and he was appointed military governor of Paris by Hitler on August 7, 1944. Called to Berlin the following day, von Choltitz met with Hitler and received a startling directive. Clearly he was to maintain order through whatever means necessary, but if Paris were to be lost to the Allies, then it fell to von Choltitz to destroy the city—to obliterate the most beautiful and historic city in the world. Would the good soldier follow this order?

By August 18 the resistance organizations inside Paris had been in heated discussions about what to do. Clearly the Allied armies were not headed for Paris anytime in the near future. The FFI had gotten clear orders not to stage a mass uprising. But many others were convinced that the Germans were in a weakened condition and the time was ripe to throw the occupiers out. If the Allied armies would not do it, they could do it themselves. This argument was most urgently pressed by the leaders of the Military Action Committee (COMAC), a division within the CNR. Its leaders were mostly communists, and it was closely linked with the communist labor and resistance organizations.[24] With COMAC resolved to take action, the FFI officers came to agree or simply saw no other choice. On August 19 their plans for the uprising went into effect. But as the printed pamphlets were being taken out to be distributed all over the city, it was seen that the police of Paris had taken a major step of their own. During the night, the police, who were on strike, had taken control of the prefecture police building, directly facing Notre-Dame Cathedral. It would prove to be a key area of fighting throughout the uprising. As the notices went out, cells all over town quickly moved into action and seized local institutions. Resistance groups moved into town halls, telephone exchanges, and any government buildings they could find that were occupied by occupation authorities. Known collaborators were taken prisoner, and many were simply put against walls and shot. The Germans began to realize they had a mass rising on their hands.

The top resistance commander was Colonel Henri Tanguy, who was known by the code name "Colonel Rol." From that point he became known as "Rol-Tanguy." He and his command staff set up their headquarters in a series of underground bunkers at the Place Denfert-Rocherau in the south Paris district of Montparnasse.[25] Rol-Tanguy had telephone service here and was in contact with all the major group actions around the city. The Germans moved immediately to challenge the seizures by the resistance, and with that, prolonged gun battles ensued. The people of Paris built barricades across the smaller streets, and those who could find arms and ammunition took up positions and fired on the Nazis. The Germans still had tanks and large guns at their disposal, but the widespread nature of the uprising had troops dispersed in all directions. There were approximately 20,000 German troops facing about 20,000 formal resistance fighters, but the civilians of Paris now poured into the ranks of the fighters, as did former Vichy police and officials. The fighting was especially vicious at the prefecture police building and across the Seine, where *résistants* eventually took the Hôtel de Ville (City Hall).

Some of the leaders of the FFI who had argued against the rising were alarmed by the scale of the fighting and the lack of central control. They began to work with the Swedish consul in Paris, Raoul Nordling, to negotiate a ceasefire with General von Choltitz. Nordling went to von Choltitz's offices in the hotel le Meurice, which overlooked the Tuileries Garden. From the general, Nordling heard of the potential for Paris's destruction, but Nordling pled with him for restraint. A ceasefire was negotiated, but fighting erupted again after only a day, and the ceasefire was abandoned. Nordling again met with von Choltitz, patiently discussing options and pleading for calm in the face of the violence. In the end, von Choltitz made the decision not to destroy the city. Preparations certainly had been made, and when the uprising was over and Paris finally was liberated, the explosives and detonator wires were found packed at the feet of Paris's most iconic monuments, like the Eiffel Tower. The true motives of von Choltitz may never be known, but it seems most probable that by this time he considered Hitler to be mad and thought the loss of Paris and the war were inevitable. In the custody of the Allies, "the man who destroyed Paris" would most certainly be executed for war crimes, and his name would live forever among history's most notorious villains. He would stand a much better chance of survival if he could position himself as "the man who saved Paris." He was somewhat successful in this, and he managed to survive the war. After a brief captivity in the United States, he was released; no formal charges were ever filed against the man who had overseen the liquidation of the Jews in his districts of the Soviet Union. It seems highly likely that his restraint in Paris saved his life.

As the fighting raged in Paris, the news made its way to the Allied commanders progressing across northern France. One French resistance officer, Roger Cocteau (code-named "Gallois"), escaped the city and went to the camp of General George S. Patton. His reports on the Parisian situation convinced the Allied High Command to change its plans and send divisions into Paris to prevent further bloodshed and chaos. To lead the armies into the city, it had long ago been decided that Free French troops should be used under the leadership of General Philippe Leclerc. Another U.S. division would accompany the Free French, but it was Leclerc's troops who made the initial entry into Paris on August 23. There was intense fighting between German, French, and American troops, but by August 25 the Germans were all but defeated. General von Choltitz faced the painful reality and went to the headquarters of General Leclerc, where he signed surrender documents. After more than four dreadful years, Paris was free once more.

Within hours General de Gaulle was driven into the city, where he immediately met with General Leclerc and leaders of the resistance. They eventually made their way to the Hôtel de Ville, where de Gaulle made a rousing speech, formally announcing the liberation of Paris and at the same time his declaration that the French state was in control. The following day a great parade was staged, which began at the Arc de Triomphe, proceeded down the Champs-Élysées, and ended at the Notre-Dame Cathedral. De Gaulle was adamant that he would lead the parade, symbolizing his government's complete control of the state, but key members of the Free French army and the resistance marched behind him. From that parade came our most iconic images of the liberation, but there was also some terror in the ceremony. Gunfire broke out during the march, sending the massive crowd rushing for cover, and briefly there was a dangerous and chaotic scramble. But de Gaulle held his place in the parade, and it was seen through to completion. In the days that followed, there would be terrifying incidents of retribution as collaborators were denounced, often by resistance members, but also simply by large mobs. Women who had dated German occupation soldiers were called "horizontal collaborators" and, if caught, had their heads shaved for public humiliation. As for the resistance organizations themselves, de Gaulle instituted a policy that immediately disbanded and disarmed the resistance groups across France with every liberated region. The fighters of the resistance were channeled immediately into the conventional Free French army, while many of the resisters, including women, now simply went back to their prewar lives and returned to the mundane tasks of everyday existence. For many, the excitement and purpose of their time in the resistance was the highlight of their lives, which made adjusting to civilian life quite difficult indeed.

When the war was over and all of France liberated, the country established a new parliamentary republic, the Fourth Republic, which took France through the 1940s and into the 1950s. A large number of key officials in the resistance became important figures in French politics. The Vichy authorities, on the other hand, were permanently discredited. Marshal Pétain and Pierre Laval were tried for high treason and sentenced to death. Laval's sentence was carried out, but Pétain's was commuted. He lived the rest of his life in prison on the tiny Île d'Yeu, just off France's Atlantic coast. He died there on July 23, 1951, at age 95 and was buried on the prison grounds. Charles de Gaulle was not impressed by the new republic, finding it too factional and left-leaning for his taste, and he retired from government to his family's estate. But in 1958, in the midst of a constitutional crisis, de Gaulle would return and take charge of the French government once again, changing its constitution and establishing the Fifth Republic. He remained the president of France until his death in 1970.

France continues to memorialize its remarkable resisters, and scholarship continues to accumulate on this rich historical subject. New works, like Robert Gildea's *Fighters in the Shadows*, are emphasizing the roles of lesser-known *résistants*, particularly communists, Jews, and women. Other

De Gaulle leads the parade down the Champs Elysee at the liberation of Paris. France's resistance leaders follow behind. (AP Photo)

works are exploring the experiences of ordinary families as they faced the harrowing choice of whether or not to take on the risks of resistance. To make the choice of active resistance meant that one would never have a moment's safety; one would face the very real prospect of arrest, torture, and execution. It is not always as well understood that one also imposed these risks on friends and family. Still, thousands of courageous men and women signed up for this terrifying responsibility and, in so doing, helped to rescue the dignity of their nation. As one French operative, the Baron de Vomécourt, one of three brothers who all worked for the SOE in France, put it so well, "Had all of us in France meekly, lawfully carried out the orders of the German master, no Frenchman could have ever looked another man in the face. Such submission would have saved the lives of many—some very dear to me—but France would have lost its soul."[26] Thanks in great part to the men and women of the resistance, it did not.

NOTES

1. Schoenbrun, *Soldiers of the Night,* p. 366.

2. In fact, this deception was even larger in scale. Known as "Operation Fortitude," the operation staged two false or phantom forces. "Fortitude North" near Edinburgh was intended to convince the Nazis of an impending attack on the

Norwegian coast. The other, "Fortitude South," was staged on Britain's southwest coast to create the illusion of a force headed for Pas-de-Calais.

3. Schoenbrun, *Soldiers of the Night*, p. 366.

4. Ibid., p. 366.

5. See Matthew Cobb, *The Resistance: The French Fight Against the Nazis* (London: Pocket Books, 2009), p. 245.

6. Lacouture, *De Gaulle: The Rebel*, pp. 525–526.

7. Schoenbrun, *Soldiers of the Night*, p. 358.

8. "SOE Assistance to Overlord," British National Archives, HS/8/300, p. 12.

9. Ibid., p. 12.

10. Ibid., p. 12.

11. Ibid., p. 12.

12. Schoenbrun, *Soldiers of the Night*, pp. 372–373.

13. Ibid., p. 374.

14. Cobb, *The Resistance*, p. 250.

15. Telegram from General Kœnig to FFI chiefs, quoted in Cobb, *The Resistance*, p. 250.

16. Ibid., p. 250.

17. Ibid., p. 251.

18. Ibid., p. 252.

19. For a thorough treatment of this remarkable episode of the war, see Paddy Ashdown, *The Cruel Victory: The French Resistance, D-Day, and the Battle of the Vercors, 1944* (London: HarperCollins, 2014).

20. Cobb, *The Resistance*, p. 257.

21. Ibid., p. 259.

22. Schoenbrun, *Soldiers of the Night*, p. 424.

23. Cobb, *The Resistance*, p. 258.

24. Schoenbrun, *Soldiers of the Night*, p. 428.

25. Today this square is the site of the Paris catacombs museum.

26. Baron de Vomécourt, quoted in Kaiser, *The Cost of Courage*, p. 43.

Conclusion

With our survey completed of the most prominent resistance movements across Europe during the Second World War, a set of questions emerges that leads us to the drawing of conclusions. First and foremost is this question: Did the resistance movements contribute in a meaningful way toward winning the war? Put another way, one might ask, was it all worth it? One wonders if a clinical "cost–benefit analysis" can ever be constructed for such an enormous set of activities across so many nations, with so much information still unknown. The *costs* of the resistance movements are difficult to add up and have yet to be quantified in total. How many people died in resistance operations? How many innocent civilians were slaughtered as a result of minor accomplishments by the resistance groups? How many military movements were betrayed by resistance members under interrogation and torture? As difficult as it is to calculate the costs of the resistance, calculating the *benefits* is surely just as difficult, perhaps more so. How can one measure the benefits of factory slowdowns, sabotaging weapons, or cutting off the supply of heavy water to the German nuclear program? Certainly some have questioned the value and the importance of the resistance movements. One historian of the SOE, Alan Milward, has concluded that the SOE's operations were "seldom effective, sometimes stultifying, frequently dangerous, and almost always too costly."[1] One of the most prestigious military historians writing in the English language, John Keegan, wrote in his 1989 book, *The Second World War*, that we should not lose sight of the fact that it was the overwhelming force of the Allied armies engaged in murderous battles against Axis armies that won the war. It was certainly not the work of the resistance effort and the SOE. Concentrating on the failed uprisings such as Warsaw and Vercors, he says that these kinds of uprisings "typify in their outcome the unintended effect of the program of subversion, sabotage, and resistance which Churchill, later abetted by Roosevelt and the European governments in exile, so ardently supported after June 1940," and hence, he goes on to say, they "must be adjudged a costly and misguided failure."[2] Set against the large-scale slaughter at places like Warsaw, Lidice, and Oradour-sur-Glane, he writes that these movements "must be seen, by any objective reckoning, as irrelevant and pointless acts of bravado."[3] But such opinions may be changing, and perhaps the expansion of the documentary evidence and the growing body of literature are helping to create that change. As the historian István Deák has recently written,

> It is nearly impossible to calculate the damage the European resistance movements caused to the enemy. Western historians, especially of the career military type, like to believe that the resistance did not seriously weaken the German war machine. Judging by the World War II experiences of Poland, the Soviet Union, and Yugoslavia as well as by the later deadly efficiency of the anti-Soviet guerrillas in Afghanistan and the Vietcong fighting the Americans in Vietnam, such arguments are no longer completely satisfactory.[4]

As we have surveyed the various shapes that resistance could take, perhaps it is worth questioning the value of the resistance beyond the damage it caused in individual operations. As Deák indicates, and as newer research is making clear, in places like Yugoslavia and the Soviet Union, the partisan movement caused a lot of damage and killed large numbers of Germans. But as we have reviewed the many areas of the occupied continent, we have seen that the resistance certainly did something else. The disorder caused by the resistance groups kept the Axis forces on constant alert in many places where they might otherwise have been able to let down their guard. We have seen that in Norway, some 300,000 German troops were used to maintain the occupation there through the end of the war—300,000 troops that could have been wreaking havoc on the Western Front. In Denmark, 40,000 German troops remained in that country rather than being sent into combat on the Western Front. We have also seen how acceleration of resistance activity was used to create diversions, convincing the Axis that landings were imminent in locations such as Greece in the summer of 1943. In response, the Nazi troop levels in Greece were increased and no troops from Greece or Yugoslavia were moved to Italy, where the actual landings took place. In Italy during the final offensive in April 1945, the partisans marched ahead of the Allied armies. The historian M. R. D. Foot quotes one Italian official as saying, "The partisans took in that month alone 40,000 German and Fascist prisoners, and liberated over a hundred towns before the Allied armies reached them . . . By armed force, they helped to break the strength and the morale of an enemy well superior to them in numbers. Without the partisans' victories there could not have been an Allied victory in Italy so fast, so complete, and with such light casualties."[5] In all these kinds of operations, the accomplishments of the resistance groups point to large numbers of conventional army lives saved.

Certainly the intelligence gathered by the resistance groups was vital as well. And it seems highly unlikely that so much key information could have been gathered only using existing intelligence networks through Britain's SIS, for instance. The development of large-scale resistance forces greatly expanded the amount of vital information passed to the Allies. As we have seen, information regarding troop levels and coastal fortifications proved crucial. Was intelligence all that important relative to sheer military force? To turn the question around, there are prominent examples of military commanders ignoring or misinterpreting pertinent information from the resistance. The most tragic cases that come to mind are Operation Market Garden in Holland during September 1944 and the Battle of the Bulge in December 1944. In Market Garden, the Dutch resistance and aerial photos provided information about German troops stationed at areas key to the operation's success. Debate, however, continues to rage about the High Command's disregard for this information.[6] In the Battle of the Bulge, the American intelligence team had accumulated information about large German troop buildups behind their lines. This was interpreted by some to mean that the Germans were preparing a major offensive. Others did not see it this way. In both cases the dismissal or misinterpretation of intelligence led to enormous casualties, and in the case of Market Garden to an utterly failed operation.[7]

This is not to say that the resistance movements' practical achievements were decisive in defeating the Axis powers. It is difficult to argue with Keegan's assessment that final victory was, and could only have been, achieved by the sacrifice and force of large-scale armies. But that the resistance made direct military contributions and saved a tremendous number of lives, though impossible to quantify, seems just as difficult to refute. But beyond the direct military contributions of the number of soldiers killed, the number of soldiers detained or diverted, the number of equipment failures caused, and the like, another area must be considered. In writing this survey, the author became increasingly aware of the contributions that resistance groups made to the psychological state of the occupied population. In places like Norway, ordinary people refused to join Nazi professional organizations, teachers refused to teach Nazi curriculums in their classes, and workers went on strike. In Denmark, the population refused to allow the Jewish population to be deported and gassed. In Greece, the knowledge of the resistance in the hills gave Ioanna Tsatsos the hope and encouragement to continue her assistance of the poor and destitute. The very fact that the resistance existed helped to sustain masses of ordinary people. In each of the occupied countries (with the notable exception of Poland), there was a small group of enthusiastic supporters of Nazism or fascism, such as Quisling's party in Norway or Pétain's Milice in France. These supporters were anxious to become part of the "New Order," and many of them would actually join the Axis military forces and fight in places like the Soviet Union. Despite this, in every occupied country the vast majority of the population did not enthusiastically embrace or even cooperate with Nazism or fascism. This is surely significant. Had the general populations of places like Norway, Denmark, the Netherlands, Belgium, France, Yugoslavia, or Greece become enthusiastic supporters of Axis rule, they almost certainly would have been integrated into the German and Italian armed forces in staggering numbers. Had the Axis been able to add these millions of additional bodies to its war machine, it is possible that the war would not have had the outcome it did. This cannot be known, and it is frivolous for the historian to engage in "what-ifs." But what is certain is that had the Nazis felt they could trust and rely on the occupied peoples enough to arm them, the Nazi military would have been enlarged by the millions. But this did not happen. The circulation of resistance information, hearing news of successful resistance operations, even listening to the BBC—all helped convince the people of occupied Europe that there *was* hope, and that resigning themselves to accept the Nazi way of life was not the only alternative.

If one accepts that the various resistance movements did make important contributions to winning the war, another question that emerges is the question of outside assistance. Could the various national groups have mounted significant movements without the outside help from the SOE, the OSS, and Soviet High Command? The accumulation of evidence suggests that the movements would have been very small indeed and could not have made nearly the contribution they did. For one thing, outside groups like the SOE provided special training in vital skills, and vital new kinds of equipment. It is possible that the various groups could have come up with a corps of experts for such training and invention, but this seems extremely unlikely. The repressive environment of the occupation authorities made this nearly impossible. For the movements that operated from the hills, they received only small amounts of food from the outside, and they generally seem to have relied on local communities and on their own enterprise. But the matter of weaponry is crucial. There seems to be no way, under the conditions of occupation, that resistance groups could have gotten anywhere near the amount and type of armaments they were provided by the SOE and the OSS. Resistance groups complained constantly of needing more and larger weapons and ammunition. This suggests that they were unable to make up any gaps on their own, and that had not the Soviets, the SOE, or the OSS helped with their supplies, their weapons would have been inadequate to create a meaningful armed challenge.

A final conclusion relates to the personal character of those who made the courageous choice to become active resisters. That these people were brave, intelligent, and enterprising is beyond question. Certainly some were more so than others, but all faced tremendous challenges on a daily basis, including the challenge of constant stress and fear. These attributes have been well documented, and deservedly so. Beyond this, though, another dimension to the experience of the resistance fighter is emerging from the growing literature. Resisters could deal easily enough with their choice to fight a vile and hateful enemy. If harm came to them, there was generally little regret about their decision. But for nearly all resisters, there was also the agonizing reality that their resistance activity endangered other people besides themselves. Resisters who were caught not only suffered severe torture and execution, but often their innocent friends or family members were put through the same hell. This book has been full of such examples, such as the innocent and clueless members of the Moravec family who paid with their lives for their mother's involvement with the Czech resistance. The assassins who killed Heydrich, of course, inspired the Nazis to wipe out an entire village full of innocent people. Another example is the resistance work of Christiane and André Boulloche in France. The Nazis, having become aware of André and Christiane's activities, arrested their parents and older brother and shipped them off to concentration camps, where they perished. Christiane and André carried this terrible knowledge for the rest of their lives. For those concerned with the history of the period and the history of this remarkable subject, it is important to understand that terrible burden of responsibility that weighed upon the shoulders of any individual who made the courageous choice to resist. We have a growing understanding of the terrors they faced and the burdens they carried, yet so many of them still made the decision to actively fight for a better future. We must surely, today, be grateful they did.

NOTES

1. Alan Milward, "The Economic and Strategic Effectiveness of Resistance," in Stephen Hawes and Ralph White, eds., *Resistance in Europe, 1939–1945* (New York: Viking, 1976), pp. 186–203.

2. John Keegan, *The Second World War* (London: Hutchinson, 1989), p. 484.

3. Ibid., pp. 484–485.

4. Deák, *Europe on Trial*, p. 149.

5. See Foot, *Resistance*, p. 228.

6. See Ryan, *A Bridge Too Far*, pp. 159–160.

7. Operation Market Garden was plagued by numerous problems involving logistics, equipment, poor maps, and at times simply bad luck; but certainly ignoring the presence of German armored divisions must be considered a contributing factor.

Bibliography

ARCHIVAL MATERIALS
British National Archives at Kew
War Office Records
Cabinet Papers
SOE Papers

DOCUMENTARY READERS

Clogg, Richard, ed. *Greece 1940–1949: Occupation, Resistance, Civil War: A Documentary History.* New York: Palgrave, 2002.
Noakes, Jeremy, and Geoffrey Pridham, eds. *Documents on Nazism, 1919–1945.* New York: Viking, 1975.
Zander, Patrick G. *The Rise of Fascism: History, Documents, and Key Questions.* Santa Barbara: ABC-CLIO, 2016.

PRIMARY SOURCES AND PERSONAL ACCOUNTS

Bialoszewski, Miron. *A Memoir of the Warsaw Uprising.* Translated by Madeleine Levine. Ann Arbor: Ardis, 1977.
Ciano, Count Galeazzo. *The Ciano Diaries, 1938–1943.* Garden City: Doubleday, 1946.
Deakin, F. W. D. *The Embattled Mountain.* New York: Oxford, 1971.
Dulles, Allen. *Germany's Underground.* New York: Macmillan, 1947.
Fourcade, Marie-Madeleine. *Noah's Ark.* Translated by Kenneth Morgan. New York: Dutton, 1974.
Giskes, H. J. *London Calling North Pole.* London: British Book Center, 1953.
Gobetti, Ada. *Partisan Diary: A Woman's Life in the Italian Resistance.* Translated and edited by Jomarie Alano. New York: Oxford, 2014.

Hitler, Adolf. *Mein Kampf.* Translated by Ralph Manheim. New York: Houghton Mifflin, 1971 [1925].

Kieler, Jorgen. *Resistance Fighter: A Personal History of the Danish Resistance Movement, 1940–1945.* New York: Gefen, 2007.

Meerlo, Thomas. *Total War and the Human Mind: A Psychologist's Experiences in Occupied Holland.* New York: International University Press, 1945.

Moravec, František. *Master of Spies: The Memoirs of František Moravec.* New York: Doubleday, 1975.

Myers, E. C. W. *Greek Entanglement.* Revised edition. London: Sutton, 1985 [1955].

Special Operations Executive Manual: How to Be an Agent in Occupied Europe. London: British National Archives, 2014 (reprint).

Tsatsos, Jeanne. *The Sword's Fierce Edge: A Journal of the Occupation of Greece, 1941–1944.* Translated by Jean Demos. Nashville: Vanderbilt, 1969.

SECONDARY SOURCES

Ashdown, Paddy. *The Cruel Victory: The French Resistance, D-Day, and the Battle for the Vercors, 1944.* London: HarperCollins, 2014.

Auty, Phyllis. *Tito: A Biography.* New York: McGraw Hill, 1970.

Beevor, Antony. *The Second World War.* New York: Little Brown, 2012.

Beevor, Antony. *The Battle for Spain. The Spanish Civil War, 1936–1939.* New York: Penguin, 2006.

Behan, Tom. *The Italian Resistance: Fascists, Guerillas, and the Allies.* New York: Pluto, 2009.

Boatner, Mark M. *The Biographical Dictionary of World War II.* Navato, CA: Presidio Press, 1996.

Borodziej, Wlodzimierz. *The Warsaw Uprising of 1944.* Translated by Barbara Harshave. Madison: Wisconsin University Press, 2006.

Boswroth, R. J. B. *The Italian Dictatorship: Problems and Perspectives in the Interpretation of Mussolini and Fascism.* London: Arnold, 1998.

Charles Rivers, ed. *The Assassination of Reinhard Heydrich.* Publishing details not included.

Cobb, Matthew. *The Resistance: The French Fight Against the Nazis.* London: Pocket Books, 2009.

Cooper, Matthew. *The Nazi War against Soviet Partisans, 1941–1944.* New York: Stein & Day, 1979.

Cornish, Nik. *Soviet Partisan, 1941–44.* New York: Osprey, 2014.

Czajkowski, Z. G. *Warsaw 1944: An Insurgent's Journal of the Uprising.* Barnsley: Pen & Sword Military, 2012.

Davies, Peter. *The Extreme Right in France, 1789 to the Present.* London: Routledge, 2002.

Davies, Norman. *Rising '44.* New York: Viking, 2006.

Deak, Istvan. *Europe on Trial: The Story of Collaboration, Resistance, and Retribution during World War II.* Philadelphia: Westview, 2015.

De Jong, Louis. *The Netherlands and Nazi Germany.* Cambridge, MA: Harvard, 1990).

Djilas, Milovan. *Tito: The Story from Inside.* London: Weidenfeld and Nicolson, 1981.

Faber, David. *Munich 1938: Appeasement and World War II.* New York: Simon & Schuster, 2008.

Foot, M. R. D. *SOE: The Special Operations Executive, 1940–1946.* London: BBC, 1984.

Foot, M. R. D. *Resistance: European Resistance to Nazism, 1940–1945.* New York: McGraw-Hill, 1977.

Foot, M. R. D., ed. *Holland at War against Hitler: Anglo-Dutch Relations, 1940–1945.* London: Frank Cass, 1990.

Galante, Pierre. *Operation Valkyrie: The German General's Plot against Hitler.* New York: Harper & Row, 1981.

Gallagher, Thomas. *Assault in Norway.* New York: Harcourt Brace Jovanovich, 1975.

Gallo, Patrick. *For Love and Country: The Italian Resistance.* Lanham, MD: University Press of America, 2003.

Gellately, Robert. *The Gestapo and German Society: Enforcing Racial Policy, 1933–1945.* Oxford: Oxford University Press, 1999.

Gerwarth, Robert. *Hitler's Hangman: The Life of Heydrich.* New Haven: Yale, 2011.

Gilbert, Martin. *The Holocaust: The Jewish Tragedy.* London: Collins, 1986.

Gildea, Robert. *Fighters in the Shadows: A New History of the French Resistance.* Cambridge, MA: Harvard University Press, 2015.

Gjelsvik, Tore. *Norwegian Resistance, 1940–1945.* London: Hurst, 1979.

Grenkivich, Leonid. *The Soviet Partisan Movement, 1941–1944.* London: Frank Cass, 1999.

Grose, Peter. *Gentleman Spy: The Life of Allen Dulles.* Boston: Houghton Mifflin, 1994.

Haasis, Hellmut G. *Bombing Hitler: The Story of the Man Who Almost Assassinated the Fuhrer.* New York: Skyhorse, 2001.

Haukelid, Knut. *Skis Against the Atom.* Minot, ND: North American Heritage Press, 1989 [1954].

Hawes, Stephen, and Ralph White, eds. *Resistance in Europe, 1939–1945.* New York: Viking, 1976.

Heineman, John L. *Hitler's First Foreign Minister: Constantine Freiherr von Neurath, Diplomat and Statesman.* Berkeley: University of California, 1979.

Hill, Alexander. *The War Behind the Eastern Front: The Soviet Partisan Movement in Northwest Russia, 1941–1944.* London: Frank Cass, 2005.

Hoffman, Peter. *The German Resistance to Hitler.* Cambridge, MA: Harvard, 1988.

Howarth, David. *The Shetland Bus: A World War II Epic of Escape, Survival, and Adventure.* Guilford, CT: Lyons, 2001 [1951].

Kaiser, Henry. *The Cost of Courage.* New York: Other Press, 2015.

Karau, Mark D. *Germany's Defeat in the First World War: The Lost Battles and Reckless Gambles That Brought Down the Second Reich.* Santa Barbara, CA: Praeger Press, 2015.

Kedward, H. R. *In Search of the Maquis: Rural Resistance in Southern France, 1942–1944.* Oxford: Clarendon Press, 1993.

Keegan, John. *The Second World War.* London: Hutchinson, 1989.

Kurapovna, Marcia Christoff. *Shadows on the Mountain: The Allies, the Resistance, and the Rivalries That Doomed WWII Yugoslavia.* Hoboken: Wiley, 2010.

Lacouture, Jean. *De Gaulle: The Rebel, 1890–1944.* Translated by Patrick O'Brien. New York: Norton, 1990.

Lampe, David. *The Last Ditch: Britain's Secret Resistance and the Nazi Invasion Plans.* London: Frontline, 2007 [1968].

Lampe, David. *Hitler's Savage Canary: A History of the Danish Resistance in World War II.* New York: Skyhorse, 2011.

Linderman, A. R. B. *Re-Discovering Irregular Warfare: Colin Gubbins and the Origins of Britain's Special Operations Executive.* Norman, OK: University of Oklahoma Press, 2016.

MacDonald, Callum. *The Killing of Obergruppenführer Reinhard Heydrich.* New York: Free Press, 1989.

Mack Smith, Denis. *Modern Italy: A Political History.* Ann Arbor: University of Michigan Press, 1997 [1959].

Mazower, Mark. *Inside Hitler's Greece: The Experience of Occupation, 1941–1944.* New Haven: Yale, 1993.

Mears, Ray. *The Real Heroes of Telemark: The True Story of the Secret Mission to Stop Hitler's Bomb.* London: Hodder & Stoughton, 2003.

O'Donnell, Patrick K. *Operatives, Spies, and Saboteurs: The Unknown Story of WWII's OSS.* New York: Citadel, 2004.

Pavone, Claudio. *A Civil War: A History of the Italian Resistance.* Translated by Peter Levy, with the assistance of David Broder. London: Verso, 2013.

Paxton, Robert O. *Vichy France: Old Guard, New Order, 1940–1945.* New York: Columbia, 1972.

Ramet, Sabrina P. *The Three Yugoslavias: State-Making and Legitimation, 1918–2005.* Bloomington: Indiana University, 2006.

Ryan, Cornelius. *A Bridge Too Far: The Classic History of the Greatest Battle of World War II*. New York: Touchstone, 1974.

Schoenbrun, David. *Soldiers of the Night: The Story of the French Resistance*. New York: Meridian, 1981.

Seaman, Mark, ed. *Special Operations Executive: A New Instrument of War*. London: Routledge, 2006.

Self, Robert. *Neville Chamberlain*. Burlington, VT: Ashgate, 2006.

Service, Robert. *Stalin: A Biography*. Cambridge, MA: Harvard, 2004.

Shirer, William L. *The Collapse of the Third Republic: An Inquiry into the Fall of France in 1940*. New York: Simon & Schuster, 1969.

Shirer, William L. *The Rise and Fall of the Third Reich*. New York: Ballantine, 1960.

Stafford, David. *Britain and European Resistance, 1940–1945*. Toronto: Toronto University, 1980.

Sweets, Jonathan F. *Choices in Vichy France: The French under Nazi Occupation*. New York: Oxford, 1986.

Thomsett, Michael. *The German Opposition to Hitler: The Resistance, the Underground, and the Assassination Plots, 1938–1945*. Jefferson, NC: McFarland, 1997.

Woodhouse, C. M. *The Struggle for Greece: 1941–1949*. London: Hart-Davis, 1976.

Index

About the Author

Dr. Patrick G. Zander received his MA in European History from Georgia State University and his MS and PhD from the Georgia Institute of Technology. He is the author of *The Rise of Fascism: History, Documents, and Key Questions* (2016) and *The Rise of Communism: History, Documents, and Key Questions* (2017). In 2009 he was awarded the Duncan C. Tanner Prize from Oxford University Press for his work on the British fascist movement in the interwar years. He is currently Associate Professor of History at Georgia Gwinnett College near Atlanta, Georgia, where he teaches modern British and European history and classes on the world wars.